PROGRAMMING TECHNIQUES FOR SOFTWARE DEVELOPMENT

PROGRAMMING TECHNIQUES FOR SOFTWARE DEVELOPMENT

Bebo White

Stanford University

 VAN NOSTRAND REINHOLD
New York

Printed in the United States of America

Van Nostrand Reinhold
115 Fifth Avenue
New York, New York 10003

Van Nostrand Reinhold International Company Limited
11 New Fetter Lane
London EC4P 4EE, England

Van Nostrand Reinhold
480 La Trobe Street
Melbourne, Victoria 3000, Australia

Macmillan of Canada
Division of Canada Publishing Corporation
164 Commander Boulevard
Agincourt, Ontario M1S 3C7, Canada

16 15 14 13 12 11 10 9 8 7 6 5 4 3 2 1

Library of Congress Cataloging-in-Publication Data

White, Bebo, 1945–
  Programming techniques for software development.

  Bibliography: p.
  1. Computer software—Development. 2. Electronic
digital computers—Programming.   I. Title.
QA76.76.D47W48 1988   005.1   87-29589
ISBN 0-442-29187-6

This book is dedicated to my family—Nancy, Andrew and Christopher. It is also dedicated to the hope that all who use it will do so for the benefit of mankind.

PREFACE

*"Often it is means that justify ends: Goals advance technique and
technique survives even when goal structures crumble."*

Alan J. Perlis
Yale University
"Epigrams on Programming"
ACM SIGPLAN Notices (Sept. 1982)

To the beginning programmer, programming techniques are clever applications usually presented by example. The study of techniques is often sacrificed in order to concentrate on the syntax and semantics of a programming language. Development of techniques is usually regarded as a talent which comes with experience.

To the experienced programmer, the word *techniques* usually implies "programming tricks." These "tricks" are part of a successful programmer's repertoire, or "toolkit." They are the subject of many short articles in programming and computer science literature and are often shared and discussed when programmers get together. Presentations of such techniques vary greatly. Some are presented as complete procedures expressed in algorithmic or pseudo-code form. Still others are more philosophical or empirical in nature, and are characterized in general terms only. Others are simply a "seed" around which the framework of a particular application may be built.

My goal in writing this book has been to cover a wide variety of programming techniques. Although areas are related, my focus is on the specific topic itself, not on its relationship to other topics. Each topic is presented independently of others in order to minimize the referencing required by the user. Chapters can be referenced as needed, and programmers with special interest can use only those sections or chapters they need. However, if the chapters are taken in sequence, a common logical thread will become visible. This thread demonstrates how seemingly diverse areas of programming relate to one another and how tools and techniques are applicable in a multitude of cases.

Programming examples are provided in the BASIC and/or Pascal programming languages where appropriate. These two languages were chosen because each represents the minimum of a set of algorithmic programming languages. BASIC represents a generic example of an unstructured language. Examples in BASIC may be translated to languages such as FORTRAN with no loss in capability. Pascal was selected as the generic example of a structured language, having additional features such as dynamic data types and recursion. Examples in Pascal may be translated in a straightforward manner to languages such as PL/1, Structured COBOL, FORTRAN 77, C, Ada, or Modula-2. All program examples have been deliberately kept small (i.e., minimal number of statements) in order to allow them to be easily converted into specialized modules which implement a specific process/technique.

The techniques presented and the organization of this book are designed to appeal to a wide range of individuals involved with computer programming. Experienced programmers will find it a source of readily available tools (program fragments and ideas useable in their real world applications); novice programmers will find it an introduction to advanced techniques, a guide to the vocabulary associated with those techniques, sources for further study, and a source of immediately useable tools.

None of the techniques presented is "hardware-dependent." As a result, the techniques should be useable on a wide variety of computers of all types. Programmers working on large mainframe systems and programmers working on microcomputers will find this book equally valuable.

The goal of this book is to present a diverse collection of programming techniques useful in a wide range of programming applications. It will be realized if the reader experiences that familiar light bulb over his or her head, and says, "Hey, that's the way I can solve my problem."

CONTENTS

PROGRAMMING
TECHNIQUES
FOR
SOFTWARE
DEVELOPMENT

1

INTRODUCTION

"And now reader—bestir thyself—for though we will always lend thee proper assistance in difficult places, as we do not, like some others, expect thee to use the arts of divination to discover our meaning, yet we shall not indulge thy laziness where nothing but thy own attention is required; for thou art highly mistaken if thou dost imagine that we intended when we begun this great work to leave thy sagacity nothing to do, or that without sometimes exercising this talent thou wilt be able to travel through our pages with any pleasure or profit to thyself."

Henry Fielding

The Random House College Dictionary* defines *technique* as:

1. The manner, methods, or ability with which a person fulfills the technical requirements of his particular art or field of endeavor.
2. The body of specialized procedures and methods used in any specific field, esp. in an area of applied science.
3. Technical skill; ability to apply procedures or methods so as to effect a desired result.
4. Method of projecting personal charm, appeal, and so forth. . . .

Programming techniques would therefore be methods, etc. that are useful in the development of computer programs.

The form that programming techniques take vary widely. The most fundamental type of technique is a specialized implementation of an *algorithm*. Algorithms should be, by definition, implementation-dependent (i.e., not dependent on the device on which they are used). This is obvious in that the concept of an algorithm predates computers. In the context of this book, when

---

*The Random House College Dictionary, Random House, Inc., New York, Revised edition, 1980, p. 1349.

1

an algorithm is described for a specific application using a computer, that algorithm may also be described as a *programming technique*.

Programming techniques are also *models*. In this sense, a technique represents a programmer's visualization of how a computer may be used to solve a problem in terms of the elements of computer science.

Programming techniques reflect *creativity*. Some programmers argue that programs are a form of literature and that the variations used to solve a problem in a program are as significant as the many ways in which an author may describe a situation. However, unlike their literary counterparts, computer programs utilizing specific programming techniques are often written to be shared with other programmers and incorporated in a variety of different program applications.

TECHNIQUES AND COMPUTER PROGRAMS

Edward Yourdon (see Note, end of chapter) has listed what he considers to be the important qualities of a good computer program:

1. It works.
2. It works according to specification.
3. It is flexible.
4. It is ready on time.
5. It has no bugs.
6. The bugs, which are inevitable, can be fixed quickly.
7. It is well documented.
8. It executes quickly.
9. It makes efficient use of memory.

These qualities appear to emphasize, with the possible exception of the first, that a program is not merely an algorithm translated into a programming language with some consideration of data structures. Writing a program that has these features becomes an involved process of design, maintenance, documentation, timing and sizing with the end result being a *good program*.

These supplementary processes, which can be language-dependent or language-independent, hardware-dependent or hardware-independent, are *techniques*.

TECHNIQUES AND COMPUTER PROGRAMMERS

Certainly, a computer programmer can be competent (i.e., write computer programs that are algorithmically correct) without a broad knowledge of techniques. Like creative writing, programming can be viewed as either an *art* or a *skill*. However, techniques with a programming language are somewhat like vocabulary with a natural one.

Edward Yourdon has also compiled a list of talents, acquired either academically or through experience, that can contribute to the success of a programmer:

1. The ability to read and understand a problem description and to grasp the formulator's desires
2. The ability to extract the difficulties and ignore irrelevancies
3. The ability to recognize where theory can be applied and to know when to seek assistance
4. The ability to break a problem into manageable pieces and to understand the relationships between these pieces
5. The ability to judge the cost of proposed solutions in programming effort, computer resources, and user satisfaction, and to balance these costs
6. The ability to build partial solutions into coherent and elegant complete solutions
7. The ability to express solutions in graceful and straightforward language, natural or artificial, that persuades both humans and computers of the solution's correctness.
8. The ability to disengage the ego and try alternate approaches (or even alternate problems) when continual attempts appear unsuccessful.

Points 1–3 can be gained from experience; points 5–7 can be developed with the selection of programming techniques. Point 8 is a psychological one, but a broad base of techniques makes alternate approaches more accessible.

Therefore, assuming the goal of a programmer is to write successful programs, techniques can aid in accomplishing this goal by providing a selection of programming tools, and increasing the programmer's competence level.

NOTE

[1]Yourdon, Edward, *Techniques of Program Structure and Design.* Englewood Cliffs, NJ, Prentice-Hall, 1975.

2
KEY TOPICS IN SOFTWARE DESIGN

"Everything should be made as simple as possible, but no simpler."

Albert Einstein

The last twenty years of the computer software industry has seen a steady procession of new software engineering philosophies and new approaches to software design problems. The cause of this influx of software design methods is unclear. Some indicators suggest that it is part of a natural evolutionary process. The increasing complexity of the problems being addressed may also be a relevant factor.

Whatever the reason for their presence, the large number of software design methodologies poses a dilemma for the programmer/analyst involved in the development of a system. The selection of a design methodology has become one of the most critical parts of the software design cycle.

A software design method is a collection of techniques based upon a particular design concept or philosophy.

GLOSSARY OF TERMS

Data Flow Diagram (DFD): A graphical representation of the transformation of data within a system, i.e., the work done in transforming input to output; DFDs are typically presented as a network of subtransformations connected by flows.

Decision Table: A table of all contingencies that are to be considered in the description of a problem together with actions to be taken for each set of contingencies.

Entity Relationship Diagram (ERD): A graphical representation of the organization of stored data within a system as a network of data objects and the relationships between them.

Flowchart: A detailed solution of a problem in terms of its logic; symbolic notation is used to represent the information and describe the input, output, arithmetic and logical operations involved; a flowchart is directed to describe the flow (hence *flowchart*) or the order in which operations are conducted. A flowchart emphasizes decision structure and flow of control and deemphasizes data structure.

Hierarchy Input/Process/Output (HIPO): A set of HIPO diagrams containing a visual table of contents, overview HIPO diagrams and detail HIPO diagrams. It may also contain related non-HIPO documentation, such as file and record layouts, system flowcharts, screen designs, decision tables, or detailed flowcharts.

HIPO Diagram: A graphic representation of the functions of processes of a system; it contains three major sections:

1. *Input*—the data items used by the process steps and connected to them by arrows.
2. *Process*—a series of numbered statements describing a given function; these statements are connected by arrows to the input needed to perform the function and the output created by the function.
3. *Output*—the data items created or modified by the process steps and connected to them by arrows.

Loop-Exitif-EndLoop: A synonym for a control structure involving the premature exiting of an active loop (LOOP, EXIT IF a condition is true, else END current iteration of LOOP);

Modular Programming: Programming in which the problem is broken down into logical subdivisions, each of which is coded and tested as a unit.

Program: The complete plan for the solution of a problem; more specifically, the complete sequence of machine instructions necessary to solve a problem.

Pseudocode: An artificial language that describes computer program algorithms without using the syntax of a particular programming language; *syn.*: structured English.

State: A mode of behavior of a system; a particular set of behaviors that has a unique combination of conditions and destinations.

State Transition Diagram (STD): A graphical representation of the dynamics of a system as a network of states connected by transitions.

Stepwise Refinement: A technique of program development that begins with an English or pseudocode description of the solution of a problem and that via a series of refinements, is transformed into the actual code itself.

Structure Theorem: A program with one entry and one exit (i.e., a *proper* program) is functionally equivalent to a program constructed from the following logic structures:

1. A sequence of two or more functions.

2. A conditional branch of the form If-Then-Else (i.e., selection).
3. Repeated execution of a function while a condition is true (i.e., repetition).

Structured Programming: An approach for constraining programs to be written using only a fixed set of flow-of-control constructs.

Transition: The movement of a system from one state to another.

Truth Table: A table that describes a logic function by listing all possible combinations of input values and indicating, for each combination, the true output values.

NOTATIONAL DESIGN TECHNIQUES

Pseudocode

CONCEPT: To define a notation that closely associates a native (spoken or written) language and a programming language

PROCESS: Pseudocode (or ''structured English'') is a free-form language that permits a programmer/analyst to think about the problem to be solved and express the logic of a program without concern for the syntax of any specific programming language. The notation allows the programmer to deal with problems at various levels of abstraction without concern about program details.

Pseudocode is also a language that can be used during a *stepwise refinement* process in order to describe the program's operation at each level of refinement. This provides a convenient way for a programmer to document the stages of program development for his or her own use, allows other programmers the opportunity to review the function of a program before it is translated into a programming language and facilitates an assessment of the development status at any stage of the refinement process.

Since pseudocode allows the designer to work with a language at a level higher than a programming language, it is easier to implement design changes in pseudocode. Further, changes in the program logic may be more visible in pseudocode than when the program is translated into a programming language. The pseudocode notation also can provide a detailed description of the completed source program; this description can be the basis for program documentation.

Summary of Pseudocode Structures.   The following is an example of a pseudocode format which could be adopted as the basis for an expanded format in a programming language:

Assignment:
> variable ← expression

Input:
> *input* variable list

Output:
> *output* variable list

If-Then-Else
> *if* condition *then* Then Part *endif*
> **Or**
> *if* condition
> > *then* Then Part
> > *else* Else Part
> > *endif*

Case:
> *case*
> > condition1 : Case 1 Part
> > condition2 : Case 2 Part
> > . . . . .
> > conditionx : Case X Part
> > *otherwise*
> > > Otherwise Part
> > *endcase*

Repeat:
> *repeat*
> > Repeat Part
> *forever*
> **Or**
> *repeat*
> > Repeat Part
> *until* condition

While:
> *while* condition *do*
> > While Part
> *endwhile*

EXAMPLE: The following is a pseudocode listing of an algorithm that adds elements of two arrays. This example uses the pseudocode format just described.

```
Procedure ARRAYADD;
  Given Arrays A and B,
  Produce Array C;

Initialize control and
  reference variables,
  and Array C;

if the dimensions of A and C conform
  then
    while maximum of index is not exceeded do
```

```
        C[index] = A[index] + B[index];
        increment index;
        endwhile;
        Return C;
        else
            output 'Improper array dimensions'
   endif;
```

Nassi-Shneiderman/Chapin Charts

CONCEPT: To define a flowcharting technique that is effective as a design tool with graphic attributes to aid in communication and conducive to maintaining top-down design

PROCESS The original concepts for this technique were developed by I. Nassi and B. Shneiderman[1] and were later expanded by N. Chapin.[2] The goals of this alternative flowcharting method as described in the original paper are:

- To allow the scope of iterative processes to be more visible and well-defined.
- To allow the scope of decision processes to be more visible and well-defined.
- To improve the visibility of processes that involve compound conditional clauses (AND, OR, etc.) to make all resultant paths visible.
- To demonstrate graphically the necessary scope of local and global variables.
- To make undesirable programming practices (e.g., arbitrary transfers of control—GOTOs) awkward or impossible to represent graphically.
- To provide an understandable representation of recursion.
- To limit the physical size of a flowchart representation, thereby forcing a logical modularization of the definition of a process.

Nassi-Shneiderman/Chapin representations of the well-known control structures are shown in Figures 2-1 through 2-4. It must be noted that "unstructured" forms such as premature loop exiting are also included. This is done in the belief that certain structures represent frequently occurring forms and can be allowed if their use is controlled. Conventions are defined with regards to the flow of control through flowcharts of this type. Flow will always pass downward through horizontal lines and never between vertical lines. Downward flow of control is interrupted in the chart only when indicated by a series of slash marks enclosed by horizontal and vertical lines. In no case will flow ever continue through the slash marks in either a horizontal or vertical direction.

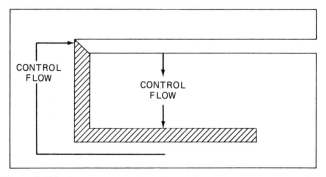

Figure 2.1(a). Representation of an interruption in downward control flow.

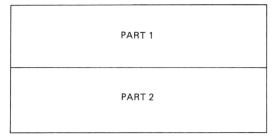

Figure 2.1(b). Representation of the sequence structure in Nassi-Schneiderman form.

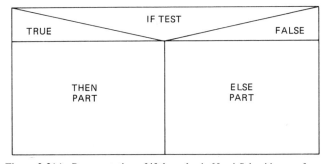

Figure 2.2(a). Representation of if-then-else in Nassi-Schneiderman form.

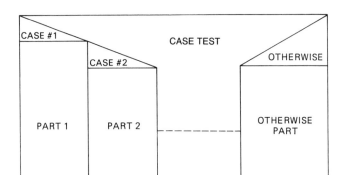

Figure 2.2(b). Representation of case in Nassi-Schneiderman form.

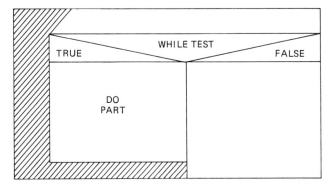

Figure 2.3(a). Representation of while-do in Nassi-Schneiderman form.

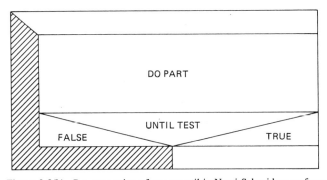

Figure 2.3(b). Representation of repeat-until in Nassi-Schneiderman form.

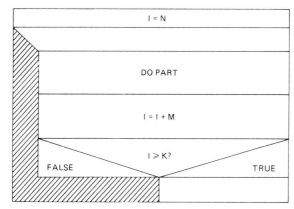

Figure 2.3(c). Representation of iterative-do in Nassi-Schneiderman form.

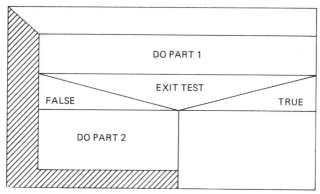

Figure 2.4(a). Representation of premature loop exiting with one exit in Nassi-Schneiderman form.

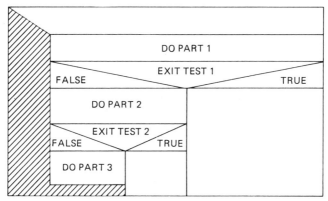

Figure 2.4(b). Representation of premature loop exiting with two exits in Nassi-Schneiderman form.

ADVANTAGES:

- Not only does this notation assist a programmer in thinking in an orderly manner, but it makes it easier to do so.
- The absence of any representation of the GOTO or branch statement forces the programmer to code in a structured manner.
- Since no more than 15 to 20 symbols can be drawn on a standard 8.5-inch × 11-inch sheet of paper, a programmer is encouraged to modularize programs into meaningful sections/procedures.
- There are no strict rules regarding the use of this convention; additional structures can be defined if necessary.

Decision Tables

CONCEPT: To represent a program or algorithm in a tabular fashion; an alternative to a sequential representation (steps) or a pictorial representation (flowcharts).

PROCESS: Decision tables are a method of documenting process flows. Constructing decision tables for a given process involves

- The identification of various conditions that impact the process.
- The identification of various actions involved in the execution of the process.
- The determination of specific combinations of conditions that result in specific combinations of actions being taken.

A decision table maps conditions and links them to actions while not necessarily specifying the implementation of that mapping.

A decision table is formatted as a four-quadrant table. The upper left, lower left, upper right and lower right quadrants contain the *condition stubs*, *action stubs*, *condition entries* and *action entries* respectively. The conditions in the stubs are to be tested to see which of the entries apply. A decision table is called *limited entry* if the condition entries are restricted to be T(rue) or F(alse); otherwise, it is called an *extended entry* table. Each column of entries is called a *rule*, which specifies the sequence of actions to be performed if the indicated combinations applies. The asterisks represent *not applicable* or *not determinable*.

Lew has also adopted two conventions not standard to the use of decision tables:[3]

1. Prior to executing a decision table for the first time, a special variable (e.g., λ) must be initialized to zero; this λ controls "entry" into the table.

2. Execution of a decision table is repeated until an exit or return action is explicitly performed.

The initialization of λ is necessary if the first execution of a decision table is to be distinguished from subsequent repetitions. This distinction is made primarily to accommodate data input.

EXAMPLE 1:   The decision table (Table 2-1) is a representation of the Euclidean algorithm to calculate the greatest common divisor (GCD) of two positive integers A and B. It provides an illustration of the kinds of process relationships and flows depicted in decision tables.

This decision table is interpreted as follows:

1. When λ = 0, obtain values for A and B and set λ = 1.
2. When A > 0, B > 0, A > B and λ ≠ 0, assign A the value of A − B.
3. When A > 0, B > 0, A < B and λ ≠ 0, assign B the value of B − A.
4. When A > 0, B > 0, A = B and λ ≠ 0, output current value of A and exit the procedure;
5. When any other relationships exist between A and B, output "error" and exit the procedure.

EXAMPLE 2:   As traditionally constructed, decision tables do not directly present functional structure. McMullen has introduced a set of notational conventions to define structured decision tables [4] (see Table 2-2).

Table 2.1

Condition Stubs	Condition Entries				
λ = 0	T	F	F	F	F
A > 0	*	T	T	T	*
B > 0	*	T	T	T	*
compare A vs. B	*	>	<	=	*
Action Stubs	Action Entries				
get A, B	x	*	*	*	*
A = A − B	*	x	*	*	*
B = B − A	*	*	x	*	*
put A	*	*	*	x	*
put 'error'	*	*	*	*	x
exit	*	*	*	x	x
λ = 1	x	*	*	*	*

Table 2.2

Sequence

Entry ⇒	1
* * *	
Action 1	x
Action 2	x
. . .	x
Action n	x
Exit	x

If-Then-Else

Entry ⇒	1	2
Condition of If Test?	T	F
* * * *		
Then Part	x	
Else Part		x
Exit	x	x

Case

Entry ⇒	1	2	3	. . .	m	Otherwise
Case Condition # Test?	T	T	T		T	*
* * * *						
Case Action #	x	x	x		x	x
Exit	x	x	x	. . .	x	x

Do-While

Entry ⇒	1	2
Condition of While Test?	T	F
* * * *		
While Part	x	
Exit		x

Do-Until

Entry ⇒	0	1	2
Condition of Until Test?	*	T	F
* * * *			
Until Part	x	x	
Exit			x

This pedagogy defines decision table forms analogous to the sequence, decision and repetition control structures indicative of structured design.

While maintaining the flexibility of the traditional decision table form, structured decision tables can also be quite useful in demonstrating the reducibility of algorithms and in the potential recognition of possible subfunction patterns.

SURVEY OF SOFTWARE PROJECT METHODOLOGIES

The features of a good structured analysis technique are that it

- Documents the problem and its alternative solutions in a way that is easily understood and verified by its users.
- Positions the problem within a larger context and clearly defines the problem's boundaries within that context.
- Breaks the problem's solutions down into progressively more detailed levels (decomposition), identifies data, specifies operations on data and supplies a documentation package that serves as a succinct yet complete lead-in to the *design phase*.

During the analysis phase, the following primary activities occur:

- Investigation, documentation and understanding of
    * The current system.
    * The *problem* or opportunity that presents itself.
    * The *requirements* placed upon the current environment by the problem or the opportunity in terms of functions, interfaces, constraints and priorities.
- Preliminary definition of *implementation alternatives* for the solution.
- Cost/benefit analysis.

The diagram in Figure 2.5 illustrates the relationships between the components of a *Software Project Methodology*.

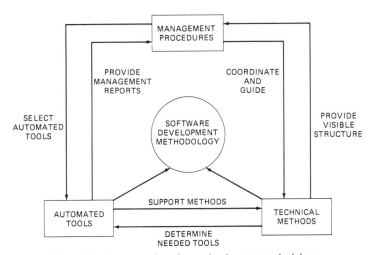

Figure 2.5. Elements of a software development methodology.

Five analysis methodologies—SADT, Yourdon/DeMarco, Gane/Sarson, Warnier-Orr, HIPO—are evaluated in this section according to the following criteria:

- Overview.
- Problem definition.
- Requirements definition.
- Implementation alternatives.
- Cost/benefit analysis.
- Documentation.
- General evaluation.

It is not the intention of this evaluation to demonstrate that a particular methodology is superior to another. Each represents an alternative means to an end— the successful building of a system. They differ with respect to the emphasis placed on different characteristics and the role those characteristics play in the operation of differing systems.

Software project methodologies should be selected according to how well they

- Fit the technology to be used in the proposed system.
- Suit the personnel who will be involved in the proposed system.
- Cover the entire software life cycle.
- Satisfy the needs of users of the proposed system.

Structured Analysis and Design Technique (SADT)

OVERVIEW: The Structured Analysis and Design Technique (SADT) provides a hierarchical model and a modeling process for logically decomposing a problem into its parts. The process is designed to

- Expose detail gradually in a controlled manner.
- Encourage conciseness and accuracy.
- Focus attention on data and activity relationships.

A complete SADT model consists of both data and activity diagrams with supporting text, and may include multiple sets of diagrams of the same system viewed from several perspectives (see Figures 2.6 and 2.7).

PROBLEM DEFINITION: The SADT model documents user interviews, helps to communicate with users, management and professional staff, and organizes and documents the problem and its boundaries. The result is a bounded functional

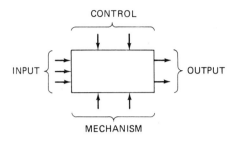

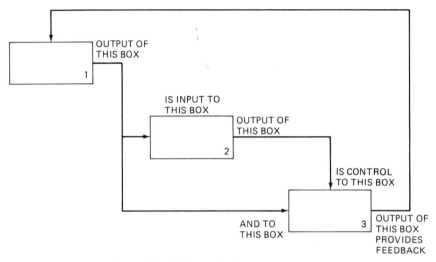

Figure 2.6. SADT activity diagram elements.

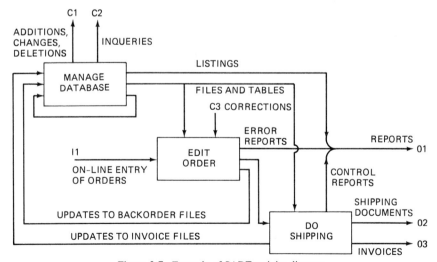

Figure 2.7. Example of SADT activity diagram.

17

model of what the problems are and what they are not. How the problems are to be solved is determined later.

The SADT methodology begins, then, with a gathering—through the study of available documents and by interviews of those familiar with the problems—of all available information about the problems to be analyzed. A formalized iterative process of "author/reader cycles" results in a general understanding of the problem, its boundaries; and a SADT model reflecting current operations, identifying issues, needs, and deficiencies.

Rectangular boxes with carefully defined inputs, outputs, controls, and mechanisms are step-wise refined to introduce detail in a manner that provides orderly comprehension of the technical information. Diagramming is done alternately for both data and activity aspects of the problem area. Each diagram is checked to make sure it shows all elements of the other diagrams and that use of the elements is consistent among them.

Recognition of when to stop diagramming a SADT model depends on the purpose of the model.

- An environmental model is complete when the analyst/programmer can precisely identify the bounded context of the problem under study.
- A current operations model is complete when issues, needs, and deficiencies in the existing systems can be precisely identified in terms of their source and impact.

In general, decomposition is stopped when a common function can be identified, or a mechanism is identified that can support a particular activity.

Another good indicator of when to stop developing a model is the recognition that a change in the "level of abstraction" is occurring (i.e., during the modelling of the "whats" of a system, when one recognizes the "hows" appearing).

The transition from analysis to design is not an evolutionary process, but rather a process whereby the design solutions are tied back to the statement of the problem or requirements.

SADT requires that each reviewer make comments in writing on the diagrams sent by the author for review, until the diagrams are officially accepted.

REQUIREMENTS DEFINITION: The same SADT methods used to state the problem are used to define the solution. That is, problem analysis leads to solution design.

The functional phase of analysis is made up of the following major steps:

1. Diagram the activity and data aspects of the *target* system.
2. Cross-reference activity diagrams and data diagrams.

3. Analyze the sequence in which activities can occur.
4. Tie the functional model back to the requirements model.

The functional model provides the basis for systems design.

IMPLEMENTATION ALTERNATIVES: If a good job of specifying the functional requirements of a system has been done (and if the specification has not been unduly influenced by software approaches), there can exist a variety of design models, each proposing one or three approaches to a solution:

1. Modification of an existing system.
2. Installation of a commercially available software package.
3. Development of a new software system.

Each of the design solutions would explicitly show the level of requirement satisfaction for each alternative.

COST/BENEFIT ANALYSIS: Use the current operations model to show existing problems, a requirements model to show *what* problems are going to be solved, and a design model to show *how* those problems are going to be solved. These models will help in the quantification of cost elements that is, operational cost of the existing system, operational cost of the future system, and development cost of the proposed system. The same procedure should be followed for benefits.

GENERAL EVALUATION: The SADT modeling process is a definite aid in analysis as well as a documentation medium. It provides for breaking a complex problem down into manageable chunks.

The real cost and effort is in the basic research and interviewing process to get information to put into SADT form.

There are three approaches to automated documentation:

1. Time-sharing editor and file system
2. Stand-alone microcomputer system with word processing
3. PSL/PSA's data dictionary function (problem statement language/problem statement analyzer)

The problem environment can be represented by a projected top level box at least one level of detail above the conceptualized problem. This process can be repeated until the context of the problem is sufficiently understood.

Structured Analysis (Yourdon/DeMarco)

OVERVIEW: The Yourdon approach to structured analysis is essentially a process of:

- Building *logical models* of the system.
- Using *functional decomposition* as the analytical technique.
- Using data flow diagrams as the primary documentation tool.

The Yourdon approach does not specify a particular methodology that must be used; rather it offers collection of tools and techniques that can be applied to any systems development methodology (see Figure 2.8 through 2.10).

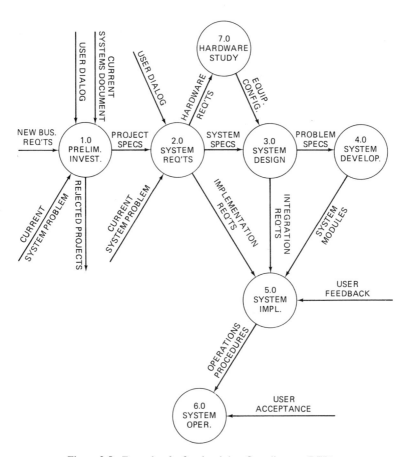

Figure 2.8. Example of a first-level data flow diagram (DFD).

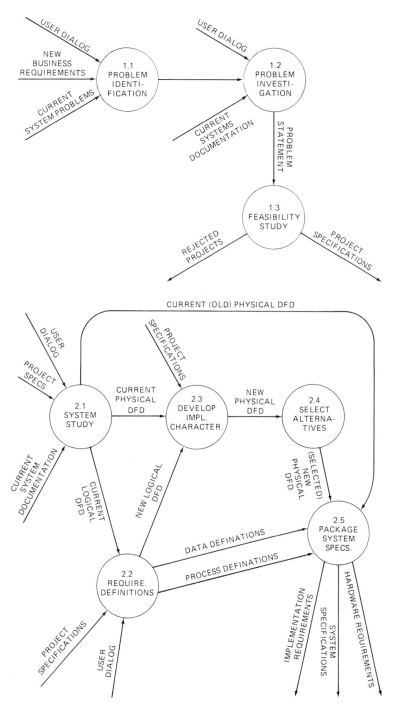

Figure 2.9. Example of second-level decomposition in a data flow diagram (DFD).

21

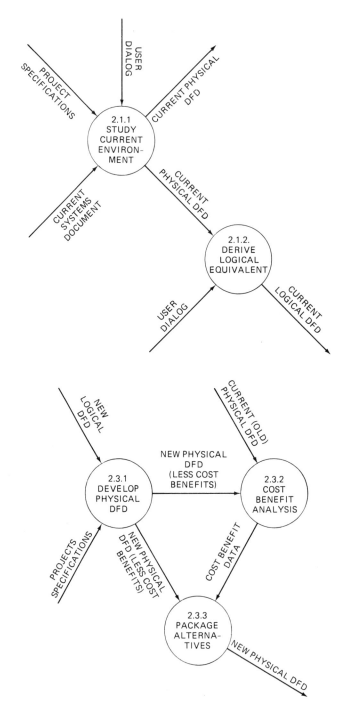

Figure 2.10. Example of third-level decomposition in a data flow diagram (DFD).

PROBLEM DEFINITION: Whether or not structured analysis applies to the area of problem definition depends on how the user structures the analysis phase:

- Tom DeMarco[5] says that the analysis phase could be preceded by a feasibility study of which problem definition is a part.
- Victor Weinberg[6] says that the tools and techniques of structured analysis apply to problem definition as well as all other phases of the system life cycle.

REQUIREMENTS DEFINITION:

1. The current environment is studied and a set of *current physical* data flow diagrams is drawn.
2. From the current physical flow diagrams, the logical equivalent is derived and is drawn as the *current logical* data flow diagrams.
3. New or changed functions are determined and merged into current logical data flow diagrams, thus creating the *new logical* data flow diagrams.
4. All data flows, files, processes (data transformations) and data elements are documented in a *data dictionary*.

The technique of functional decomposition from the viewpoint of the data is used to develop these diagrams.

Feedback is particularly important in the *requirements definition* phase, for it is *here, near the beginning of a project, where errors can be corrected most cheaply*. Instant feedback is obtained when the analyst/programmer uses data flow diagrams to document user interviews. This is made possible by the ease with which data flow diagrams can be explained to the user, and because the analyst/programmer is drawing the data flow diagrams even as the user interview is occurring.

It is possible to derive acceptance test data from the data flow diagrams.

IMPLEMENTATION ALTERNATIVES: Different means of satisfying the system requirements are studied. These studies should focus on how much of the system will be automated and how quickly the system will respond to its environment.

A set of *new physical* data flow diagrams are created as follows:

1. Draw a man-machine boundary using the new logical data flow diagrams produced in the requirements definition phase. The functions within this boundary are the functions that will be automated.
2. Add any implementation dependent features.
3. Perform a cost/benefit study.
4. Repeat steps 1 through 3 until all reasonable alternatives have been covered.

COST/BENEFIT ANALYSIS: The cost/benefit study is the primary means of selecting the implementation alternative and is performed only after the new physical model is complete.

Structured analysis does not provide new tools nor processes for conducting the cost/benefit study; however, a complete and understandable model of the system will have a positive effect on the accuracy and completeness of the study.

GENERAL EVALUATION: The communication tool of structured analysis, the data flow diagram, is quickly understood and easy to use. The pictorial nature of the data flow diagram and the use of data dictionaries to define terms helps to eliminate redundant discussions and decisions, and also helps to minimize misunderstandings.

Structured Systems Analysis (Gane/Sarson)

OVERVIEW: Structured systems analysis, as presented by Chris Gane and Trish Sarson,[7] consists of an integrated collection of tools and techniques to help in systems analysis and specification. The data flow diagram (DFD) is the primary tool in building a logical model of the system (see Figure 2-11). It illustrates what data flow through the system, where data originate, what processes transform the data, and most importantly, the interrelationships of all the system parts. A DFD represents the functions and requirements of the system, not the implementation of those functions and requirements. Gane and Sarson outline a typical systems development methodology, with appropriate management review checkpoints.

The four graphic symbols used in constructing Data Flow Diagrams are shown in Figure 2.12.

PROBLEM DEFINITION: The problem is defined in the first two phases of the typical methodology: the initial study and the detailed study. In the initial study, the analyst/programmer gathers information about the current situation, and may develop an overview DFD to aid in understanding the current system. In the detailed study, the analyst/programmer analyzes current system to a degree sufficient to specify a replacement system. The logical model in this phase consists of an overall DFD supported by lower level DFDs, a data dictionary, and process logic represented in various ways.

When it is no longer useful to decompose a process, the logic of that process is specified with a combination of decision trees, decision tables, structured English (pseudocode), and *tight* English (a more readable form of structured English).

A *data dictionary* is established to define the data of the current system. The items identified and described in the data dictionary are data *elements* and data

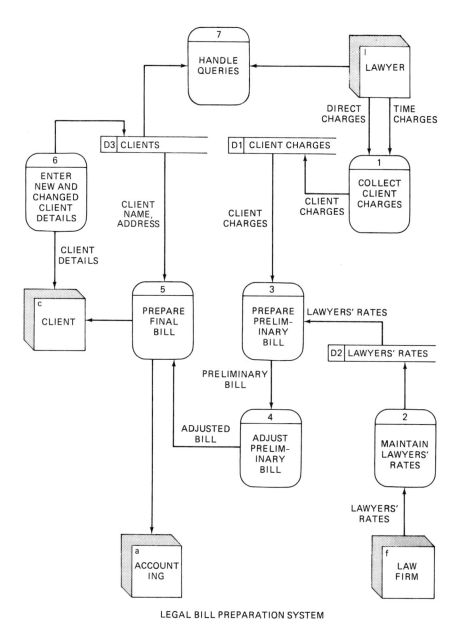

LEGAL BILL PREPARATION SYSTEM

Figure 2.11. Example of structured systems analysis data flow diagram (DFD).

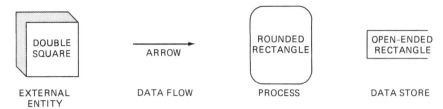

Figure 2.12. Graphic symbols used for constructing data flow diagrams.

structures (logically related groups of data elements). In addition, the data dictionary may contain data *flows*, data *stores*, *process definitions*, *external entities*, and *glossary* entries.

The logical model, consisting of the overall DFD, lower level DFDs, the data dictionary, and the detailed process logic, serves to document the work that has been accomplished and the information that has been uncovered, as well as to organize and structure the details.

The logical model will also help expose errors and misconceptions; redundant functions and unnecessary inputs and outputs typically are uncovered. The logical model also helps to determine the boundaries of the system under study. Furthermore, the logical model contributes to the analyst/programmer's perception of the system's true functions and requirements, which are frequently obscured by the system's physical implementation.

Common sense best decides how much detail should be analyzed and recorded.

REQUIREMENTS DEFINITION: The general requirements are defined in two stages:

1. Determination of the objectives for the new system.
2. Development of the logical functional specifications for the new system from the objectives and the logical model of the current system.

The logical model of the new system is produced by incorporating the objectives into the logical model of the current system, then expanded further by the use of two more tools and techniques:

1. The data immediate access diagram (DIAD) is used to specify the requirements for real-time responses and the attributes by which the data stores are to be accessed (see Figure 2.13).
2. The technique of *normalization* (removing redundancy and grouping truly related data elements together) is used to represent each data store in its simplest form, totally free of physical considerations.

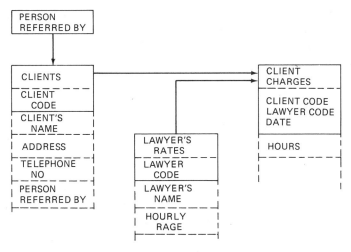

Figure 2.13. Example of structured systems analysis data immediate access diagram (DIAD).

At this point, the logical model of the new system is composed of:

1. The overall DFD.
2. Lower-level DFD's.
3. The data dictionary.
4. The recorded process logic.
5. The DIAD.
6. The simplified data stores.

An analysis of the elements of this logical model provide a sufficient description of function and design features to constitute a logical functional specification for the new system.

The logic of the processes is detailed only to the degree necessary to estimate the time required to implement them.

The logical DFD converts fairly smoothly into a hierarchical model (i.e., structure charts), which lends itself to top-down design, testing, and implementation. In addition, the data dictionary can be a source for generating acceptance test data.

IMPLEMENTATION ALTERNATIVES: After the logical model of the new system has been developed to a sufficient level of detail, the analyst/programmer working with the designer uses the logical DFD and DIAD to formulate several diverse physical implementation alternatives. A wide selection of possible implementation alternatives can easily be envisioned, since the DFD is free of physical assumptions.

The DFD aids visually but does not define the criteria for narrowing down and evaluating this wide selection of alternatives to a few varying investments in time and money. However, the logical DFD helps communicate alternatives to users and management.

COST/BENEFIT ANALYSIS: Gane and Sarson's tools and techniques indirectly support cost/benefit analysis. First, the logical DFD can aid visually during analysis of alternatives. Second, the precision and clarity of the logical functional specifications should contribute to the accuracy of this activity.

GENERAL EVALUATION: Gane and Sarson's structured systems analysis offers a definite improvement over traditional methods of systems analysis.

The logic model promotes a clearer understanding, among the user, the analyst/programmer, and the designer, of what the system does, or will do, than has been traditionally been achieved. The graphic nature of the logical model furnishes the analyst/programmer a visual aid for use during conferences with the user, designers, or managers. The detail recorded in the data dictionary and *tight* English is precise and thus reduces the number of ambiguities traditionally encountered.

The DIAD is not readily apparent to someone unfamiliar with its use. Also, it seems reasonable that the DIAD requirements would be more clearly understood if the data stores have been previously simplified (i.e., "normalized"). No criteria are given for determining at what point processes on the DFDs should no longer be exploded. Also, there is little guidance on how much detail should be recorded.

Warnier-Orr

OVERVIEW: The Warnier-Orr method is a combination of tools and procedures that develop detailed information, especially system outputs, according to the model shown in Figure 2.14.

Developing a new system creates version 1; each enhancement creates a new version. Each version completes four stages:

- *Initiation*—request and set priorities for a system's versions.
- *Development*—create a fully tested and installed system version.
- *Operation*—create and use the version's data.
- *Evaluation and Audit*—monitor and evaluate the version's operation.

The *development stage* is subdivided into five phases:

- Planning and problem analysis.
- Requirements definition.

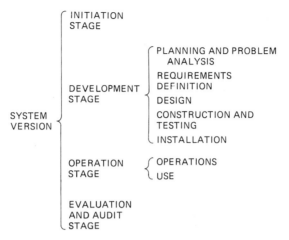

Figure 2.14. Elements of the system model used in the Warnier-Orr method.

- Design.
- Construction and testing.
- Installation.

The first two phases within Warnier-Orr's development process pertain to analysis, which begins with the *needed system* and ends with the *defined system*, as illustrated in the Warnier-Orr model of the version's life cycle shown in Figure 2.15.

Warnier-Orr uses three analysis tools: (1) Warnier-Orr diagrams, (2) entity diagrams, and (3) problem matrices.

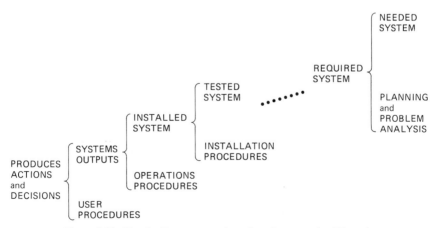

Figure 2.15. Warnier-Orr representation of a software version life cycle.

A *Warnier-Orr diagram* graphically represents hierarchy, sequence, alternation, repetition and concurrence. The levels of the hierarchy are represented from left to right. (Figure 2-16). Subordinate levels are placed to the right of superior levels. Braces separate levels. Sequence flows from top to bottom within the same brace. Alternation is the selection of exactly one alternative, A or not A (Figure 2.17). A plus sign within a circle represents an "exclusive OR." A (0, 1) indicates that the alternative occurs zero or one times. Repetition is indicated by (1, N) to the left of the brace enclosing the body of the loop. (Figure 2.18). Concurrence (i.e., two events occurring at the same time) is shown with the plus sign (+) (Figure 2.19).

Entity diagrams are used to define data flowing into or out of an organization or entity (Figure 2.20). Only two symbols are used for entity diagrams:

1. A circle which represents an entity (an organization or an individual).
2. An arrow which indicates data flow or a line of communication.

The third tool, *problem matrices*, (Figure 2.21) helps the analyst/programmer organize, document, and present

Symptom(s)	Cause(s)
Problem(s)	Solution(s)
Should be (objective)	Benefit(s)
Actually is	Risk(s)

PROBLEM DEFINITION: Warnier-Orr defines a problem as a difference between what is and what should be. The analyst/programmer uses three tools to define problems and establish project mission, purpose and scope: (1) Warnier-Orr diagrams. (2) Entity diagrams. (3) Problem matrices.

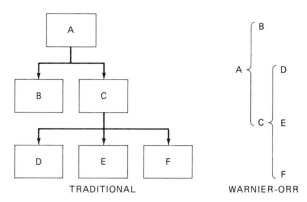

Figure 2.16. Representations of hierarchical relationships.

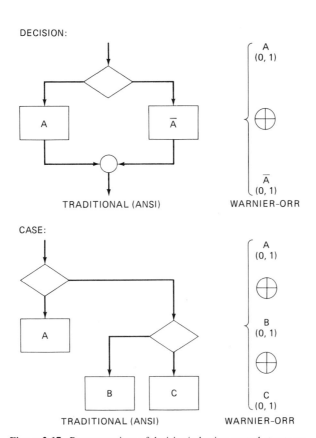

Figure 2.17. Representations of decision/selection control structures.

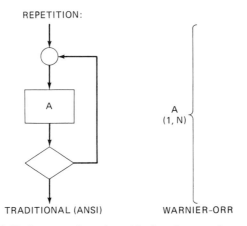

Figure 2.18. Representations of repetition/iteration control structures.

CONCURRENCE:

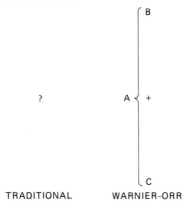

TRADITIONAL   WARNIER-ORR

Figure 2.19. Representations of concurrence.

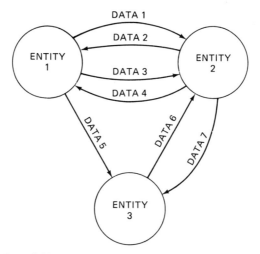

Figure 2.20. Data flow as represented in an entity diagram.

PROBLEM MATRIX

SYMPTOM	PROBLEM	SHOULD BE	ACTUALLY IS	CAUSE(S)	SOLUTION	BENEFITS	RISKS

Figure 2.21. The elements of a problem matrix.

This analysis method can handle the worst case: that is, when the user does not know the problem and the analyst/programmer is unfamiliar with the user's organization. An explicit assumption is that the initial problem defined by the user may be a symptom, not a problem.

The analyst/programmer must interview various individuals in the subject organization, draw entity diagrams to define data flow, draw Warnier-Orr diagrams to define organizations and tasks, complete a problem matrix, and verify the accuracy of these documents with the users (Figure 2.22).

Statements of symptoms are collected through an interviewing process. Immediate solutions based on the symptoms are discouraged. Little or no attempt is made to talk in terms of general project functions in the *planning and problem analysis* phase. A thorough analysis of the existing organizational structure is encouraged.

Several documents are used to model the findings from this phase. The organization is defined by drawing a Warnier-Orr diagram (Figure 2-23).

Data flows are documented by drawing an entity diagram for each interviewee, and then consolidating all the entity diagrams onto one large entity diagram (Figure 2.24).

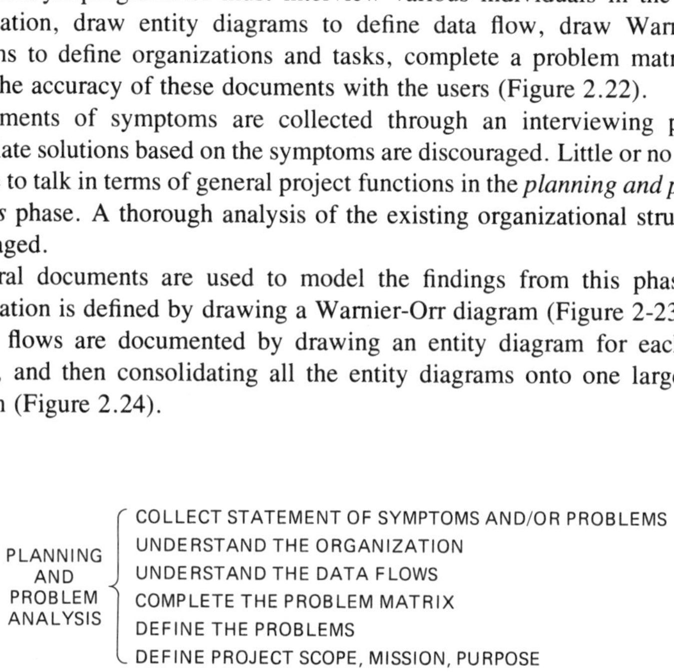

Figure 2.22. Warnier-Orr representation of the elements of planning and problem analysis.

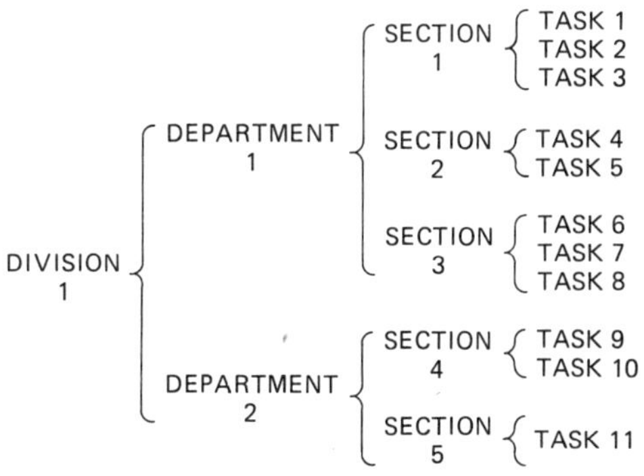

Figure 2.23. Organization definition used during the planning and problem analysis phase.

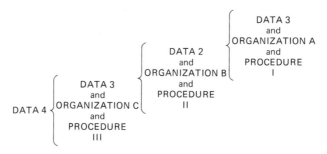

Figure 2.24. Hierarchical representation of data flow.

Hierarchy Input/Process/Output (HIPO)

OVERVIEW: HIPO expresses the subject in terms of a hierarchy of processes, (Figure 2.25) which are represented in a chart similar to a corporate organizational chart. These processes are logically divided into more and more detail as one reads from the top of the chart to the bottom. IPO graphically describes the processes which convert input into output.

PROBLEM DEFINITION: HIPO merely states the logical hierarchy as observed, with no specific rules or tricks for this activity. HIPO asks for a great deal of detail; therefore, it is quite thorough. The only real rule-of-thumb is the overriding admonition to state *what*, not *how*.

Complexity is reduced by HIPO by way of logically dividing the problem into functions, and subsequently breaking the functions into subfunctions.

The graphics of HIPO are in two parts:

- A tree of lines and boxes resembling an organization chart. (HIPO)
- A detail chart divided into thirds for input, processes, and outputs. (IPO)

The graphics well support the results of analysis but do not necessarily guarantee a single correct approach. They are quite flexible; modification, however, can become extensive due to the amount of detail that may be present. There are no alternative forms or views provided and no choice is offered by the specific rules.

The tool offers a fairly good communications medium but may require rewriting if presented to different audiences; it does allow a high level of detail or merely an overview if desired. It can be the medium for all activities—user manuals and all.

REQUIREMENTS DEFINITION: The HIPO method fits better with a ''functional decomposition'' method than with a data structure method; in fact, it tempo-

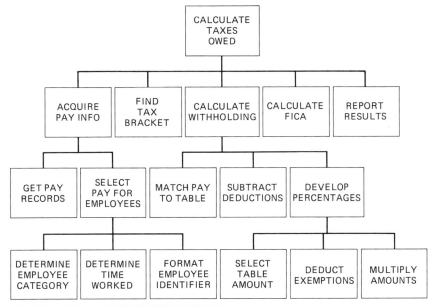

(A) HIERARCHICAL DECOMPOSITION OF TASKS

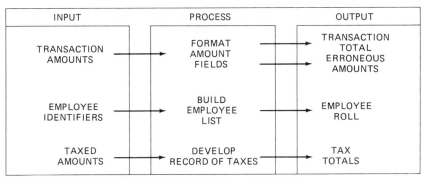

(B) INPUT/PROCESS/OUTPUT (IPO) ANALYSIS

Figure 2.25. Example of HIPO/IPO.

rarily hides data structures until appropriate. The following are some notes and cautions:

- Complexity is reduced by dealing with one function at a time, postponing detailed resolution until appropriate.
- HIPO does seem to facilitate isolating changes, although major policy changes may cause extensive HIPO changes.

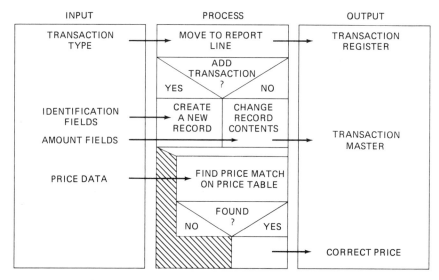

Figure 2.26. Example of detailed process definition in the IPO.

- HIPO does facilitate documentation, but not if done after the fact of specification.
- HIPO aids in understanding the subject. It shows the hierarchical division of thinking used in the method. The designer can use it as a working paper.

The graphics form the structure and interrelationships while text provides the details.

Figure 2.26 illustrates how the processes described in an IPO chart (Figure 2.25(B)) can be logically and functionally defined using a graphical flowcharting technique such as Nassi-Shneiderman charts.

IMPLEMENTATION ALTERNATIVES: Alternatives are provided only if the analyst/programmer produces alternate HIPO packages—a significant task if done in detail. The only suggestions for comparing HIPO solutions is to look for omissions, incorrect repetition, too little or too much decomposition at each level, or failure to ''parse'' at all.

COST/BENEFIT ANALYSIS: The overview charts could be used to show, function by function, the cost savings resulting on each.

GENERAL EVALUATION: The hierarchy diagram and the decomposition idea stand out as very useful and worthwhile tools. However, to do a correct HIPO is not an intuitively obvious operation in every situation.

RESTRUCTURING UNSTRUCTURED PROGRAMS/ALGORITHMS

Although not always recognized as such, an important design decision involves the reuse, redesign or rewriting of existing software. The opportunities to reduce system cost and fault rate that exist with existing software must be recognized as part of the design activity.

The evolution of programming languages and current programming philosophies very closely impact the reuse of existing software. Rewriting existing programs in a new language should involve using the new language to the fullest of its capabilities—not just converting from one syntax to another. Design features such as information hiding and data abstraction should be considered.

One of the most fundamental rewriting efforts involves the conversion of software written in an "unstructured" language such as BASIC or FORTRAN IV into a "structured" language such as Pascal, Ada, or FORTRAN 77.

Three techniques for restructuring unstructured programs or algorithms are discussed in this section. Each uses the premature exiting of a loop as an example of an unstructured control sequence.

Duplication of Code

CONCEPT: To define a technique for restructuring an algorithm or program that violates the "single-entry, single-exit" philosophy involves a minimal use of repetition.

PROCESS: Duplication of code is, perhaps, the most brutally forceful of the restructuring techniques. The process, which is simple, consists of

- Identifying those program modules or processes which violate *single-entry, single-exit*.
- Replacing each of these modules or processes with sufficient copies of itself so that each copy has a single entry and single exit.
- Insuring that the modified form contains the same logical sequences as the original form.

The premature exiting of a loop is an *unstructured* process as demonstrated in the flowchart in Figure 2.27. This loop is defined as being unstructured in that it cannot be readily reduced, without modification, into some form of the fundamental iteration structures while-do or repeat-until. It is, in fact, the first of the non-one-in, one-out generalizations of these structures described by Bohm and Jacopini.[8]

In that fundamental structures are not involved, the process represented by block A in Figure 2.27 has two distinct entry points (from the preceding struc-

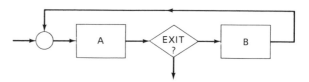

Figure 2.27. Traditional representation of premature exiting of a loop.

ture and from the process described by block B). The flowchart in Figure 2.28 demonstrates how this process can be restructured using the duplication-of-code technique.

Duplication of block A allows the redefinition of this process in terms of a sequence structure followed by a While-Do structure. Duplicates of A occur as the sequence process and in the repetition process. The placement of A within the While-Do is critical in order to maintain the same logical flow represented in the unstructured definition (Figure 2.27).

The duplication of code technique generally will not work extremely well for programs or algorithms that are heavily loop-oriented (i.e., contain complex structures of nested loops). Under such circumstances, duplication of code can become quite cumbersome and other techniques for restructuring such programs and algorithms should be explored. Duplication of code is especially well-suited for programs and algorithms containing network or lattice structures (i.e., with a major emphasis on branching and alternative paths).

There is an obvious disadvantage to the technique of duplicating code in that it artificially increases program size (the number of program statements) thereby leading to greater program memory requirements. However, in many cases, the code duplicated consists of a small number of statements and code duplication may be viewed as a worthwhile design trade-off. For larger segments of duplicated code, this process results in a natural modularization of a program or algorithm. Such modules can then be implemented as "callable" subprograms rather than being duplicated in-line.

State Variable Approach

CONCEPT: To define a technique for restructuring an unstructured algorithm or program that can contain any use of selection and repetition processes.

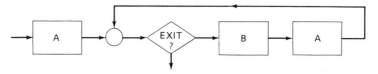

Figure 2.28. Premature loop exiting as a structural process using duplication of code.

PROCESS: Another technique for structured conversion has been suggested in a paper by Ashcroft and Manna.[9] This technique attempts to define the *process states* of a program and insure that the program flow has access to each of these states. Flow control through these states is accomplished using a *state variable*.

The state variable approach is an algorithmic process that may be applied to any unstructured flowchart or algorithm.

1. Each block of the unstructured flowchart is assigned an integer label; this label represents the "state" of the flowchart at that block during processing. The value of these labels (or states) is completely arbitrary, although the usual convention is to assign the label 1 to the first executable operation and the successive integers to successive operations. The label 0 is then assigned to the last executable operation. An example of this labelling is shown in Figure 2.29.
2. A new variable is introduced into the flowchart. The purpose of this "state variable" is to record the state of the process (as indicated by the process

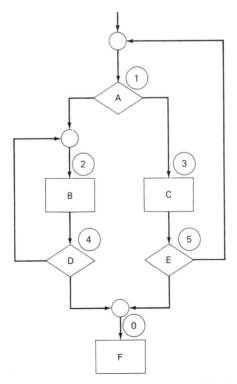

Figure 2.29. Process labelling of an unstructured flowchart.

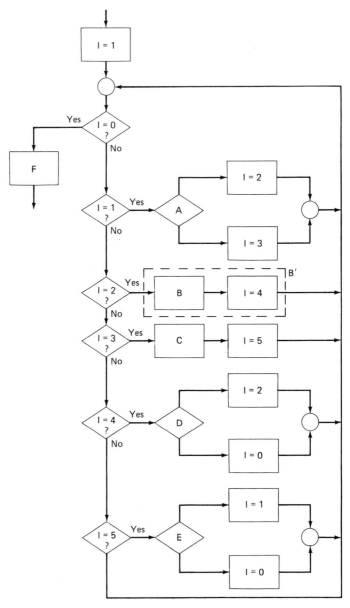

Figure 2.30. Restructuring using the state variable approach.

labels) at any point during processing. The name of this variable is arbitrary, but in this example "I" will be used.

3. The process blocks in the unstructured flowchart are replaced by new process blocks that perform the same operation but also assign to the state variable the label value of the *succeeding* operation (i.e., next state). Thus, process B in Figure 2.30 apparently branches in all cases to process D. A new process B′ is now defined. This process is identical to that of B except that it contains an additional step of assigning the state variable the value 4 (I = 4), the value of the label of process D.

4. The decision blocks in the unstructured flowchart are converted in a similar fashion. The processes following the alternative conditions are replaced by processes that assign to the state variable the label values of the alternative process in the unstructured flowchart. Figure 2.30 illustrates how each process of the original unstructured flowchart is amended to contain state information.

5. The entire flowchart is driven by values of the state variable. If this variable is allowed to step through all process label values, then it can be seen that the logical sequence of the original flowchart is unchanged. The resulting "structured" flowchart is always equivalent to a case logical structure within a while-do loop.

EXAMPLE: In this manner the premature exiting of a loop may be restructured as shown in Figure 2.31.

Boolean Flag Technique

CONCEPT: To define a technique for converting a loop-oriented program or algorithm into a structured form.

PROCESS: Restructuring with this technique is accomplished by means of a variable flag within the program to be restructured. This variable may be introduced solely for this technique or it may be present in the program already. This flag is initialized at some point prior to the loop. A while-do or repeat-until structure is then used to control the execution of the loop until the flag is reset appropriately.

Finally, some conditions *inside* the loop determine when the flag should be set. Figure 2.32 shows the correction of the premature loop exit problem, accomplished by introducing a new flag into the loop as part of the redesign process.

It is not always necessary to add a flag to a program in order to restructure it. The flowchart in Figure 2.33 illustrates how the example in Figure 2.32 can

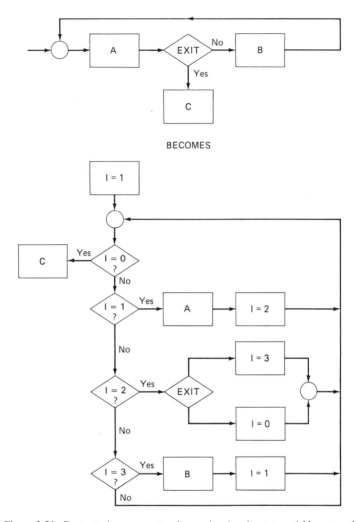

Figure 2.31. Restructuring a premature loop exit using the state variable approach.

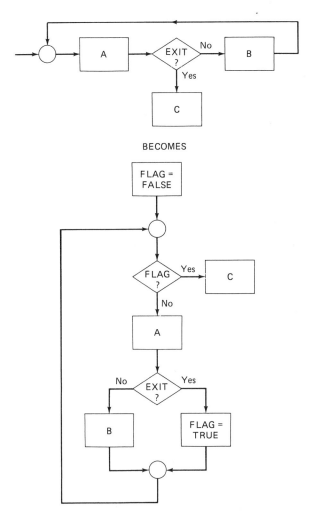

Figure 2.32. Restructuring a premature loop exit using the Boolean flag technique.

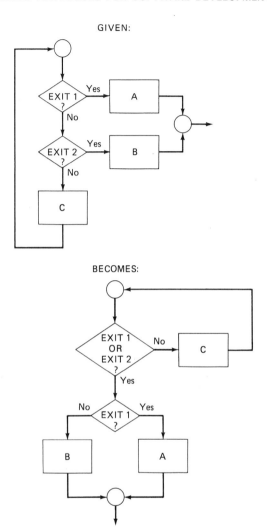

Figure 2.33. Restructuring with Boolean expression reorganization.

be "structured" by rewriting the predicates of the decision blocks. This solution appears to be much cleaner and more elegant than the other solution. However, if the loop were to contain several different exits instead of just the two, this approach could become quite clumsy.

STRUCTURED TECHNIQUES IN UNSTRUCTURED LANGUAGES

Many proponents of structured programming have argued that it is not possible in unstructured languages like FORTRAN IV and BASIC to accomplish the systematic development of algorithms in a proper manner. A counter-opinion is that structured programming, while concerned with control structures, is primarily concerned with the design process. Therefore, algorithm design should, in fact, be language-independent, except, of course, for the final coding step.

It is quite likely that an unstructured language would not be the programming language of choice of a programmer/analyst involved with structured design. However, if the programmer is faced with the necessity of using an unstructured language, many of the benefits of the design may still be applicable.

Structured BASIC

CONCEPT: To establish a mechanism whereby the scheme of structured programming may be accomplished in an *unstructured programming language* (such as BASIC) so that the advantages of structured design such as readability and maintainability may be realized.

PROCESS: The six programming control structures identified with structured programming may be emulated using BASIC statement fragments. Such code fragments then may provide a template into which relevant program processes may be inserted. These templates would then provide to the BASIC programmer the utility and structure of the structured statements in a structured programming language.

The following BASIC statement fragments are representative of the six control structures. "aaa", "bbb", "ccc", etc. Represent BASIC program line numbers. Text following "→" are descriptors of the processes and would not appear in a program.

IF-THEN-ELSE

```
aaa IF ⟨Boolean Expression⟩ THEN bbb  → Entry Point
    . . . . .
    . . . . .  → Statements which comprise ELSE part
    . . . . .
    GOTO ddd→ Exit point from ELSE part
bbb . . . . .
    . . . . .  → Statements which comprise THEN part
ccc . . . . .→ Exit Point from THEN part
ddd . . . . .→ First Statement following exit
```

The order of the THEN and ELSE parts may be changed by negating the Boolean expression.

CASE

Simple CASE using COMPUTED GOTO:

```
aaa GOTO bbb,ccc,ddd,... ON ⟨expr⟩ → Entry Point
bbb. . . .→ First Statement of CASE 1     ,
    . . . .→ CASE 1 part
    GOTO xxx → Exit Point from CASE 1
ccc. . . .→ First Statement of CASE 2
    . . . . → CASE 2 part
    GOTO xxx → Exit Point from CASE 2
ddd. . . .→ First Statement of CASE 3
    . . . . → CASE 3 part
    GOTO xxx → Exit Point from CASE 3
    . . . . → other CASE parts
xxx. . . .→ First Statement after CASE exit
```

CASE as series of IF-THEN-ELSEs:

```
aaa IF ⟨Case 1 Test⟩ THEN bbb → Entry Point

    . . . .
    . . . . → CASE 1 part
    GOTO xxx→ Exit Point from Case 1
bbb IF ⟨Case 2 Test⟩ THEN ccc

    . . . .
    . . . . → CASE 2 part
    GOTO xxx→ Exit Point from Case 2
ccc IF ⟨Case 3 Test⟩ THEN ccc

    . . . .
    . . . .→ CASE 3 part
    GOTO xxx→ Exit Point from Case 3
    . . . .→ Other CASE parts and tests
xxx. . . .→ First Statement following CASE exit
```

DO WHILE

```
aaa IF ⟨While Test⟩ THEN xxx→ Entry Point

    . . . .
    . . . . → Statements which comprise Do part
    . . . .
    GOTO aaa
xxx. . . . → First Statement following DO WHILE exit
```

DO UNTIL

```
aaa. . . .→ Entry Point
    . . . .→ Statements which comprise Do part

    . . . .
    IF ⟨Until Test⟩ THEN aaa
xxx. . . .→ First statement following DO UNTIL exit
```

EXAMPLE: The following BASIC program demonstrates the structured coding of an algorithm to convert some number of days into its equivalent form of weeks and days:

```
10 INPUT D
20 W = 0
30 IF D < 7 THEN 70
40    D = D - 7
50    W = W + 1
60 IF D >= 7 THEN 40
70 PRINT W,D
80 STOP
90 END
```

Statements 40–60 represent the *Else part* of the If-Then-Else structure defined in Statement 30. Statements 40–60 also represent an implementation of a Repeat-Until in BASIC.

SUMMARY: THE GOALS OF SOFTWARE PROJECT METHODOLOGIES

Each of the software design methodologies discussed in this chapter have as a goal the top-down design and modular refinement of software in such a way as to provide programmers and system designers with a disciplined approach towards defining and refining program specifications.

Simply stated, such approaches allow programmers to "*. . . .identify the major functions to be accomplished and then. . . . .proceed from there to an identification of the lesser functions that derive from the major ones.*"[10]

This identification process means that the problem to be solved is subdivided into a series of smaller and easier-to-handle processing steps (program modules). By isolating and defining the processing steps required, the programmer or system designer is confined to establishing *what* processing has to be done, not *how* it is done. The programmer or system designer is, in fact, creating *abstractions* of processes. The details of these processes may encompass an infinite variety of applications utilizing techniques such as those described in later chapters of this book.

BIBLIOGRAPHY

Agarwal, K. K., *Programming with Structured Flowcharts*. New York, Petrocelli, 1984. Comprehensive description on use of Nassi-Shneiderman flowcharts.

Ashcroft, E., and Manna, Z., "The Translation of GOTO Programs to WHILE Programs," *Information Processing 71*, 1, 250–255. Amsterdam, North-Holland, 1972.

Dahl, O. J., Dijkstra, E. W., and Hoare, C. A. R., *Structured Programming*. New York, Academic Press, 1972.

DeMarco, Tom, *Structured Analysis and System Specification*. New York, Yourdon Press, 1985.

Gane, Chris, and Sarson, Trish, *Structured Systems Analysis: Tools and Techniques*. New York, Improved System Technology, 1977.

Higgins, David, *Program Design and Construction*. Englewood Cliffs, NJ, Prentice-Hall, 1979. This reference discusses the Warnier-Orr technique in detail.

Hughes, J. K., and Michtom, J. I., *A Structured Approach to Programming*. Englewood Cliffs, NJ, Prentice-Hall, 1977.

IBM, *HIPO—A Design Aid and Documentation Technique*. IBM Manual GC20-1851.

McGowan, C. L., and Kelly, J. R., *Top-down Structured Programming Techniques*. New York, Van Nostrand Reinhold, 1975.

Linger, R. C., Mills, H. D., and Witt, B. I., *Structured Programming Theory and Practice*. Reading, MA, Addison-Wesley, 1979.

Myers, Glenford J., *Composite/Structured Design*. New York, Van Nostrand Reinhold, 1978.

Orr, Ken, *"Structured Requirements Definition,"* Topeka, Kansas, ORR, 1981.

Page-Jones, Meilir, *The Practical Guide to Structured Systems Design*. New York, Yourdon Press, 1980.

Softech, *An Introduction to SADT Structured Analysis and Design Technique*.

Ward, Paul T. and Mellor, Stephen J. *Structured Development for Real-time Systems*. 3 volumes, N.Y., Yourdon Press, 1985.

Weinberg, Victor, *Structured Analysis*. New York, Yourdon Press, 1978.

Yourdon, Edward, *Techniques of Program Structure and Design*. Englewood Cliffs, NJ, Prentice-Hall, 1975.

NOTES

[1]Nassi, I. and B. Schneiderman, "Flowcharting Techniques for Structured Programming, *ACM SIGPLAN Notices, 8,* 8, 12–26 (1973).

[2]Chapin, N., "New Format for Flowcharts, *"Software: Practice and Experience, 4,* 341–357, (1974).

[3]Lew, Art, *Decision Tables for General-purpose Scientific Programming. Software-Practice and Experience*, Vol. 13, pp. 181–188 (1983).

[4]McMullen, W. L., Jr., *"Structured Decision Tables," SIGPLAN Notices, 19,* 4 (April 1984).

[5]DeMarco, Tom, *Structured Analysis and System Specification*. New York: Yourdon Press, 1985.

[6]Weinberg, Victor, *Structured Analysis*. New York: Yourdon Press, 1978.

[7]Gane, Chris and Sarson, Trish, *Structured Systems Analysis:* Tools and Techniques. New York, Improved System Technology, 1977.

[8]Bohm, C., and Jacopini, G. "Flow Diagrams, Turing machines and languages with Only Two Formation Rules." *Comm. ACM 9,* 5 366–371, May 1966.

[9]Ashcroft, E. and Manna, Z., "The Translation of GOTO programs to WHILE Programs," *Information Processing 71,* 1, 250–255. Amsterdam: North-Holland, 1972.

[10]Yourdon, E. *Techniques of Program Structure and Design*. Englewood Cliffs, NJ, 1975, p. 38.

3
ORGANIZATION OF DATA

*"Finding the deep simplicities in a complicated collection of things
to be done is the creativity in programming."*

Harlan Mills

If the task of computer programs is to manipulate data, then the goal of the study of data structures is to make that task easier. Organization of the data to be operated upon by a program is often as important as the choice of algorithm used in the program. In many cases, data organization drives software development—especially when a body of data exists prior to the program which uses it. As Pascal inventor and computer science theorist Niklaus Wirth has said, ". . .one has an intuitive feeling that data precede algorithms: You must have some objects before you can perform operations upon them."[1]

The study of data structures thus yields a firm conceptual grasp of the structural relationships within data and the techniques available for representing and manipulating such structures in a computer. Specifically, important to the understanding of data structures are the definitions of the static and dynamic properties of different data structure types and the methods for data allocation and representation within those types. Once a software designer understands these factors, it is easier for him or her to make sense of algorithms—the means programmers use to deal with data structures.

The role of data structures in the programming discipline then becomes a critical part of a two-step procedure:

1. Establishing and/or understanding the relationships (structure) of the *problem*—the algorithm; establish and understand the relationships (structure) of the *data* necessary to a satisfactory solution to the problem.
2. Assembling the units of information (i.e., data) in the computer's memory in the most efficient way for access and retrieval. "Some data structures exist, others must be invented."[*]

This chapter deals with the organizational idea that makes programming easier by making the details of a program directly analogous to the details of the

*Ibid, note 1.

problem to be solved. The idea is to recognize some of the structure (relationships between subparts) of a problem and then assemble units of information in the computer memory into that structure.

Stafford Beer[2] says that a pattern is a pattern because someone declares a concatenation of items to be meaningful or cohesive. He continues by saying that a viable system is something we detect and understand and that our brains themselves impose a structure on reality.

Similarly, a data structure is essentially a *spatial* or *patterned* concept. The relationships between the elements of a structure can be ultimately reduced to and explained by a map of how that information is organized in the computer's memory.

Data structures are typically divided into two categories: the *static* structures and the *dynamic* structures. Static structures are defined as having a fixed size and shape. Interpretation as to the meaning and applicability of these attributes usually lies within the mind of the programmer. All use of these structures must be accomplished within these fixed attributes. On the other hand, dynamic structures can vary in size and/or shape. In fact, it is often difficult to assign these attributes at all.

Static structures usually represent structured data types within a particular programming language definition. Examples of static structures are arrays, sets, records, and files. Dynamic structures are usually built from programming language primitives or emulated using static data structures.

GLOSSARY OF TERMS

Array: A collection of variables, each having a separate value just like scalar variables, but with *all the variables of the collection sharing a common identifier*. A *subscript* is added to this common identifier to produce a unique name for each individual element (value) of the collection.

Column Major Form: The representation of a two-dimensional array as a one-dimensional array with mapping based on the second-array parameter (i.e., column); as such, an array with m rows and n columns is mapped into a vector with $m \times n$ elements. This vector may be logically divided into n sections, each section containing m elements and representing one column.

Data Attribute: A characteristic of a unit of data such as data type, length, and so forth.

Database: A collection of shareable data.

Dequeue: To remove items from a queue.

Dimension: An actual or notational axis of storage locations in an array.

Dynamic Allocation: To allocate system resources (e.g., storage) to meet the changing needs of a program during execution.

Element: A single member of a data structure; *syn.*: node.

FIFO: A queueing technique in which the next item to be retrieved is the item which has been in the queue for the longest period of time; first-in-first-out. *Syn.*: push-up storage.

File: A set of related records treated as a unit.

File Attribute: An item that identifies a file.

Heap: A vector with a well-defined relationship between elements such that it may be used to emulate a binary tree.

Hierarchical Database: A collection of data (usually tables) that must be scanned in a predetermined order to retrieve information.

LIFO: A queueing technique in which the next item to be retrieved is the item most recently placed in the queue; last-in-first-out. *Syn.*: push-down storage.

List: An ordered set of data items; *syn.*: string, one-dimensional array, vector.

Map: To establish a one-to-one relationship between the entities of different data sets.

Multiple Precision Format: A scalar numeric value represented as a vector in which each element contains a single digit of the represented value. For example, if a positive, base-10 integer value X is represented in multiple precision format using vector Y, then

$$X = \sum_{i=1}^{i} Y_i 10^{i-1}$$

where $i \geq$ the number of digits in X.

Node: A single member of a data structure; *syn.*: element.

Pop: To remove an item from the top of a push-down stack.

Push: To add an item to the top of a stack.

Queue: An inherently first-in-first-out (FIFO) data structure containing two or more items awaiting service or attention. *Syn.*: double-ended queue.

Relational Data-base: A collection of data in which each entry is composed of a list of connected (or related) items; any subset of the items in the entire list can readily be retrieved.

Row Major Form: The representation of a two-dimensional array as a one-dimensional array with mapping based on the first array parameter (i.e., row); As such, an array with m row and n columns is mapped into a vector with $m \times n$ elements. This vector may be logically divided into m sections, each section containing n elements and representing one row.

Sparse Array: An array with size greater than initially required, thereby containing many ''empty'' elements.

Stack: A data structure in which data items can be added or removed at one end only (LIFO).

Stack Pointer: The address of the storage location holding the item of data most recently stored in push-down storage.

Table: An array of data, each item of which may be unambiguously identified by means of one or more arguments, labels, and so forth.

Tree: A term applied to a hierarchical data structure.

Unpack: To recover the original form of the data from packed data.

Vector: Generalized term for a one-dimensional array.

STATIC DATA STRUCTURES

The common three characteristics of static data structures are:

1. Elements are directly addressable according to a scheme characteristic of the data structure
2. The data structure is fixed in size—elements may not be added or deleted
3. Element values are stored in nondynamic memory, usually sequentially.

ODD-SHAPED ARRAYS

Most, if not all, high-level programming languages offer an array data structure. In many cases, it is the only facility for structured data that is available. This section will discuss the many ways of using arrays. It will also attempt to dispel the notion that arrays are suitable only for collections of data formatted as lists or tables.

The concept of a multidimensional array is a data abstraction of convenience to the programmer. Such arrays must ultimately be transformed into one-dimensional arrays (vectors) in order to accommodate the sequential form of computer storage. An example of this transformation, performed by the compiler, can be visualized as follows for the declaration of a two-dimensional array:

1 A two-dimensional array, $A(M,N)$ contains $M \times N$ elements and is therefore equivalent in storage capacity to a one-dimensional array, $B(M \times N)$;
2. Logically, the internal structure of B can be viewed as consisting of N sections, each section having M elements. Therefore, each of these logical sections represents a column of the two-dimensional model.
3. The location of element $A(I, J)$ is equivalent to the "Ith" element of the "Jth" section of B or:

$$A(I, J) = B\big(M \times (J - 1) + I\big)$$

This transformation for two-dimensional arrays is referred to as storage (or organization) in *column major form*. A comparable process could be described which performs the transformation in row major form.

These transformation functions are based on the logical model of a two-dimensional array as represented by a table with a constant number of rows and columns. However, the definition of specialized transformation functions allows the definition of two-dimensional (or greater) arrays that conform to other logical models. These models provide the basis for *odd-shaped arrays* (for example, Figures 3.1 through 3.6).

Right Triangular Array

CONCEPT: To accurately and efficiently represent operations between data elements whose logical relationship resembles the physical configuration of a right triangle

PROCESS: Figure 3.1 illustrates 10 data elements whose logical relationship is described by a 4 × 4 right triangular array. The transformation function for this array is the summation function of positive integers from 1 to k:

$$\sum_{i=1}^{k} i = \frac{k(k+1)}{2}$$

Each row of a right triangular array has one more element than the previous row. Therefore, the total number of elements up to and included in a particular row is equal to the sum of the positive integers to that row number.

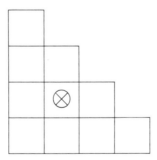

Figure 3-1. Mileages between selected European Cities.

This transformation function maps the array of Figure 3.1 into the vector shown in Figure 3.2. A particular element of this vector is identified by the number of complete rows which precede it plus its column location within the incomplete row which contains it.

Therefore, $A_{i,j} = B_k$ where

$$k = \frac{(i-1)(i-1+1)}{2} + j = \frac{i(i-1)}{2} + j$$

Figure 3-2. Vector-mapped from a 4 × 4 right triangular array.

Therefore, the element of Figure 3.1 containing the $\otimes$, $A_{3,2}$ is equivalent to B_5 of Figure 3.2 since

$$\frac{3 \times 2}{2} + 2 = \frac{6}{2} + 2 = 3 + 2 = 5$$

APPLICATION: To represent relationships between two parameters that are symmetric, i.e., $A_{i,j} = A_{j,i}$ while avoiding the use of a two-dimensional tabular array containing $i \times j$ elements.

The right triangular array reduces the number of elements required by 50%.

RESTRICTIONS: The transformation function requires the two independent parameters i and j have the following relationship:

$$i \geq j$$

Since the array they represent is symmetric, this presents no difficulty.

SAMPLE APPLICATION: The following chart (Figure 3.3) provides mileage information between selected European cities:

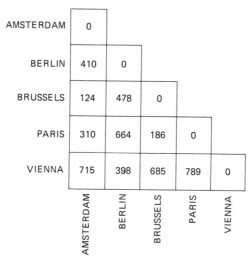

Figure 3-3. Vector-mapped from a 5 × 5 right triangular array.

The relationship between this data is clearly that of a right triangular array. To use a 5 × 5 array data structure in this case would clearly include redundant data entries.

The following BASIC program illustrates how data within this structure may be accessed as a right triangular array:

```
10 PRINT 'THIS PROGRAM PROVIDES MILEAGE BETWEEN EUROPEAN CITIES'
20 PRINT 'INTEGER CODES REPRESENT THE FOLLOWING CITIES'
30 PRINT '1 - AMSTERDAM'
40 PRINT '2 - BERLIN'
50 PRINT '3 - BRUSSELS'
60 PRINT '4 - PARIS'
70 PRINT '5 - VIENNA'
80 DIM M(15)
90 MAT READ M
100 PRINT 'INPUT INTEGER CODES FOR THE INTER-CITY MILEAGE REQUIRED'
110 INPUT M1, M2
120 IF M1 >= M2 THEN 160
130 T = M1
140 M1 = M2
150 M2 = T
160 M3 = M1*(M1-1)/2 + M2
170 PRINT 'INTERCITY MILEAGE IS ';M(M3)
180 DATA 0,0,410,0,124,478,0,310,664,186,0,715,398,685,789,0
190 STOP
200 END
```

Isosceles Triangular Array

CONCEPT: To accurately and efficiently represent operations between data elements having a relationship resembling the physical configuration of an isosceles triangle.

PROCESS: Figure 3.4 illustrates 16 data elements whose logical relationship is described by a 4 × 7 isosceles triangular array.

The transformation function for this array is the summation function of first k positive odd integers.

$$\sum_{i=1}^{k} (2i - 1) = k^2$$

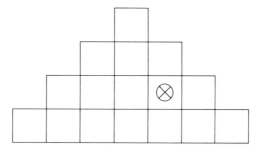

Figure 3-4. A 4 × 7 isoceles triangular array.

The first row of an isosceles triangular array has one element. Each subsequent row has two more elements than the previous row. Therefore, the total number of elements up to and included in a particular row is equal to the sum of the positive, odd integers to that row number.

This transformation function maps the array of Figure 3.4 into the vector shown in Figure 3.5. A particular element of this vector is identified by the number of complete rows that precede it plus its column location within the incomplete row that contains it.

Figure 3-5. Vector-mapped from a 7 × 4 isoceles triangular array.

Therefore, $A_{i,j} = B_k$ where

$$k = (i - 1)^2 + j$$

Therefore, the element of Figure 3.3 containing the $\otimes$, $A_{3,4}$ is equivalent to B_8 of Figure 3.4 since

$$(3 - 1)^2 + 4 = 2^2 + 4 = 4 + 4 = 8$$

RESTRICTIONS: The transformation function requires the two independent parameters i and j have the following relationship:

$$j \leq 2 \times i - 1$$

SAMPLE APPLICATION: The BASIC program shown in Figure 3.6 demonstrates the access of data whose relationship is as follows:

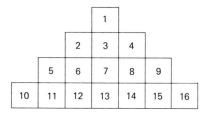

Figure 3-6. Data arranged as an isoceles triangular array.

```
10 PRINT 'THIS PROGRAM DEMONSTRATES THE ACCESS OF DATA'
20 PRINT 'REPRESENTED AS AN ISOSCELES TRIANGULAR ARRAY'
30 DIM I(16)
40 MAT READ I
50 PRINT 'INPUT THE ROW AND COLUMN OF THE DATA ELEMENT DESIRED'
60 INPUT R, C
70 IF C > (2*R - 1) THEN 110
80 M = (R-1)**2 + C
90 PRINT 'DATA VALUE IS ';I(M)
100 DATA 1,2,3,4,5,6,7,8,9,10,11,12,13,14,15,16
110 STOP
120 END
```

MULTIPLE PRECISION ARITHMETIC USING VECTORS

Every so often the news media will pick up a story that describes a new discovery in numerical analysis made with the assistance of computers. These discoveries usually involve the determination of very large (thousands of digits), exotic numbers (e.g., Mersenne primes). Such stories tend to reinforce in the public mind the impact that computers have on the advancement of sciences such as mathematics.

In one sense, these stories actually emphasize the limitations of computers, for the discovery of such values may occur more frequently were it not for the limits on numerical representation present on all systems.

The range of numerical values (size) that can easily be manipulated by a computer system depends upon that system's architecture. The word length characteristic of a system determines the maximum number of digits allowable in an integer value and the number of significant digits (accuracy) in a real (decimal) value. These numbers can be small compared to the range of values or the types of calculations desired.

Discoveries in numerical analysis are an extreme case of this numerical limitation. A more familiar application may involve calculations of large sums of money such as may be done by banks. These sums may easily exceed the number of significant digits allowable in a fixed decimal format and floating point format, thereby involving a loss of accuracy, *not a desirable factor in banking transactions!*

Multiple precision arithmetic is a technique that allows accurate calculations involving large numbers. This technique is accomplished by representing a value in *multiple precision format*, whereby each digit of a value is represented as an element of a vector. In this representation, the computer word length has no impact on the length of a number. The number of digits is only limited by the maximum allowable size of a vector (i.e., available memory).

However, by adapting numerical values in multiple precision format, the programmer loses the ability to perform the primitive numeric operations available to values *not* in that form. Therefore, the fundamental operations of addition, subtraction, multiplication and division must be emulated in order to accomplish calculations involving values in multiple precision format. The definition of multiple precision format is given in the Glossary of Terms at the beginning of this chapter.

Multiple Precision Addition

CONCEPT: To emulate the addition of integers represented in the multiple precision format, i.e., each digit contained within a vector array element;

GIVEN: A and B are vectors containing integer values in the multiple precision format. A and B each have k elements.

C is a vector to contain the sum of A and B in the multiple precision format. C has $k + 1$ elements in order to accommodate the maximum sum possible.

ALGORITHM:

1. Let i represent the index counter; it should be initialized to 1.
2. Assign C_i the value of $A_i + B_i$.
3. Increment i by 1 and repeat until $i > k$.
4. Reinitialize i to 1.
5. If $C_i \geq 10$, then subtract 10 from C_i and add 1 to C_{i+1}; this emulates the addition "carrying" process.
6. Increment i by 1 and repeat step 5 unless $i = k + 1$.
7. Stop.

Multiple Precision Subtraction

CONCEPT: To emulate the subtraction of integers represented in the multiple precision format, i.e., each digit contained within a vector array element;

GIVEN: A and B are vectors containing integer values in the multiple precision format. A and B each have k elements.

C is a vector to contain the difference of A and B in the multiple precision format. C has k elements in order to accommodate the maximum difference possible.

ALGORITHM:

1. Let i represent the index counter; it should be initialized to 1.
2. Assign C_i the value of $A_i - B_i$.
3. Increment i by 1 and repeat until $i > k$.
4. Reinitialize i to 1.
5. If $C_i < 0$, then add 10 to C_i and subtract 1 from C_{i+1}; this emulates the subtraction "borrowing" process.
6. Increment i by 1 and repeat step 5 unless $i = k$.
7. Stop.

Multiple Precision Multiplication

CONCEPT: To emulate the multiplication of integers represented in the multiple precision format, i.e., each digit contained within a vector array element;

GIVEN: A and B are vectors containing integer values in the multiple precision format. A and B each have k elements.

C is a vector to contain the product of A and B in the multiple precision format. C has $2 \times k$ elements in order to accommodate the maximum product possible.

The integer represented by A can be expressed by the following series expansion:

$$A = a_1 + 10a_2 + 100a_3 + \cdots + 10^{k-1}a_k = \sum_{m=1}^{k} 10^{m-1}a_m$$

Likewise the integer represented by B can be expressed as

$$B = \sum_{n=1}^{k} 10^{n-1} b_n$$

The product of A and B can also be represented in terms of these series:

$$A \times B = \sum_{m=1}^{k} 10^{m-1} a_m \times \sum_{n=1}^{k} 10^{n-1} b_n$$

$$A \times B = \sum_{m=1}^{k} \sum_{n=1}^{k} 10^{m+n-2} a_m b_n = C$$

ALGORITHM:

1. Let m represent an index counter; it should be initialized to 1.
2. Let n represent an index counter; it should be initialized to 1.
3. Increment the current value of C_{m+n-1} by $A_m \times B_n$.
4. Increment n by 1 and repeat Step 3 unless $n > k$.
5. Increment m by 1 and repeat Step 2 unless $m > k$.
6. Let i represent an index counter; it should be initialized to 1.
7. If $C_i \geq 10$, then increment C_{i+1} by the number of times C_i is divisible by 10; this emulates the multiplicative "carrying" process; Replace C_i by C_i modulo 10.
8. Increment i by 1 and repeat step 7 unless $i = 2 \times k$.
9. Stop.

Multiple Precision Division

CONCEPT: To emulate the division of integers represented in the multiple precision format, i.e., each digit contained within a vector array element;

GIVEN: A and B are vectors containing integer values in the multiple precision format. A and B each have k elements. C is a vector that contains the quotient of A and B in the multiple precision format.

Donald Knuth[3] describes a method of calculating the quotient of two power series, $U(z)$ and $V(z)$ where

$$U(z) = U_0 + U_1 z + U_2 z^2 + \cdots$$

$$V(z) = V_0 + V_1 z + V_2 z^2 + \cdots$$

the resultant power series, $W(z)$ is also of the form:

$$W(z) = U(z)/V(z) = W_0 + W_1 z + W_2 z^2 + \cdots$$

The coefficients of the $W(z)$ series can be calculated using the recurrence relation

$$W_n = (U_n - W_0 V_n - W_1 V_{n-1} - \cdots - W_{n-1} V_1)/V_0$$

when $V_0 \neq 0$.

Unfortunately, this relationship does not describe multiple precision division in the circumstance where $A = U(z)$, $B = V(z)$, $C = W(z)$ and $z = 10$. This is because the coefficients of W are unlikely to be integral (since they are the result of real divisions) and therefore would not conform to multiple precision format. Calculation of real coefficients would actually contribute to an error in each digit of the result.

It appears that the only *closed* solution is a rather *brute force* interpretation of the division process described by the following algorithm. Steps within this algorithm are implemented using the algorithms described for multiple precision addition and subtraction and are therefore less detailed in their description.

1. If the value represented by vector A is greater than or equal to the value represented by vector B, then subtract B from A using multiple precision subtraction. Assign vector A the result of this subtraction and increment the value represented by vector C; else go to step 3.
2. Repeat step 1.
3. Multiply the value represented by vector A by 10 by shifting the elements of A and assigning A_1 the value 0.
4. If the value represented by the vector A is greater than the value represented by the vector B, then go to step 1; else multiply the value represented by the vector C by 10 and go to step 3.

This process can be repeated until the desired accuracy (i.e., the length of vector C) is attained. In this process, the position of the decimal point in vector C is implied. Designation of the decimal point occurs at the first application of step 3 in the above algorithm.

Examples

The following are listings of four Pascal procedures that implement the algorithms described for multiple precision addition, subtraction, multiplication and division.

```
Type Vector = Array[1..10] of Integer;
     AddResult   = Array[1..11] of Integer;
     MultResult  = Array[1..20] of Integer;
```

$\star$ $\star$ $\star$

```
Procedure MultAdd(X,Y : Vector; Var Z : AddResult);
Var Index : 1..11;
Begin
  For Index := 1 to 10 do
   Z[Index] := X[Index] + Y[Index];
  For Index := 1 to 10 do
   If Z[Index] >= 10 then
      begin
        Z[Index] := Z[Index] - 10;
        Z[Index+1] := Z[Index+1] + 1
      end
End{MultAdd};


Procedure MultDif(X,Y : Vector; Var Z : AddResult);
Var Index : 1..11;
Begin
  For Index := 1 to 10 do
   Z[Index] := X[Index] - Y[Index];
  For Index := 1 to 10 do
   If Z[Index] < 0 then
      begin
        Z[Index] := Z[Index] + 10;
        Z[Index+1] := Z[Index+1] - 1
      end
End{MultDif};


Procedure MultMult(X,Y : Vector; Var Z : MultResult);
Var Index, M, N : 1..20;
Begin
  For M := 1 to 10 do
   For N := 1 to 10 do
    Z[M+N-1] := Z[M+N-1] + X[M]*Y[N];
  For Index := 1 to 19 do
   If Z[Index] >= 10 Then
                   Begin
                     Z[Index+1] := Z[Index+1] + Z[Index] DIV 10;
                     Z[Index] := Z[Index] MOD 10
                   End
End{MultMult};


Procedure MultDiv(X,Y : Vector; Var Z : AddResult);
 Var Unit, Copy : Vector;
     Q : AddResult;
     Index : Integer;
```

```
Function Compare(X,Y : Vector) : Boolean;
 Var Index : 0..11;
     Flag : Boolean;
 Begin {Compare}
   Index := 11;
   Flag := False;
   Repeat
     Index := Index - 1;
     If X[Index] > Y[Index] Then Flag := True
   Until (Index = 1) Or Flag;
   Compare := Flag
 End;{Compare}




Function Equal(X,Y : Vector) : Boolean;
 Var Index : 1..10;
     Flag : Boolean;
 Begin {Equal}
   Flag := True;
   For Index := 1 to 10 Do
     If X[Index] <> Y[Index] Then Flag := False;
   Equal := Flag
 End;{Equal}




Begin {MultDiv}
  For Index := 1 to 10 Do
   Begin
    Z[Index] := 0;
    Unit[Index] := 0;
    Copy[Index] := 0
   End;
  Z[11] := 0;
  Unit[1] := 1;
  While Compare(X,Y) Or Equal(X,Y) Do
   Begin
    MultDif(X,Y,Q);
    MultAdd(Copy,Unit,Z);
    For Index := 1 to 10 Do
     Begin
      Copy[Index] := Z[Index];
      X[Index] := Q[Index]
     End
   End
End {MultDiv};
```

MultAdd accepts two 10-element vectors representing the sum in multiple precision format.

MultDif accepts two 10-element vectors representing positive integers in multiple precision format. It returns an 11-element vector representing the difference in multiple precision format.

MultMult accepts two 10-element vectors representing positive integers in multiple precision format. It returns a 20-element vector representing the product in multiple precision format.

MultDiv accepts two 10-element vectors representing positive integers in multiple precision format. It returns an 11-element vector representing the *integer quotient* in multiple precision format. The functions *Compare* and *Equal* defined in this procedure determine the numeric relationship between values represented in multiple precision format.

Limitations of the Examples

- MultAdd, MultDif, MultMult and MultDiv only support addition, subtraction, multiplication and division of *positive* integers.
- MultDif assumes a positive result from its subtraction process; i.e., the first vector in its parameter list, X, is greater than the second vector in its parameter list, Y.
- MultDiv performs only integer division.
- None of these procedures provide any mechanism for the suppression of leading zeroes in the display of results.

Partial Multiple Precision

CONCEPT: To obtain the advantages of multiple precision arithmetic in a situation where only one of the operands in the arithmetic process is in the multiple precision format.

GIVEN: A is a vector containing integer values in the multiple precision format. B is a scalar integer value.

C is a vector to contain the result of the operation between A and B. C is in the multiple precision format.

The operations between the value of B and the value of each element of A is the same as in the previously described multiple precision arithmetic operations.

Examples

The following is a listing of a BASIC program demonstrating the concept of partial multiple precision multiplication.

```
100 DIM F(50)
110 L = 50
120 PRINT 'INPUT NUMBER WHOSE FACTORIAL IS TO BE COMPUTED'
130 INPUT N
140 FOR I = 2 TO L
150 F(I) = 0
160 NEXT I
170 F(1) = 1
180 P = 1
190 FOR M = 1 TO N
200 C = 0
210 FOR I = 1 TO P
220 F(I) = F(I)*M + C
230 C = INT(F(I)/10)
240 F(I) = F(I) - 10*C
250 NEXT I
260 IF C = 0 THEN 320
270 P = P+1
280 F(P) = C
290 C = INT(F(P)/10)
300 F(P) = F(P) - 10*C
310 GO TO 260
320 NEXT M
330 S = 0
340 FOR I = P TO 1 STEP -1
350 IF F(I) > 0 THEN 370
360 IF S=0 THEN 390
370 PRINT F(I);
380 S = 1
390 NEXT I
400 STOP
410 END
```

This program is designed to calculate the factorial of an input value N. Intermediate values and the final result are stored in multiple precision format in the vector F.

$N!$ is calculated by multiplying the vector F by all scalar positive integer values which are less than or equal to N.

The program also illustrates two additional concepts of interest in multiple precision operations.

Variable P has been introduced in an attempt to minimize operations on vector elements. P "points" to the leftmost, *i.e.* highest indexed, non-zero element of the result vector. Therefore, operations on this vector may be limited to the first P elements instead of all elements of the result vector.

In lines 330–390 of this program, a variable S is introduced to aid in the suppression of leading zeroes in the display of the result vector. S operates as a "flag" to control the printing of the element values of F, the result vector.

This example demonstrates only the use of multiple precision multiplication.

The next example demonstrates the use of multiple precision techniques for all four arithmetic processes (addition, subtraction, multiplication and division).

The following program calculates π to 50 decimal places:

```
100 REM PROGRAM NAME IS PI
110 REM MULTIPLE PRECISION CALCULATION OF PI
120 DIM A(51), B(51)
130 REM FIXED DECIMAL POINT BETWEEN 2 AND 3
140 REM FIND B = ARCTAN(1/5)
150  A(2), B(2) = 2
160 FOR N = 1 TO 65 STEP 2
170 GOSUB 830
180  L = N + 2
190 IF L < 10 THEN 220
200 GOSUB 1130
210 GOTO 230
220 GOSUB 1040
230  L = 25
240 GOSUB 1130
250  T = ((N - 1)/4) - INT((N - 1)/4)
260 IF T = 0 THEN 290
270 GOSUB 630
280 GOTO 300
290 GOSUB 730
300 NEXT N
310 REM FIND B = 4 * ARCTAN(1/5)
320 GOSUB 950
330 REM FIND B = -ARCTAN(1/239) + 4 * ARCTAN(1/5)
340  A(1), A(51) = 0
350 FOR J = 2 TO 44 STEP 7
360  A(J), A(J+1) = 0
370  A(J+2), A(J+5) = 4
380  A(J+3), A(J+6) = 1
390  A(J+4) = 8
400 NEXT J
410 GOSUB 730
420 FOR N = 1 TO 17 STEP 2
430 GOSUB 830
440  L = N + 2
450 IF L < 10 THEN 480
460 GOSUB 1130
```

```
470 GOTO 490
480 GOSUB 1040
490 GOSUB 1230
500  T = ((N - 3)/4) - INT((N - 3)/4)
510 IF T = 0 THEN 540
520 GOSUB 630
530 GOTO 550
540 GOSUB 730
550 NEXT N
560 REM WE NOW HAVE PI/4
570 GOSUB 950
580 FOR I = I TO 51
590 PRINT B(I);
600 NEXT I
610 STOP
620 REM SUBPROGRAM TO ADD B + A
630 FOR K = 51 TO 1 STEP -1
640 IF A(K) + B(K) > 9 THEN 670
650  B(K) = B(K) + A(K)
660 GOTO 690
670  B(K) = B(K) + A(K) - 10
680  B(K-1) = B(K-1) + 1
690 NEXT K
700 RETURN
710 REM END OF ADDITION SUBPROGRAM
720 REM SUBTRACTION B - A
730 FOR K = 51 TO 1 STEP -1
740 IF B(K) < A(K) THEN 770
750  B(K) = B(K) - A(K)
760 GOTO 790
770  B(K) = B(K) - A(K) + 10
780  B(K-1) = B(K-1) - 1
790 NEXT K
800 RETURN
810 REM END OF SUBTRACTION SUBPROGRAM
820 REM SUBPROGRAM FOR MULTIPLICATION BY N
830  C = 0
840 FOR I = 51 TO 1 STEP -1
850  A(I) = A(I) * N + C
860  C = INT(A(I)/10)
870  A(I) = A(I) - 10 * C
880 NEXT I
890 IF C = 0 THEN 920
900 PRINT "MUST REDIMENSION"
910 GOTO 1330
920 RETURN
930 REM END OF MULTIPLICATION SUBPROGRAM
940 REM SUBPROGRAM TO MULTIPLY B BY 4
950  C = 0
```

```
960 FOR I = 51 TO 1 STEP -1
970  B(I) = B(I) * 4 + C
980  C = INT(B(I)/10)
990  B(I) = B(I) - 10 * C
1000 NEXT I
1010 RETURN
1020 REM END OF SUBPROGRAM TO MULTIPLY B BY 4
1030 REM DIVISION BY ONE DIGIT L
1040 FOR I = 1 TO 50
1050  C = INT(A(I)/L)
1060  A(I+1) = A(I+1) + 10 * (A(I) - C * L)
1070  A(I) = C
1080 NEXT I
1090  A(51) = INT(A(51)/L)
1100 RETURN
1110 REM END OF DIVISION SUBPROGRAM
1120 REM DIVISION BY TWO DIGIT L
1130  D = A(1)
1140  A(1) = 0
1150 FOR I = 2 TO 51
1160  C = INT((10 * D + A(I))/L)
1170  D = 10 * D + A(I) - C * L
1180  A(I) = C
1190 NEXT I
1200 RETURN
1210 REM END OF DIVISION SUBPROGRAM
1220 REM DIVISION BY 57121
1230  D = 10000*A(1)+1000*A(2)+100*A(3)+10*A(4)+A(5)
1240  A(1), A(2), A(3), A(4) = 0
1250 FOR I = 5 TO 50
1260  C = INT(D/57121)
1270  D = 10 * (D - C * 57121) + A(I+1)
1280  A(I) = C
1290 NEXT I
1300  A(51) = INT(D/57121)
1310 RETURN
1320 REM RETURN OF DIVISION BY 57121
1330 END
```

The algorithm used in this program is a result of the following mathematical analysis.

Calculation of π to 50 decimal places may use the formula (due to John Machin):

$$(1) \quad \frac{\pi}{4} = 4 \arctan\left(\frac{1}{5}\right) - \arctan\left(\frac{1}{239}\right)$$

The arctan function may be described as an infinite series of the form:

$$\arctan(x) = x - \frac{x^3}{3} + \frac{x^5}{5} - \frac{x^7}{7} + \frac{x^9}{9} - \frac{x^{11}}{11} + \cdots$$

$$\arctan(x) = \sum_{i=1}^{\infty} (-1)^{i+1} \frac{x^{2i-1}}{2i - 1}$$

In particular,

$$(2) \quad \arctan\left(\frac{1}{5}\right) = \left(\frac{1}{5}\right) - \frac{1}{3}\left(\frac{1}{5}\right)^3 + \cdots - \frac{1}{67}\left(\frac{1}{5}\right)^{67}$$

Since the next term of the series is $(1/5)^{69} \approx 8.5 \times 10^{-51}$, it may be considered insignificant due to the 50-decimal place accuracy specified.

If elements of an array A contain the values of each term of this series, then the following iteration expression is true:

$$A_{n+1} = \frac{-n}{n + 2} \times \frac{1}{25} \times A_n$$

Likewise,

$$(3) \quad \arctan\left(\frac{1}{239}\right) = \left(\frac{1}{239}\right) - \frac{1}{3}\left(\frac{1}{239}\right)^3 + \cdots - \frac{1}{19}\left(\frac{1}{239}\right)^{19}$$

Since the next term is equal to $(1/21)(1/239)^{21} \approx 5.3 \times 10^{-52}$ the desired level of accuracy has been attained.

The iteration expression of successive terms of this expression is

$$A_{n+1} = \frac{-n}{n + 2} \times \frac{1}{57121} \times A_n$$

The combination of expressions (2) and (3) in the form described by (1) results in the value of $\pi/4$ from which the value of π easily follows.

DYNAMIC DATA STRUCTURES

Dynamic data structures can expand or contract or even be reorganized under the direction of the algorithmic part of a program. The data elements of such structures are usually referred to as *nodes*. These nodes are typically records that contain the data stored in the structure *and* pointers that permit access to other nodes. The concept of "adjacency" so essential to the use of static data structures is not explicitly defined for dynamic data structures.

The simplest dynamic data structure is the *linked list*.

Singly Linked Lists

CONCEPT: To design a sequential-access dynamic data structure that can be traversed in only one direction.

PROCESS: The linked list is a dynamic data structure that can readily be created from nodes and pointers. Each element of the list is generally implemented as a record. One of the fields of this record is a pointer to the next record/node/ element. The other fields of the record contain data relevant to that element. The pointer of the last element has a value NIL.

A linked list is entered (i.e., initially accessed) via a scalar pointer value directed to the first element of the data structure. This value is typically referred to as the *list pointer*.

Graphically a singly linked list may be viewed as shown in Figure 3.7.

This structure is referred to as a *singly linked* list because each element has a single pointer—to the next list element.

Singly linked lists are defined by the operations used to add and delete elements.

To logically add an element to a singly linked list is to insure that the value of that element will be "pointed to" at the proper location in the traversal of the list.

This process is accomplished by having the element logically preceding the element to be added point to the new element. The pointer field of the added

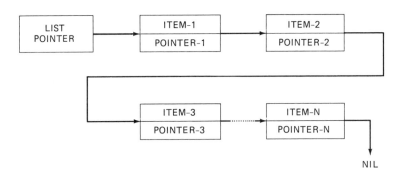

Figure 3-7. Graphical representation of a singly linked list.

element is assigned the old value of the pointer field of the preceding element in order to assure continuity in traversal of the list.

Via an extension of the previous graphical representation of a linked list, a new element ("item 2'") may be added between elements "item 2" and "item 3" as shown in Figure 3.8.

The new value of "pointer-2" in this graphic is dependent upon the definition of the new element added to the linked list ("item-2'"). The value of "pointer-2'" in this graphic is the old value of "pointer-2" in the previous graphic, insuring that "item-3" follows "item-2')".

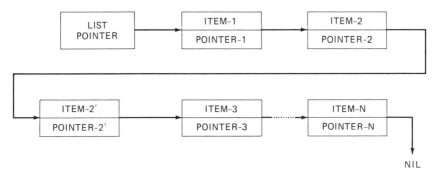

Figure 3-8. The addition of an element to a singly linked list.

Traversal of a Singly Linked List. Linked list traversal is the fundamental operation key to all linked list functions. The following Pascal procedure demonstrates the traversal of a linked list. Note that the linked list is defined solely in terms of the list pointer that controls access to the elements of the list.

```
Type Ptr = ^Element;
Element = Record
          ElementData : SomeDataType;
          Link : Ptr;
          End {Element Definition}


. . . . . . .


Procedure Traverse(ListPtr : Ptr);
Var x : Ptr;
Begin
  x := ListPtr;
  While x ≠ NIL Do
    Begin
      {Operation to be performed at each node};
    End
End;
```

In this procedure, parameter ListPtr is the identifier of the list pointer which controls access to a linked list. Once the list pointer is identified, traversal of the linked list becomes the repetitive assignment of pointers to each of the individual elements.

Examples. Linked list operations are most easily implemented in programming languages with support dynamic data types (pointers). Such languages include Pascal, Ada, C, and Modula-2.

Following is a listing of three Pascal procedures that implement the algorithms described for insertions to and deletions from singly linked lists:

```
Program LinkList(Input,Output);
Type Ptr = ^Element;
     Element = Record
                   ElementData:Integer;
                   Link:Ptr
                   End {Element Definition};


Var Head, Temp : Ptr;
    Data : Integer;

Procedure Traverse(ListPtr:Ptr);
Var X : Ptr;
Begin
  X := ListPtr;
  While X <> Nil Do
   Begin
    WriteLn(X^.ElementData);
    X := X^.Link
   End
End;


Procedure Add(Var Ptr1, Ptr2:Ptr; RefData:Integer);
Var X : Ptr;
Begin
  X := Ptr1;
  If X = Nil Then Begin
                      Ptr1 := Ptr2;
                      Ptr2^.Link := Nil;
                   End
              Else
                If X^.ElementData = RefData Then
                    Begin
```

```
                            Ptr1 := Ptr2;
                            Ptr2^.Link := X
                         End

                                              Else

Add(X^.Link,Ptr2,RefData)
End {Procedure Add};

Procedure Delete(Var Ptr1, Ptr2:Ptr; RefData:Integer);
Var X : Ptr;
Begin
  X := Ptr1;
  If X <> Nil Then
     If X^.ElementData = RefData Then
                                 Begin
                                   Ptr2 := X;
                                   Ptr1 := Ptr2^.Link
                                 End
                                 Else

Delete(Ptr1^.Link,Ptr2,Refdata)
End {Delete Procedure};

Begin {LinkList}
 Termin(Input);
 Termout(Output);
 Head := Nil;
 New(Temp);
 Data := 5;
 Temp^.ElementData := 10;
 Add(Head,Temp,Data);
 Traverse(Head);
 WriteLn;
 New(Temp);
 Data := 10;
 Temp^.ElementData := 15;
 Add(Head,Temp,Data);
 Traverse(Head);
 WriteLn;
 New(Temp);
 Data := 10;
 Temp^.ElementData := 12;
 Add(Head,Temp,Data);
 Traverse(Head);
 WriteLn;
 New(Temp);
 Data := 40;
 Temp^.ElementData := 7;
```

```
Add(Head,Temp,Data);
Traverse(Head);
Writeln;
Temp := Nil;
Data := 10;
Delete(Head,Temp,Data);
Traverse(Head);
Writeln;
Temp := Nil;
Data := 7;
Delete(Head,Temp,Data);
Traverse(Head)
End.
```

Add adds a new element to a linked list under the following conditions:

1. The element may be added (inserted) at any point within the linked list.
2. The point within the linked list where the element is to be added is identified by the data field of the element that *follows* the added element in the linked list.
3. If the linked list is empty (i.e., has no elements: the list pointer points to Nil), the element is added, becoming the sole element of the linked list.
4. If the list element whose data field serves to indicate where the new element is added is *not* present, the new element is added at the *end* of the linked list. This condition follows from condition (3) in that the pointer field of the added element points to Nil.

Conditions (3) and (4) are arbitrary and may be subject to change based upon application.

In this procedure, parameter Ptr1 is used to point successively to each item of the linked list (traverse) until the data field of the element that succeeds the element pointed to by Ptr1 contains the data value indicating the point of insertion. This data value is passed to the procedure through parameter RefData. Parameter Ptr2 points to the value to be added as an element of the linked list.

This procedure can be expressed recursively in that it represents the recursive examination of adjacent pairs of elements of the linked list. The first element of the pair is that element whose pointer field would point to the added element if the data field of the second element indicates that addition should occur between this pair. If addition does occur, the pointer field of the added element then points to the second element of the original pair.

Delete deletes an element from a linked list under the following conditions:

1. The element may be deleted from any point within the linked list.

2. The element within the linked list to be deleted is identified by the value of its data field.
3. If the linked list is empty (i.e., has no elements, the list pointer points to Nil), or if none of the data fields of the elements in the linked list contain the specified value, then no operation occurs.

In this procedure, parameter Ptr1 is used to point successively to each item of the linked list (traverse) until the data field of that element contains the data value designating deletion. This data value is passed to the procedure through parameter RefData. Parameter Ptr2 points to the item deleted from the linked list after the deletion operation has occurred. With the deletion of this item from the linked list, Ptr2 thereby provides the only access to the value of this dynamic variable.

This procedure can be expressed recursively in that it represents the recursive examination of adjacent pairs of elements of the linked list. The first element of this pair is that element whose pointer field would be modified if the element which succeeds it in the linked list were to be deleted.

Push-down Stack

CONCEPT: To design a dynamic data structure based upon the linked list for which elements may be added or deleted only at the top of the list (i.e., via the list pointer)

PROCESS: The push-down stack is a special application of a singly linked list. It is commonly referred to as a last-in-first-out (LIFO) stack in that elements may be deleted from the list only in the reverse order in which they were added to the list.

Adding an element to a push-down stack is commonly referred to as *pushing* that element onto the stack.

Deleting (removing) an element from a push-down stack is commonly referred to as *popping* that element from the stack.

The traversal of a push-down stack is accomplished as with any linked list data structure and is unaffected by the stack's specialized addition/deletion operation.

Examples.   As with generalized singly linked lists, the implementation of a push-down stack is most easily accomplished in a programming language that supports dynamic data types.

The following is a listing of four Pascal procedures that implement operations defined for a push-down stack.

```
Type Ptr = ^Element;
     Element = Record
                  ElementData:Integer;
                  Link:Ptr
                  End {Element Definition};


               *  *  *  *


Procedure Push(Var ListPtr, NewPtr : Ptr);
Begin
  NewPtr^.Link := ListPtr;
  ListPtr := NewPtr
End {Push Procedure};

Procedure Pop(Var ListPtr, PopPtr : Ptr);
Begin
  If ListPtr <> Nil Then
                       Begin
                         PopPtr := ListPtr;
                         ListPtr := ListPtr^.Link
                       End
End {Pop Procedure};

Procedure Traverse(ListPtr : Ptr);
Var X : Ptr;
Begin
  X := ListPtr;
  While X <> Nil Do
                   Begin
                     WriteLn(X^.ElementData);
                     X := X^.Link
                   End
End {Traverse Procedure};

Procedure SeqSearch(ListPtr : Ptr);
Var X : Ptr;
    Large : Integer;
Begin
  Large := 0;
  X := ListPtr;
  While X <> Nil Do
                   Begin
                     If X^.ElementData > Large
                        Then Large := X^.ElementData;
                     X := X^.Link
                   End;
  WriteLn(Large)
End {SeqSearch Procedure};
```

The following parameters are defined for use by these procedures:

- Parameter ListPtr is the list pointer to the stack.
- Parameter NewPtr is the pointer to a dynamically allocated value of type 'Element.' In Pascal this dynamic allocation is accomplished using the predefined procedure NEW. This operation and the assignment of a value to the ElementData field of this element would occur prior to the invocation of the Push procedure.

Parameter PopPtr is the pointer to the value popped from the stack. With the removal of this value from the stack, PopPtr provides the only access to this dynamic variable. If the data field of this popped element is to be accessed, it can only be done using PopPtr.

PopPtr may be used by the predefined Pascal procedure DISPOSE to deallocate this value after its removal from the stack.

Push adds a new element to a stack under the following conditions:

1. The element may be added (inserted) only at the top of the stack.
2. The top of the stack is identified by the stack pointer (variable ListPtr).
3. If the stack is empty (i.e., has no elements: the stack pointer points to Nil), the element is added becoming the sole element of the stack.

Pop removes or deletes an element from a stack under the following conditions:

1. The element may be removed or deleted only from the top of the stack.
2. The top of the stack is identified by the stack pointer (variable ListPtr).
3. If the linked list is empty (i.e., has no elements: the stack pointer points to Nil), no action occurs (the value of variable PopPtr is unchanged).

Traverse operates in the same manner as for traversal of the generalized singly-linked linear list.

Queue

CONCEPT: To design a dynamic data structure based upon the linked list for which elements may only be added at one end and deleted at the other end.

PROCESS: The queue is a special application of a singly linked list. It is commonly referred to as a first-in-first-out (FIFO) stack in that elements may be deleted from the queue only in the order in which they were added to the queue.

In order to accomplish the addition and removal procedures associated with a queue, two list pointers are required. One pointer identifies the latest element added to the queue (i.e., points to the rear), while the other pointer identifies the next element that may be removed from the queue (i.e., points to the front).

The traversal of a queue is accomplished as with any linked list data structure and is unaffected by the queue's specialized addition/deletion operation.

Examples. The following is a listing of three Pascal procedures which implement operations defined for queues.

```
Type Ptr = ^Element;
     Element = Record
                  ElementData:Integer;
                  Link:Ptr
                  End {Element Definition};

              *  *  *  *

Procedure EnQueue(Var RearPtr, FrontPtr, NewPtr : Ptr);
Begin
   If FrontPtr = Nil Then FrontPtr := NewPtr;
   NewPtr^.Link := RearPtr;
   RearPtr := NewPtr
End {EnQueue Procedure};

Procedure DeQueue(Var RearPtr, FrontPtr, DataPtr : Ptr);
Var X : Ptr;
Begin
   If RearPtr = FrontPtr Then
                      If RearPtr = Nil Then DataPtr := Nil
                                       Else
                                         Begin
                                           DataPtr := FrontPtr;
                                           RearPtr := Nil;
                                           FrontPtr := Nil
                                         End
                   Else
                   Begin
                     X := RearPtr;
                     While X^.Link <> FrontPtr Do
                       X := X^.Link;
                     DataPtr := FrontPtr;
                     FrontPtr := X;
                     If FrontPtr = Nil Then RearPtr := Nil
                   End
End {DeQueue Procedure};
```

```
Procedure Traverse(ListPtr : Ptr);
Var X : Ptr;
Begin
  X := ListPtr;
  While X <> Nil Do
                    Begin
                      WriteLn(X^.ElementData);
                      X := X^.Link
                    End
End {Traverse Procedure};
```

The following parameters are defined for use by these procedures:

- Parameter RearPtr is the list pointer to the "rear" of the queue, where elements can be added.
- Parameter FrontPtr is the list pointer to the "front" of the queue, where elements can be removed.
- Parameter NewPtr is the pointer to a dynamically allocated value of type 'Element'. Again, in Pascal this dynamic allocation is accomplished using the predefined procedure NEW. This operation and the assignment of a value to the ElementData field of this element would occur prior to the invocation of the Push procedure.
- Parameter DataPtr is the pointer to the value removed from the queue. With the removal of this value from the queue, DataPtr provides the only access to this dynamic variable. If the data field of this removed element is to be accessed, it can be done only via DataPtr. DataPtr may also be used by the predefined Pascal procedure DISPOSE to deallocate this value after its removal from the queue.
- Parameter ListPtr is used for entry into the queue for traversal. Assignment of RearPtr or FrontPtr to ListPtr thereby allows the queue to be traversed in both the forward and backward directions.

EnQueue adds a new element to a queue under the following conditions:

1. The element may be added (inserted) only at the rear of the queue.
2. The rear of the queue is identified by the rear pointer (variable RearPtr).
3. If the queue is empty (i.e., has no elements: the rear pointer points to the front pointer, which points to Nil), the element is added, becoming the sole element of the queue.

DeQueue removes or deletes an element from a queue under the following conditions:

1. The element may be removed or deleted only from the front of the queue.

2. The front of the queue is identified by the front pointer (variable FrontPtr).
3. If the queue is empty (i.e., has no elements: the rear pointer points to the front pointer which points to Nil), no action occurs (the value of DataPtr is set to Nil).

Traverse operates in the same manner as for traversal of the generalized singly linked linear list. However, since a queue has a list pointer at both ends, this procedure can be used to accomplish traversals in both the forward and backward directions.

Priority Queue

CONCEPT: To design a ''queue-like'' data structure accessible on a basis depending on some ordering of the data that its elements contain, rather than on a FIFO basis.

EXAMPLE: A Pascal implementation of a priority queue designed to operate in a particular manner is accomplished as follows:

```
Program PriQueue (Input,Output);
Type Ptr = ^Element;
     Element = Record
                   Index:Integer;
                   ElementData:Integer;
                   Link:Ptr
                   End {Element Definition};

          * * * *

Procedure PrEnQueue (Var RearPtr, NewPtr : Ptr);
Begin
   If RearPtr = Nil Then Begin
                      RearPtr := NewPtr;
                      RearPtr^.Link := Nil
                   End
                Else
                  If NewPtr^.Index < RearPtr^.Index Then
                     Begin
                       NewPtr^.Link := RearPtr;
                       RearPtr := NewPtr
                     End
                                                    Else
                     PrEnQueue (RearPtr^.Link,NewPtr)
End {PrEnQueue Procedure};

Procedure PrDeQueue (Var RearPtr, DataPtr : Ptr);
```

```
Begin
  If RearPtr = Nil Then DataPtr := Nil
                   Else
                     Begin
                       DataPtr := RearPtr;
                       RearPtr := RearPtr^.Link
                     End
End {PrDeQueue Procedure};
```

The following parameters are defined for use by these procedures:

- Parameter RearPtr is the list pointer to the "rear" of the queue, where elements can be added.
- Parameter NewPtr is the pointer to a dynamically allocated value of type Element. As noted, in Pascal this dynamic allocation is accomplished with the predefined procedure NEW. This operation and the assignment of a value to the ElementData field of this element would occur prior to the invocation of the Push procedure.
- Parameter DataPtr is the pointer to the value removed from the queue. With the removal of this value from the queue, DataPtr provides the only access to this dynamic variable; the data field of this "removed" element is accessible only through DataPtr, which may also be used by DISPOSE to deallocate this value after its removal from the queue.

PrEnQueue adds a new element to a queue under the following conditions:

1. The element may be added (inserted) at any point within the queue.
2. The queue is identified (entered) via the rear pointer (variable RearPtr).
3. The position within the queue where the element is added is determined by a traversal of the queue and a comparison between specific characteristics of the element to be added and each element traversed.
4. If the queue is empty (i.e., has no elements: the rear pointer points to the front pointer, which points to Nil), the element is added becoming the sole element of the queue.

PrDeQueue removes or deletes an element from a queue under the following conditions:

1. The element may be removed or deleted only from the rear of the queue.
2. The rear of the queue is identified by the rear pointer (variable RearPtr).
3. If the queue is empty (i.e., has no elements: the rear pointer points to Nil), no action occurs (the value of DataPtr is set to Nil).

MULTIPLY LINKED LISTS

While extremely useful in many applications, singly linked data structures are limited in the information they provide regarding the relationships between data elements. This limitation is evident in the sequential access methods required to specify particular elements and in the processes of insertion and deletion.

In a singly linked linear list, traversal is possible only in one direction and an element has access solely to its successor because of the presence of only one pointer field per element. It therefore follows that if additional pointer fields are added to each element, then more complex relationships between elements (including new data structures) can be defined. Such elements comprise multiply linked lists in the sense that each element now has access to a multiple of other elements. The number of pointer parts defined for each element determines the number of possible links to other elements.

While the advantages of multiply linked lists may be obvious in the increased data descriptions that can occur, the equally obvious disadvantages lie in an increased storage requirement for each element and the additional processing associated with multiple links.

Doubly Linked Linear Lists

The simplest example of a multiply linked list is the *doubly linked linear list*. The data relationships between elements of this structure are the same as with the singly linked list except that the multiply linked list can be traversed in *both* the forward and backward directions instead of just the forward direction as in the singly linked list.

This additional feature is made possible by the inclusion of an additional pointer field in the definition of each list element. The generalized datatype definition of each element can then be represented as follows:

```
Type Ptr = ^Element;
      Element = Record
                    ElementData : SomeDataType;
                    ForwardLink, BackwardLink : Ptr
                  End { Element Definition }
```

Algorithms describing the operation of a doubly linked list can be defined based upon this element definition. That each element has access to the elements both preceding and following it in the list allows the entire list to be traversed in either direction. Since two forms of traversal are possible, doubly linked lists have two list pointers, one associated with each traversal scheme.

Trees

The *tree* is perhaps the best known of the multiply linked data structures. The addition of multiple links in each data element allows the definition of data relationships that cannot be described otherwise.

The tree is a data structure defined in computer science to express a hierarchical relationship between the data elements stored in the structure. In static data structures, the relationships between elements are primarily described in terms of *addressing* (i.e., by means of the subscripts). In dynamic data structures such as the linked list (including stacks and queues), the item relationship is *linear* or *sequential* in that items are dependent upon all items that precede them in the structure in order to be accessible. In a tree structure, elements reside within well-defined hierarchies and may or may not be related to other elements in the structure based upon their location within those hierarchies.

Figure 3-9 shows typical hierarchical, tree-like structure. In this illustration, each of the elements (nodes) has an explicit hierarchical relationship to one another.

Trees are best implemented as dynamic data structures, thereby affording them the opportunity to vary in size and shape as circumstances require. It follows that trees can be examples of multiply linked lists, wherein each node points to other nodes of the tree.

Unlike their natural counterparts, tree data structures grow upside-down (i.e., from the root *down*). As in the case of other dynamic data structures, entry to the tree is controlled through a special-purpose pointer called the *root pointer*. The root pointer is similar in its purpose to the list, stack, and queue pointers with respect to those data structures.

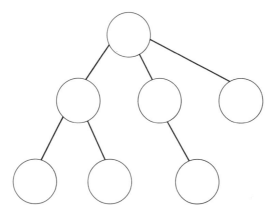

Figure 3-9. A collection of nodes defined with a tree-like relationship.

The relationships defined for trees has given rise to an amusing (and informative) vocabulary.

Root node is the term applied to the tree element (node) at the highest hierarchical level. The *root pointer* points to the *root node*.

The *children* of an element (node) are those elements (nodes) to which that node points; therefore, the children of a node are in the next lower hierarchical level from that of their parent node. The children of a node are typically identified in some sequential manner (e.g., first child, second child, left child, right child).

Parent is a term applied to an element (node) when referenced with respect to its children.

The *ancestors* of an element (node) are those elements (nodes) that lie in higher hierarchical levels and are part of a pointer path to that node.

A *leaf* is an element (node) that has no children (i.e., its pointers point to Nil).

The *depth* (or *height*) of a tree is the number of links that have to be traversed to go from a tree's root to the element (node) farthest away from the root. A tree with only one element (node) is of depth zero.

Trees are recursive data structures in that the hierarchical levels they represent give rise to the definition of *subtrees*. Therefore, any element (node) can be considered to be a *root node* of the subtree that contains its children, its children's children, and so forth. As a result, any operation that defines a process for a simple tree (a node and its children) can be applied recursively to the complete tree data structure.

The following is a generalized type definition of a single tree element (node):

```
Type Ptr = ^Element;
     Element = Record
                  ElementData : SomeDataType;
                  Child1,Child2,....ChildN : Ptr
               End { Element Definition }
```

A perfectly balanced tree is one in which the distance from the root node to all leaves is the same.

Binary Trees.   The binary tree is a tree data structure of special significance in programming applications.

As the name *binary* implies, each node of a binary tree has a single data part and two pointer parts (called the left and right branches respectively) that point to left and/or right children and possible subtrees. In a binary tree, a specific relationship exists between the left and right children of a node, making them *not* interchangeable.

A generalized type definition of a single binary tree element (node) can be expressed as follows:

```
Type Ptr = ^Element;
    Element = Record
                ElementData : SomeDataType;
                LeftBranch,RightBranch : Ptr
                End { Element Definition }
```

It follows that the number of elements (nodes) in a *perfectly balanced binary tree* is $2^n - 1$, where n is the lowest hierarchical level (or the tree depth $+ 1$). Therefore, perfectly balanced binary trees would have 1, 3, 7, 15, 31, etc., elements.

A primary application of binary trees is to accommodate the *searching* and the *sorting* of the elements stored within them. Consequently, the *building* (i.e., adding elements to a binary tree) of a tree must reflect this application by establishing a specific relationship between the elements (nodes) and their children and subtrees. These relationships become apparent in the process by which binary trees are *traversed*.

Because of the recursive definition of a trees, a traversal technique defined for a simple tree (i.e., a node and two children) can be applied recursively to traverse the complete tree.

Three ways of traversing a binary tree become apparent:

- *Pre-order traversal:* Visit the node; traverse the subtrees; (Figure 3-10).
- *In-order traversal:* Traverse the left subtree; visit the node; Traverse right subtree; Figure 3-11).
- *Post-order traversal:* Traverse subtrees; visit the node (Figure 3-12).

Pre-order and post-order traversal do not specify the order in which the respective subtrees are traversed.

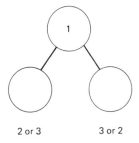

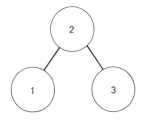

Figure 3-10. The order in which tree nodes are visited in a pre-order traversal.

Figure 3-11. The order in which tree nodes are visited in an in-order traversal.

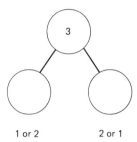

Figure 3-12. The order in which tree nodes are visited in a post-order traversal.

If a binary tree is built such that the value of the data part of the left child is less than or equal to the data part of the parent and the data part of the right child is greater than or equal to the data part of the parent, then an *in-order traversal* of the tree yields an ascending sequence of the values of all the data parts of all nodes in the tree. This particular tree configuration is called a *binary search tree* (Figure 3.13).

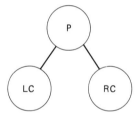

'P' IS DEFINED AS THE PARENT NODE
'LC' IS DEFINED AS THE LEFT CHILD
'RC' IS DEFINED AS THE RIGHT CHILD

THE VALUE OF LC IS LESS THAN OR EQUAL TO
    THE VALUE OF P
THE VALUE OF RC IS GREATER THAN OR EQUAL TO
    THE VALUE OF P

Figure 3-13. The relationships between nodes in a binary search tree.

Following is a listing of three Pascal procedures implementing operations defined for *binary search trees*.

```
Type Info = Packed Array[1..3] of Char;
     Branch = ^Tree;
     Tree = Record
            Word : Info;
            Left,Right : Branch
     End;
                * * * *
```

```
Procedure Traverse (T:Branch);
Begin
  If T <> Nil Then
                Begin
                 Traverse (T^.Left);
                 WriteLn(T^.Word);
                 Traverse (T^.Right)
                End
End;


Function NewNode( Item : Info ) : Branch;
  Var P : Branch;
  Begin
   New(P);
   With P^ Do
     Begin
      Word := Item;
      Left := Nil;
      Right := Nil;
     End;
   NewNode := P
  End;


Procedure Insert(Item : Info; Var T : Branch);
  Var P, Q : Branch;
      Found : Boolean;
  Begin
   P := T;
   Q := Nil;
   Found := False;
   While (P<>Nil) And Not Found Do
      If Item = P^.Word Then Found := True
                        Else
                          Begin
                           Q := P;
                           If Item<P^.Word Then P := P^.Left
                                           Else P := P^.Right
                          End;

    If Not Found Then
              Begin
               P := NewNode(Item);
               If Q = Nil Then T := P
                          Else If Item < Q^.Word Then Q^.Left := P
                                                 Else Q^.Right:= P
              End
  End;
```

New Node is a function that dynamically allocates the space for a new node and initializes its values. This function is used by the Insert procedure prior to the insertion of a new node into a specified binary tree.

Insert is a procedure to generate a new node dynamically, assign to its data part the value specified in parameter Item, and then to insert that node into its proper location in the binary tree whose root pointer is identified by parameter T. This insertion process assumes that the binary tree is to be traversed (searched) in the *in-order* fashion. As a result, the tree is searched until a node is located that will satisfy the proper parent-child relationship with the new node. The new node is then inserted as the left or right child of the found node.

Traverse performs an *in-order traversal* of the binary tree whose root pointer is specified as parameter T of the procedure. This example simply outputs the data part of the node currently visited. Other traversal forms are obtained by permuting the two recursive Traverse invocations and the WriteLn statement. Preorder traversals would result from

WriteLn(T^.Word);		WriteLn(T^.Word);
Traverse(T^.Left);	or	Traverse(T^.Right);
Traverse(T^.Right);		Traverse(T^.Left).

Post-order traversals would result from

Traverse(T^.Left);		Traverse(T^.Right);
Traverse(T^.Right);	or	Traverse(T^.Left);
WriteLn(T^.Word);		WriteLn(T^.Word).

A procedure for deleting elements (nodes) from a tree (binary or otherwise) is more complex and raises additional issues. In that any tree element is a potential root node for a subtree, the deletion of an element disrupts the relationship existing between its children, grandchild, and so forth. Therefore, various strategies can be defined for dealing with the subtrees of deleted elements. The following is one possible algorithm:

1. Determine the parent of the node to be deleted (it should exist unless the root node is being deleted).
2. If the node to be deleted has either a left or right subtree (but not both), then the parent of the node being deleted (determined in step 1) becomes the root node of the subtree.
3. If step 2, is successful, then stop (the node has been logically deleted from the tree).
4. Determine the in-order successor of the node to be deleted. Append the right subtree of this successor node to its grandparent. Replace the node to be deleted by its in-order successor.

EMULATING DYNAMIC DATA STRUCTURES

Operations involving dynamic data structures may be emulated in programming languages that do not support dynamic data types. This emulation is accomplished by using the static array type as the principal data structure, but also while addressing elements of the array as though they were elements of a dynamic structure. Because the constraints of the array data structure, the dynamic size of these data structures cannot be emulated; therefore, the array must be defined to accommodate the maximum number of elements expected in the structure.

Emulated dynamic data structures can provide distinct advantages over static arrays in specific operations.

- For operations involving frequent element addition and/or deletion, the direct addressing capability of arrays can have visible disadvantages. The addition or deletion of elements in an array usually requires a "shift" of the array elements that follow the element being processed. This shift is necessary either to create a space for the element to be added or to fill the space left by a deleted element. The use of an emulated structure eliminates the need for such shift operations.
- Emulated dynamic structures can conform to some specific processes better than arrays. For example, the use of an emulated binary tree structure eliminates the necessity of the calculations required for subscript processing in a binary search.

A common technique used in these emulations involves an *availability list*. This is a list of all unused storage (i.e., empty array elements) and is used to simulate the allocation/de-allocation process.

Singly Linked Lists

The following is a BASIC program which emulates the fundamental operations of a singly-linked list.

```
10    REM LIST PROCESSING PROGRAM
20    REM
30    REM [L] IS THE LINK ARRAY
40    REM [D$] IS DATA ARRAY OF STRINGS
50    REM [A] IS FREE SPACE POINTER LIST
60    REM [T] IS NAME LIST POINTER
70    REM [N] IS NEW NODE POINTER
80    REM [O] IS OLD LIST POINTER
90    REM
100   REM DECLARATIONS
110   REM
120   DIM L(50), D$(50)
130   REM
140   REM INITIALIZE THE LINK LIST
```

```
150  REM
160  FOR I = 1 TO 49
170  L(I) = I+1
180  D$(I) = ""
190  NEXT I
200  REM
210  REM INITIALIZE THE END LINK
220  REM
230  REM INITIALIZE THE FREE SPACE POINTER
240  REM
250  A = 1
260  REM
270  REM PROMPT FOR FUNCTION DESIRED
280  REM
290  INPUT "FUNCTION DESIRED? ADD, DELETE, PRINT OR QUIT":Z$
300  F = 0
310  IF Z$ = "ADD" THEN F = 1
320  IF Z$ = "DELETE" THEN F = 2
330  IF Z$ = "PRINT" THEN F = 3
340  IF Z$ = "QUIT" THEN F = 4
350  REM
360  IF F = 0 THEN 290
370  IF F = 4 THEN 9999
380  REM
390  ON F GOSUB 1000, 2000, 3000
400  GOTO 290
1000 REM ADD A NAME TO THE NAME LIST
1010 REM
1020 INPUT "NAME":B$
1030 REM GET A FREE NODE
1040 REM
1050 IF A = 0 THEN PRINT "LIST FULL" : RETURN
1060 N = A
1070 A = L(A)
1080 REM STORE DATA IN NODE
1090 D$(N) = B$
1100 REM LINK NODE TO NAME LIST
1110 L(N) = T
1120 T = N
1130 RETURN
2000 REM DELETE A NAME FROM THE NAME LIST
2010 REM
2020 INPUT "NAME": B$
2030 REM
2040 REM FIND NODE
2050 REM
2060 J = T
2070 IF J = 0 THEN PRINT "EMPTY LIST" : RETURN
```

```
2080 IF B$ = D$(J) THEN 2410
2090 IF J = 0 THEN 2360
2100 IF L(J) = 0 THEN 2360
2110 IF B$ = D$(L(J)) THEN 2210
2120 REM
2130 REM NO MATCH
2140 REM
2150 J = L(J)
2160 IF J = 0 THEN 2360
2170 GOTO 2090
2180 REM
2190 REM MATCHED!!
2200 REM
2210 O = L(J)
2220 L(J) = L(L(J))
2230 REM
2240 REM RETURN NODE TO FREE SPACE LIST
2250 REM
2260 L(O) = A
2270 A = O
2280 REM
2290 REM NULL DATA FIELD
2300 REM
2310 D$(O) = ""
2320 RETURN
2330 REM
2340 REM NOT IN NAME LIST
2350 REM
2360 PRINT "NOT ON NAME LIST"
2370 RETURN
2380 REM
2390 REM DELETE TOP NAME
2400 REM
2410 O = T
2420 T = L(T)
2430 REM
2440 REM RETURN NODE TO FREE SPACE LIST
2450 REM
2460 L(O) = A
2470 A = O
2480 REM
2490 REM NULL DATA FIELD
2500 REM
2510 D$(O) = ""
2520 RETURN
3000 REM PRINT CONTENTS OF NAME LIST
3010 REM
3020 J = T
```

```
3030 IF J = 0 THEN PRINT "EMPTY LIST" : RETURN
3040 PRINT D$(J)
3050 J = L(J)
3060 IF J = 0 THEN RETURN
3070 GOTO 3040
3080 REM
3090 REM
9999 END
```

Stacks

Push-down stack operations may be emulated in languages without dynamic data types. The following is a BASIC program which demonstrates this capability.

```
100    REM SOFTWARE STACK
110    REM
120    REM [S$] IS THE STACK
130    REM [T] IS THE STACK POINTER
140    REM [D$] IS THE DATA TO BE PUSHED/POPPED
150    REM
160    DIM S$(128)
170    REM
180    REM INIT [T]
190    REM
200    T = 128
210    REM
220    REM PUSH DATA ONTO STACK
230    REM
240    INPUT "HOW MANY ITEMS TO PUSH?" : X
250    FOR Y = 1 TO X
260    INPUT D$
270    GOSUB 430
280    NEXT Y
290    REM
300    REM
310    REM POP DATA OFF THE STACK
320    REM
330    INPUT "HOW MANY ITEMS TO POP?" : X
340    FOR Y = 1 TO X
350    GOSUB 490
360    PRINT D$
370    NEXT Y
380    REM
390    STOP
400    REM
410    REM
420    REM
```

```
430   REM PUSH ONTO THE STACK
440   REM
450   S$(T) = D$
460   T = T-1
470   RETURN
480   REM
490   REM POP OFF THE STACK
500   REM
510   T = T+1
520   IF T < = 128 THEN 540
530   PRINT "STACK EMPTY" : RETURN
540   D$ = S$(T)
550   RETURN
560   REM
570   END
```

Queues

Queue operations may be emulated in languages without dynamic data types.
The following BASIC program demonstrates this capability.

```
3000 REM THIS IS A SUBROUTINE TO ADD TO QUEUE Q
3010 REM MOVE BACK
3020 B = B + 1
3030 REM WRAP AROUND?
3040 IF B <= 500 THEN 3060
3050 B = 1
3060 REM TEST FOR OVERFLOW
3070 IF B <> F THEN 3110
3080 PRINT USING 3090, A
3090 : QUEUE OVERFLOW WHEN ADDING ##
3100 STOP

4000 REM THIS IS A SUBROUTINE TO MOVE FROM QUEUE Q
4010 REM FRONT MOVES ONE PLACE
4020 F = F + 1
4030 REM WRAP AROUND?
4040 IF F <= 500 THEN 4070
4050 F = 1
4060 REM INSERT VALUE
4070 A = Q(F)
4080 RETURN
```

Trees

As with stacks and queues, trees are most easily emulated in unstructured
languages using vectors. In such an implementation of a binary tree, the fields

which constitute a node (left pointer, data part and right pointer) are represented as a set vectors. This method allows nodes to contain different data types (especially important in the case of the data field). So typically the elements of a binary tree structure can be stored in three equal-length vectors. The length of these vectors is determined by an estimate of the maximum tree population. These vectors share a common indexing scheme allowing them to reference different entities of the same tree node they equally define. The value zero in the pointer vectors is defined to be equivalent to Nil (i.e., pointing to nothing).

As with the emulations of stacks and queues, dynamic allocation is emulated using an *availability list*. This is a linked list of all unused storage and simulates the allocation/deallocation process. In the emulation of a binary tree, the availability list contains a list of all positions in the three parallel vectors defining a tree node that are not currently in use. When a new tree node is required, the first node is removed from the top of the availability list.

The following BASIC program is an example of the in-order traversal of a binary tree defined in this manner.

```
100 REM IN-ORDER TRAVERSAL OF A BINARY TREE
110 REM ADAPTED FROM 'STRUCTURED FORTRAN WATFIV-S PROGRAMMING'
120 REM BY TREMBLAY AND BUNT, MCGRAW-HILL, 1980
130 DIM L(50),I(50),R(50),S(50)
140 REM ARRAY L IS THE LEFT POINTER VECTOR
150 REM ARRAY I IS THE DATA PART VECTOR
160 REM ARRAY R IS THE RIGHT POINTER VECTOR
170 REM ARRAY S IS THE AVAILABILITY LIST
180 REM VARIABLE R1 IS ROOT
190 IF R1 <> 0 THEN 230
200 PRINT 'EMPTY TREE'
210 GOTO 390
220 REM INITIALIZE
230 T = 0
240 P = R1
250 REM TRAVERSE TREE IN INORDER
260 REM STACK ADDRESS ALONG A LEFT CHAIN
270 IF P = 0 THEN 330
280 T = T + 1
290 S(T) = P
300 P = L(P)
310 GOTO 270
320 REM PROCESS NODE AND RIGHT BRANCH
330 IF T <= 0 THEN 390
340 P = S(T)
350 T = T - 1
360 PRINT I(P)
370 P = R(P)
```

```
380 GOTO 270
390 STOP
400 END
```

Vector emulation of binary trees in the manner described above has two obvious disadvantages:

- If the tree is sparsely populated, the vector contains many Nil links (value zero);
- The traversal of such a tree structure is best accomplished using an additional stack emulation. This additional requirement can be wasteful in terms of processing time and quantity of space required.

A technique developed to address this problem is to replace the Nil links with *threads*. A thread is a pointer that gives information about either the predecessor or the successor of a node in a tree during a particular traversal scheme. For the in-order traversal of a binary tree, threads are pointers that point to the higher nodes in the tree. These threads permit the examination of a node's ancestors (parent, etc.) without having to store the addresses of nodes in a stack. Since the left and right links of a node can be either a *structural* link or a thread, a convention of identification must be adopted. One strategy for making this distinction is to use negative values for thread links.

QUASI-STATIC DATA STRUCTURES

A *quasi-static data structure* incorporates properties of static and dynamic data structures. Such structures are usually designed to overcome a constraint associated with a defined structure or to define features not associated with a known structure configuration.

Quasi-Static Arrays

CONCEPT: To define a quasi-dynamic data structure that has the logical configuration associated with the static array structure, but with more flexible-sized properties.

PROCESS: It is often advantageous to define an array as an array of pointers to one-dimensional arrays. This definition allows a multidimensional array to be used in applications in which one of the dimensions is variant.

EXAMPLE: The following example describes a quasi-static array with two interesting features:

1. It defines a array (to be used as a matrix) which can be as large as 20 × 10, but it only uses 5 × 5. Instead of allocating 200 locations for the maximum possible size, it allocates 20 pointers and 5 × 10 objects. The economy becomes increasingly larger the greater the worst cast to be handled. This fact plus the use of the volatile nature of variables in subprograms makes it possible to reserve space for worst cases without actually wasting a lot of memory.

2. It demonstrates how easy it is to exchange two rows of a matrix (a rather common operation in matrix algebra). In languages without pointers, the normal process would be to copy a row into a temporary storage area; copy the second row into the first; and finally copy the temporary storage into the second. Using pointers, it is only necessary to copy the pointers instead of the whole row.

```
Program MatOps (output);

{Reproduced with permission of Harvey Lynch }
{Stanford Linear Accelerator Center          }

Const
    N_Rows = 20;        { Maximum number of rows }
    N_Cols = 10;        { Maximum number of columns }

Type
    rows = 1..N_Rows;
    cols = 1..N_Cols;
    row = array [cols] of real;     { A single row }
    matrix = array [rows] of ^row;  { Array of pointers to a row }

Var
    mat : matrix;
    r : rows;
    c : cols;

Procedure dump_mat (Var mat : matrix; rl : rows; cl : cols);

    { Dump matrix to output }

    Var
        r : rows;
        c : cols;

    Begin { dump_mat }
        for r := 1 to rl do
        begin
```

```
          for c := 1 to cl do
              Write (mat [r]^[c] :6:1);
          WriteLn;
       end;
       WriteLn;
    End    { dump_mat } ;

Procedure swap_rows (Var mat : matrix; r1, r2 : rows);

    { Swap rows of a matrix }
    Var
        temp : ^row;

    Begin { swap }
       temp := mat [r1];
       mat [r1] := mat [r2];
       mat [r2] := temp;
    End    { swap } ;

Begin { MatOps }
    { Allocate the matrix required }
    for r := 1 to 5 do
       new (mat [r]);

    { Fill mat with some random numbers }
    for r := 1 to 5 do
       for c := 1 to 5 do
          mat [r]^[c] := N_Rows * (r - 1) + c;
    dump_mat (mat, 5, 5);

    { Exchange 2 rows of mat }
    swap_rows (mat, 2, 4);
    dump_mat (mat, 5, 5);
End   { MatOps } .
```

REFERENCES

1. Baron, Robert J., and Shapiro, Linda G., *Data Structures and Their Implementation*. New York, Van Nostrand Reinhold, 1980.
2. Bertziss, A. T., *Data Structures: Theory and Practice*. New York, Academic Press, 1975.
3. Brillinger, Peter C., and Cohen, Doron J., *Introduction to Data Structures and Non-Numeric Computation: Featuring the WATFOR and WATFIV Compilers*. Englewood Cliffs, NJ, Prentice-Hall, 1972.
4. Coleman, Derek, *A Structured Programming Approach to Data*. New York, Springer-Verlag, 1979.
5. Dahl, O. J., Dijkstra, E. W., and Hoare, C. A. R., *Structured Programming*. N.Y., Academic Press, 1972. (*APIC Studies in Data Processing, 8*)
6. Date, C. J., *An Introduction to Database Systems*. Reading, MA, Addison-Wesley, 1985.

7. Flores, Ivan, *Data Structure and Management.* Englewood Cliffs, NJ, Prentice-Hall, 1977.
8. Horowitz, Ellis, and Sahni, Sartaj, *Fundamentals of Data Structure*, 9th printing with corrections ed. Rockville, MD, Computer Science Press, 1982.
9. Martin, Johannes J., *Data Types and Data Structures.* Englewood Cliffs, NJ, Prentice-Hall, 1986.
10. Maurer, Herman A., *Data Structures and Programming Techniques.* Englewood Cliffs, NJ, Prentice-Hall, 1977.
11. Harrison, Malcolm C., *Data Structures and Programming.* New York: New York University, Courant Institute of Mathematical Sciences, 1970.
12. Stone, Harold, S., *Introduction to Computer Organization and Data Structures.* New York, McGraw-Hill, 1972.
13. Wirth, Niklaus, *Algorithms + Data Structures = Programs.* Englewood Cliffs, NJ, Prentice-Hall, 1976.
14. Wirth, Niklaus, *Algorithms & Data Structures.* Englewood Cliffs, NJ, Prentice-Hall, 1986.

NOTES

[1]Quote is from "Algorithms + ..." which is already cited as Reference 13. (The quote is on page xiii of that book).

[2]Beer, Stafford, "Before the Twilight Arch: A Mythology of Systems," *Society for General Systems Research 5,* (1960), p. 12.

[3]Knuth, Donald E. "The Art of Computer Programming, Vol. 2: Semi-Numerical Algorithms". 2nd ed., Reading, Mass., Addison-Wesley, 1981.

4

GENERATION AND VALIDATION OF PSEUDO-RANDOM NUMBER SEQUENCES

"The generation of random numbers is too important to be left to chance."

Robert R. Coveyou
Oak Ridge National Laboratory

GENERATING SEQUENCES OF PSEUDO-RANDOM NUMBERS

Fundamental to the operation of many programs is the availability of a pseudo-random number generator. This section will describe techniques used to produce pseudo-random number sequences, the characteristics of such sequences, and techniques for testing the ''randomness'' of such sequences.

Applications of pseudo-random sequences are certainly not limited to the stochastic simulation of nondeterministic models. The concepts discussed in this section are therefore applicable to a wide variety of applications requiring such sequences.

What Numbers Are Random?

Almost everyone has a private notion of what constitutes randomness. Sometimes the criterion is uniformity of distribution, sometimes its unpredictability, and sometimes low correlations between adjacent or nearly adjacent members of a sequence. Unfortunately, most of these notions of randomness are difficult to quantify, thus it becomes difficult to obtain or produce numbers that will satisfy everyone's notion of how a sequence of random numbers should appear. Usually it is sufficient if only a few of the properties of ''truly random'' numbers are satisfied.

Table 4.1 is a familiar type of table of random numbers.

In most computers, numbers cannot be random in the sense of being indeterminate, since a computer inherently performs deterministic processes. What is

Table 4.1   Random Numbers (as per M. G. Kendall and B. B. Smith*)

29935	06971	63175	52579	10478	89379	61428	21363
15114	07126	51890	77787	75510	13103	42942	48111
03870	43225	10589	87629	22039	94124	38127	65022
79390	39188	40756	45269	65959	20640	14284	22960
30035	06915	79196	54428	64819	52314	48721	81594
29039	99861	28759	79802	68531	39198	38137	24373
78196	08108	24107	49777	09599	43569	84820	94956
15847	85493	91442	91351	80130	73752	21539	10986

*See note at end of chapter

usually accomplished is the production of sequence of "pseudo-random" numbers that satisfy a variety of tests for acceptable simulation of randomness. Paradoxically, this sequence is usually produced by a carefully selected deterministic process. (Some sequences may also be obtained nondeterministically by sampling an established random source such as noise on an electrical power line.)

The most commonly used method is to generate a sequence of pseudo-random integers X_k uniformly distributed in the range $0 < X_k < M$ is the *mixed congruential method* (or sometimes referred to as Lehmer's multiplicative congruential method):

$$X_{k+1} = X_k \times A \,(\text{modulo } M)$$
$$X_{k+1} = \big((X_k \times A) + C\big)\,(\text{modulo } M)$$

where:

M = limit of the desired sequence.
A = a constant of the form $2^N + 1$.
C = a positive prime number.
X_k = the most current pseudo-random number in a sequence.
X_{k+1} = the next pseudo-random number of the sequence.

The constants A, C and M are chosen to yield "good" behavior for the machine on which the sequence is generated. The choice of these constants is a subtle and difficult art, and great caution must be exercised in taking "random advice" on the subject, or in accepting "conventional wisdom."

The congruential generators are designed to be uniform and return either the integer value X_k or a pseudo-random "real" $U_k = X_k/M$ on the interval $0.0 < U_k < 1.0$, or both.

GLOSSARY OF TERMS

Frequency Test: When applied to a random or pseudo-random number sequence, examines whether the numbers in that sequence are equally likely to occur. This test is most often applied to sequences that should be uniformly distributed over a specific range.

Period: The number of values in a pseudo-random number sequence that occur before any repetition of values occurs. This is a particularly important feature of the linear congruential generators because of their recursive definition. In such generators, the sequence must repeat itself with a period no longer than its modulus term. *Syn.* sequence length.

Pseudo-random Number Sequence: An ordered set of numbers defined by an arithmetic process, but satisfying specific tests for randomness.

Random Number: A number selected from a known set of numbers in a way such that each number in the set has the same probability of occurrence; a number obtained by chance; one of a sequence of numbers considered appropriate for satisfying certain statistical tests or believed to be free from conditions that might bias the result of a calculation.

Random Number Sequence: A sequence of numbers each of which cannot be predicted from only a knowledge of its predecessors.

Range: The set of constants from which the values in a random or pseudo-random number sequence will be selected.

Sampling: Various methods of deducing properties of a large set of elements by studying only a small random subset.

Sequence Length: see Period.

Serial Test: when applied to a random or pseudo-random number sequence, determines whether pairs, triples, and so forth, of digits occur randomly.

TESTS OF RANDOMNESS

No deterministic program/algorithm such as the family of multiplicative congruential methods can generate truly random numbers, thus it is necessary to establish methods that may be used to determine whether a sequence of numbers is "random enough."

Frequency Tests

CONCEPT: To determine whether the members of a random or pseudo-random number sequence occur with the frequency that would be probabilistically expected given the definition of their range of value.

PROCESS: The chi-square test is commonly used in statistical applications to determine the agreement between a series of *observed* values O_i and corresponding *expected* values E_i. When a random or pseudo-random or pseudo-random sequence of numbers is being evaluated, O_i represents the actual number of times a specific value occurs within a sequence of determinate length. E_i represents the number of times that value would be expected to occur given the distribution function defined for that range.

For large numbers of observations (i.e., unique values), n ($n \gg 1$), the chi-square test can be expressed in a simplified form:

1. For each unique value i, compute $O_i - E_i$
2. Square these values, divide by the corresponding value of E_i, and sum the quotients over all observations
3. Divide the result by the number of observations, obtaining:

$$\chi^2 = \left(\frac{1}{n}\right) \Sigma \frac{(O_i - E_i)^2}{E_i}$$

This χ^2 value represents the relative total variation of the represented values. The larger the χ^2 value, the worse the fit. In order to determine whether the pseudo-random number sequence constitutes a sample that is randomly distributed over the desired range, the calculated χ^2 value is compared to a table χ^2 value at a significance level, α, with the appropriate number of degrees of freedom. The number of degrees of freedom in this case is equal to the number of distinct allowable value (range of i in the above equation) minus one. The significance level, α, represents the number of times one may reject randomness when indeed randomness occurs.

If the resulting quantity lies between 0.5 and 2.0, the scatter of the observations is consistent with random numbers. If $\chi^2 < 0.5$, the observations are suspiciously close to average values; if $\chi^2 > 2.0$, they are too far from an average range. This test is applicable only to quantities that are expected to obey the classic law of errors.

EXAMPLE: The following is a Pascal program that tests the frequency of the sequence produced by a random number generator, RND, using the chi-square test. The range of values produced by this sequence is [0, 99] inclusive. It is expected that the values will be uniformly distributed over this range (i.e., all values are equally likely to occur). Therefore, the expected number of observations (E_i) is constant and equal to the number of items in the sequence (in this case, 1000) divided by the number of possible values (in this case, 100). The result is $E_i = 10$ for all values of i. The array Actual in this program contains the values O_i.

```
Program Chi (Output);

Const N = 100;
     Expected = 10;

Type Bins = Array [0. .99] of Integer;
     Sequence = Array [1. .1000] of Integer;

Var Actual : Bins;
    R : Sequence;
    ChiSqrd : Real;
    i : Integer;

Begin {Program Chi}
   For i : = 0 to 99 do
      Actual[i] : = 0;
   R[1] : = Trunc(RND*100);
   Actual[R[1]] : = Actual[R[1]] + 1;
   For i : = 2 to 1000 do
      Begin
         R[i] : = Trunc(RND*100);
         Actual[R[i]] : = Actual[R[i]] + 1
      End;
   ChiSqrd : = 0.0;
   For i : = 0 to 99 do
   ChiSqrd : =ChiSqrd+(Actual[i]-Expected)*(Actual[i]-Expected)/Expected;
   ChiSqrd : = ChiSqrd/N;
   WriteLn(' The Chi Squared is ', ChiSqrd : 5 : 2)
End {Program Chi}.
```

Serial Tests

CONCEPT: To determine whether serial combinations of members in a random or pseudo-random number sequence occur with the frequency that would be probabilistically expected given the definition of their range of values.

PROCESS: The frequency tests are used to determine whether the values in a pseudo-random number sequence are distributed according to theory. The tests do not indicate if there exists within the sequence a bias associated with the order in which the values are produced. The function of serial tests is to determine whether pairs, triples, and so forth, of values occur randomly.

It is characteristic of multiplicative congruential generators that they perform poorly on serial tests of randomness. This is because the same series of values are produced by these generators over their associated sequence length. Therefore, only if the sequence produced has a long sequence length within which the sampling of values occurs will positive results for serial correlation be indicated.

The χ^2 test is an effective means of testing the serial correlation of a pseudo-random number sequence.

Tests on Sequence Length

CONCEPT: To determine the effects of the sequence length of a pseudo-random number generator on the applications with which it is used

PROCESS: Most generators will create very long sequences of numbers, usually on the order of $M/4$ (where M is the modulus), or $M - 1$. For ordinary applications, this is usually sufficient.

Occasionally, however, longer sequences are needed; this might occur if K successive numbers are used to generate points in a K-dimensional space. It can be seen that the multiplicative congruential generators have essentially no "memory" (i.e., each number is uniquely determined by its predecessor). This means that a sequence of length L generates exactly L distinct points, but it also means that with L points, the longest sequence has length L rather than the much longer sequence that would occur if each point could be followed by more than one of the other points.

This defect can be quite troublesome and is one of the major problems with the multiplicative congruential method. If K values from a sequence of length L are grouped to form points in K-space, an 'ideal' generator would deliver L^K distinct points. But, because each value delivered by the generator determines its successor, L distinct points *at most* are created; thus there are at least L^{K-1} "unavailable" points. That is, a given value can occur only once in *any* coordinate (unless more than L/K points are generated).

To illustrate: Suppose a generator delivers a sequence of 5 points (.5, .1, .7, .3, .9). In 2-space, only the five points (.5, .1), (.7, .3), (.9, .5), (.1, .7) and (.3, .9) of a possible 25 are generated; and in three (or four) dimensions, only 5 of a possible 125 (or 625) are generated. As a rule of thumb, for k-tuples derived from a congruential generator, keep $K < (1/3) \log_2 (L)$.

Even if this "thinness" of distribution in many dimensions is acceptable, some care must be exercised in the generator to ensure the points are reasonably evenly distributed along *each* dimension.

Periodicity Tests

CONCEPT: To determine whether the values produced by a pseudo-random number generator exhibit periodicity.

PROCESS: For pseudo-random number sequences produced by multiplicative congruential methods, the period is synonomous with the sequence length. This factor is due to the dependence of each value in the sequence on the preceding value. This period can be determined by noting the first value of the sequence and then either generating subsequent values or traversing the values of the existing sequence until that first value recurs (i.e., until $R_n = R_1$). Then $n-1$ is defined as the period of the sequence.

Sequences resulting from other sources may also exhibit periodic behavior. This behavior is not as easy to detect as that within sequences resulting from the multiplicative congruential methods, since the relationships between subsequent values may not be so well-defined.

One technique for detecting such *hidden* periodicity is to perform a Fourier spectrum analysis on the values in the sequence. The Fourier series is a representation of a series of data points (values), $F(t)$, as a sum of harmonic terms in the form

$$F(t) = \sum \left[a_n \sin (nwt) + b_n \cos (nwt) \right]$$

When $F(t)$ is specified at a discrete set of points, such as values in a random number sequence, the coefficients a_n and b_n can be found by summing products of the data and the trigonometric functions. These coefficients comprise the amplitude spectrum, and the quantity, $\sqrt{a_n^2 + b_n^2}$, is a measure of the importance of harmonic frequency nw in the data. Large values of a_n and b_n indicate that the sequence has a significant component of variation with a period $2\pi/(nw)$.

Tests of Multi-Dimensional Distribution

CONCEPT: To determine whether the values produced by a pseudo-random number generator are randomly distributed in multidimensional space

PROCESS: The following form of the mixed congruential method has enjoyed great popularity on 32-bit computer systems:

$$X_{k+1} = X_k \times 65539 (\text{modulo } 2^{31})$$

The choices of values for A and M reflect some knowledge of the architecture of the computer upon which this generator is used. A and M refer to the coefficients used in the definition of the mixed congruential method.

The sequences produced by this generator satisfy the usual tests for randomness. However, further analysis reveals that while in one or two dimensions the distribution of the sequence is quite acceptably uniform, in three dimensions *all* the numbers in the sequence lay on only 16 distinct planes in the unit cube. This means that sequences generated for problems such as Monte Carlo simulations in three dimensions sample only a very small portion of the available space.

Unfortunately, this behavior is common to *all* generators of the multiplicative congruential type; all the generated numbers will lie on lines, planes, or hyper-planes in spaces of two, three, or higher numbers of dimensions.

Table 4.2 shows the *maximum* number of planes on which the generated numbers can lie in a N-dimensional unit cube for various values of the moduli M.

For poor choices of A and M, the actual number of resulting planes can be far smaller, as demonstrated by the values of A and M in the previous example. The values of A, C, and M should be chosen such that the following criterion are met:

1. The number of planes upon which the sequences reside is large.
2. The pseudo-random number sequence is as long as possible (i.e., maximum number of members before any member is repeated);
3. When successive k-tuples of numbers are used to form points in a k-dimensional space, the distribution of these points is as "uniform" as possible;
4. And the "unit cube" (in whatever number of dimensions) is adequately densely populated with points for the application in which the sequence is to be used.

The family of congruential methods has been criticized as unreliable because of their plane behavior, but they can be quite satisfactory in specific, controlled applications. The suitability of such a method is one of the many trade-offs that

Table 4.2 Correlations of Planar Distribution

M	N=3	N=4	N=5	N=6	N=7	N=8	N=9	N=10
2^{15}	58	29	20	16	14	13	13	12
2^{16}	73	35	23	19	16	15	14	13
2^{24}	465	141	72	47	36	30	26	23
2^{31}	2344	476	191	107	72	55	45	38
2^{32}	2953	566	220	120	80	60	48	41
2^{35}	5907	952	333	170	108	78	61	51
2^{36}	7442	1133	383	191	119	85	66	54
2^{47}	94519	7623	1760	682	354	220	154	117
2^{48}	119086	9065	2021	766	391	240	167	126

are necessary when defining the specifications of the model within which it may be applied.

Correlations and Other Measures of 'Quality'

There have been many weighty analyses of various properties of pseudo-random number generators. Unfortunately, two things seem to occur:

1. A method is extensively analyzed because mathematical tools exist to analyze that particular method, not because the method is inherently good or bad;
2. On the basis of these analyses, definitive statements are made regarding ''optimal'' values or parameters or techniques.

Therefore the following guidelines may be useful:

1. The adequacy or appropriateness of a generator depends on the application in which it will be used. The generator should be tested with respect to that application.
2. A generator is useful only within the bounds of its sequence. Testing should insure that these bounds are not exceeded.
3. Be wary of sequences that when tested give distributions either too rough or too smooth.
4. Avoid long ''lags'' where many points are skipped over. (Almost all generators exhibit a correlation of -1 at lags of $L/2$).

PITFALLS IN PSEUDO-RANDOM NUMBER GENERATION

A number of generation techniques that have enjoyed popularity in the past can be proven unreliable. Among these techniques are

1. The ''mid-square method,'' where X_k is squared, and the middle digits of the product are taken as the value of X_{k+1};
2. The ''Fibonacci method,'' where $X_{k+1} = X_k + X_{k-1}$ (modulo M);
3. The contents of something changed in computer memory, such as a program timer;
4. ''Scrambling methods,'' where X_{k+1} is produced by shifting and/or mixing the bit representation of X_k.

Mixing Generators

One common idea is that if generated numbers are random, then the sequence of numbers will be even more random if it is generated by a method selected at random. Unfortunately, such numbers aren't usually very random, since they can't be guaranteed to have the statistical properties that are known for any one of the generators. Furthermore, pathological behavior may occur; the sequence may degenerate to a constant value, or may display a distinct bias.

These simple problems can be overcome by suitable precautions, but the real dangers have not been prevented. For example, suppose three routines are called to generate triples of points to be used as points in ordinary three-dimensional space. It may be found that the three generators called for the x, y, and z coordinates happen to have been written with the same values as the constants A and M, and differ only in their values of C. This means that the variations of the three values will be very highly correlated; a low value of the x-coordinate might always be accompanied by a high value of the y- and z-coordinates.

The point of this warning is that a random number generator may be presumed to have tolerable properties of randomness *only* when it is used by itself, and not in combination with *any* other generator. It should not be assumed that because of access to several generators of "good" quality that some clever combination of calls to some or all of them will produce even "better" numbers.

A second popular idea is to save effort by using the bits from a random number generator singly or in small groups. *This is dangerous!* To see why, consider a typical multiplicative congruential generator in which

$$X_{k+1} = X_k \times A(\text{modulo } M)$$

with M even, A odd and X_1 odd. Then *every* X_k will be odd, and the lowest-order bit is perfectly nonrandom! The other low-order bits will display periodic behavior also, but the periodicity becomes less evident toward the high-order end of the number.

It is much better to "use the whole number." If a small integer K in the range $[1, N]$ is required then

$$K = \text{RANDOM} (0) \times \text{FLOAT} (N) + 1$$

where RANDOM is a generator that returns REAL values on (0, 1). It is *not* recommended to use the integer values (modulo N) from a generator, because it is necessary that N is prime to both the multiplier A and to the modulus M of the generator.

Portable Uniform Generators

Occasionally the need arises for a program containing a random number generator that is portable between multiple computer systems. While generators of pseudo-random numbers are almost invariably machine-dependent, there exist a few techniques for writing generators that will

1. Produce a usable sequence on different machines so long as the words are long enough, or
2. Produce the identical sequence on different machines, or
3. Compute their own values of A, C and M so that the generated sequence is likely to be of high quality.

Portable generators of machine-independent sequences are difficult to write. Such routines sometimes involve concessions and compromises that make the sequences very short and the statistical properties "merely adequate." But they can be quite useful if portability is a strong requirement, or if code must be run on a mini- or micro-computer with short word length.

Non-Uniform Distributions

CONCEPT: To define techniques by which sequences of pseudo-random values that are not uniformly distributed may be generated

PROCESS: Nonuniform distributions of random or pseudo-random values may often be obtained by identifying a specific transformation function that maps uniformly distributed values onto a non-uniform distribution.

Normal (Gaussian) Distribution.   An interesting technique for generating normally distributed random values is the Box-Muller method. Given two uniform $(0, 1)$ values, R_1 and R_2, two normal $(0, 1)$ values X_1 and X_2 can be generated with the following relations:

$$X_1 = \text{sqrt}\left(-2.0 \times \text{alog}\left(R_1\right)\right) \times \sin\left(2.0\pi R_2\right)$$
$$X_2 = \text{sqrt}\left(-2.0 \times \text{alog}\left(R_1\right)\right) \times \cos\left(2.0\pi R_2\right)$$

While this method produces precise values (assuming the generator of R_1 and R_2 is adequate), it is slow due to the need to reference the square root (sqrt), inverse logarithm (alog) and trigonometric (sin and cos) functions.

Exponential/Poisson Distribution.   The following is a general method for generating a sequence of pseudo-random numbers with a given continuous (cumulative) distribution function $F(x)$.

Given a uniform $(0, 1)$ value, R_1, if the equation $F(X) = R_1$ or $F(x) = 1 - R_1$ is solved then the value of x will represent the value of R_1 transformed by $F(x)$.

Consider, for example, a desired sequence of exponentially distributed pseudo-random numbers described by the distribution function

$$F(x) = 1 - e^{-\lambda x}$$

where the mean of the function is equal to $1/\lambda$.
The solution of the equation

$$1 - e^{-\lambda x} = 1 - R_1$$

yields

$$x = -\lambda^{-1} ln R_1$$

The following Pascal program then yields the desired sequence.

```
Program ExpRand (Input, Output);
Var x, y, lambda : Real;
    i : Integer;
Begin
   ReadLn(lambda);
   y : = Random(5);
   for i : = 1 to 10 do
      Begin
         x : = -(1.0/lambda)*Ln(Random(0));
         WriteLn(x)
      End
End.
```

User-Defined Distributions. It is often desirable to produce sequences of random or pseudo-random values that are not described by a known distribution function. A good example may be empirical values resulting from observation.

The following example demonstrates a general method for describing such a desired sequence. The histogram shown in Figure 4-1 presents the observed frequency of occurrence of values between 0 and 10 over a sample of 25 observations. The values observed do not conform to a well-known distribution function. From the histogram the Table 4-3 can be constructed.

This table represents a *cumulative distribution function* for a user-defined distribution of values. Given a uniform (0, 1) value, R_1 random values (R_2) in the range [0, 10] reflecting the user-defined distribution can be generated by way of the following case analysis:

If $R_1 \leq 0.04$ then $R_2 = 0$
If $0.4 < R_1 \leq 0.16$ then $R_2 = 1$
If $0.16 < R_1 \leq 0.20$ then $R_2 = 2$
If $0.20 < R_1 \leq 0.40$ then $R_2 = 3$
If $0.40 < R_1 \leq 0.44$ then $R_2 = 4$
If $0.44 < R_1 \leq 0.56$ then $R_2 = 5$

Table 4-3. Cumulative Distribution Analysis of Values Displayed in Figure 4-1.

Value	Number of Occurrences	Cumulative Number of Occurences	Value Probability	Cumulative Fractile
0	1	1	0.04	0.04
1	3	4	0.12	0.16
2	1	5	0.04	0.20
3	5	10	0.20	0.40
4	1	11	0.04	0.44
5	3	14	0.12	0.56
6	1	15	0.04	0.60
7	5	20	0.20	0.80
8	1	21	0.04	0.84
9	3	24	0.12	0.96
10	1	25	0.04	1.00

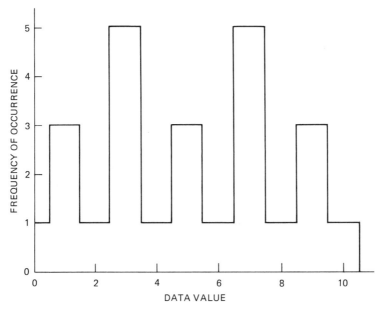

Figure 4-1. The frequency of occurrence of sample arbitrary integer values.

If $0.56 < R_1 \leq 0.60$ then $R_2 = 6$
If $0.60 < R_1 \leq 0.80$ then $R_2 = 7$
If $0.80 < R_1 \leq 0.84$ then $R_2 = 8$
If $0.84 < R_1 \leq 0.96$ then $R_2 = 9$
If $0.96 < R_1 \leq 1.00$ then $R_2 = 10$

REFERENCES

1. Ahrens, J. H., Dieter, U., and Grube, A., "Pseudo-Random Numbers: A New Proposal for the Choice of Multiplicators", *Computing 6* (1970), 121–138; and "Computer Methods for Sampling from the Exponential and Normal Distributions", *Comm. ACM 15* (Oct. 1972), 873–882.

2. Ahrens, J. H., and Dieter, U., "An Exact Determination of Serial Correlations of Pseudo-Random Numbers," *Numer. Math. 17* (1971), 101–123.

3. Christiansen, H. Dalgas, "Random Number Generators in Several Dimensions. Theory, Tests, and Examples," The Institute of Mathematical Statistics and Operations Research, The Technical University of Denmark (October 1975).

4. Everett, C. J., and Cashwell, E. D., "A Monte Carlo Sampler," Los Alamos Scientific Laboratory Informal Report LA-5061-MS, Oct. 1972.

5. Everett, C. J., and Cashwell, E. D., "A Second Monte Carlo Sampler," Los Alamos Scientific Laboratory Informal Report LA-5723-MS, Sept. 1974.

6. Hull, T. E., and Dobell, A. R., "Random Number Generators," *SIAM Review 4* 3 (July 1964), 230–239.

7. Hutchinson, David W., "A New Uniform Pseudorandom Number Generator," *Comm. ACM 9* 6 (June 1966), 432–433. (This is the first widely known reference to the Lehmer method.)

8. Knuth, Donald E., The Art of Computer Programming. Reading, MA: Addison-Wesley; Vol. 1 [2nd ed.], 1974; Vol. 2 [2nd ed.], 1981; Vol. 3, 1973

9. Marsaglia, George, "Random Numbers Fall Mainly in the Planes," *Proc. Nat. Acad. Sci. 61* 1 (Sept. 1968), 25–28.

10. Marsaglia, George, "The Structure of Linear Congruential Sequences," in *Applications of Number Theory to Numerical Analysis*, S. K. Zaremba, ed. New York: Academic Press (1972), 249–285.

11. Marsaglia, G., "The Structure of Linear Congruential Sequences," in Applications of Number Theory to Numerical Analysis, S. K. Zaremba, ed. New York: Academic Press, 1972.

12. Niederreiter, Harald, "Quasi-Monte Carlo Methods and Pseudo-Random Numbers," *Bull. AMS 54*, 6 (Nov. 1978), 957–1041. (This is a very extensive and rather mathematical review of the entire field, and is worth browsing for the advice at the end of each section.)

13. Niederreiter, Harald, and Borosh, Itshak, "Optimal Multipliers for Pseudo-Random Number Generation by the Linear Congruential Method," preprint.

14. Payne, W. H., Rabung, J. R., and Bogyo, T. P., "Coding the Lehmer Pseudo-Random Number Generator," *Comm. ACM 12* 2 (Feb. 1969), 85–86.

15. Press, W., Flannery, B., Teukolsky, S., and Vetterling, W., *Numerical Recipes—The Art of Scientific Computing*. New York: Cambridge University Press, 1986.

16. Smith, C. S., "Multiplicative Pseudo-Random Number Generators with Prime Modulus," *J. ACM 18*, 4 (Oct. 1971), 586–593. (Smith recommends the generator $X(k + 1) = X(k) * 3432$ (modulo 9973), with 9972 elements in the sequence.)

17. Sowey, E. R., "A Chronological and Classified Bibliography on Random Number Generation and Testing," *Int. Stat. Rev. 40*, 3 (1972), 335–371.

18. Sowey, E. R., ''A Second Classified Bibliography on Random Number Generation and Testing,'' *Int. Stat. Rev. 46* (1978), 89–102.
19. Whitney, Charles A., ''Generating and Testing Pseudorandom Numbers,'' *BYTE*, Oct. 1984.
20. Whittlesey, John R. B., ''On the Multidimensional Uniformity of Pseudorandom Generators,'' *Comm. ACM 12*, 5 (May 1969), 247.

NOTE

Kendall, M. G. and Smith, B. B., ''Randomness and Random Sampling Numbers.'' *J.R. Statis. Soc., 101* pp. 147–166, (1938).

5

SIMULATION AND MONTE CARLO TECHNIQUES

> *". . .What we're doing in trying to understand nature is to imagine that the gods are playing some great game and you don't know the rules of the game, but you're allowed to look at the board, at least from time to time. And in a little corner perhaps and from these observations, you try to figure out what the rules are of the game, what the rules of the pieces moving."*
>
> Richard Feynman

Simulation can, in general, be described as the technique of constructing and operating ("in vitro" using a computer) a model of a real system in order to study the behavior of that system without disrupting the environment of the real system. In fact, the system in question may be either a real (i.e., existing) system, or one that is proposed. Such a system's behavior and response to stimuli may be modeled by a computer program designed to react to various conditions in a manner quantitatively similar to the system itself. The results of such an exercise may be used to gain insights, make decisions, test hypotheses, demonstrate or verify new ideas, establish feasibility, compare alternatives, design systems, or train personnel.

The algorithmic nature of most high-level scientific programming languages typically makes them unsuitable for writing nondeterministic or stochastic programs of a type expected by these models. As a result, specific simulation languages such as GPSS and SIMSCRIPT have been developed that incorporate characteristics of such models as primitives. However, such primitives can effectively be emulated.

When it is not possible to express the interrelations of a model in a convenient closed form because the system is too complex or because responses are subject to random variation, it is necessary to formulate operating rules and to study behavior by simulation.

114

A process or model is *deterministic* if for every value of input, the output can be determined in some reproducible fashion, i.e., by an algorithm.

A process or model is *stochastic* if it is random or the interrelationships among all components cannot be defined. In such a process, when sufficient observations have been made, it may be possible to determine the statistical basis or set of rules which govern the behavior of that system.

Given the nature of these definitions, systems can be either deterministic or stochastic. Likewise, the models of these systems can be either deterministic or stochastic. The relationships between components of a model or system do not dictate the relationships between the components of their associated models or systems. Table 5.1 gives examples of the possible combinations of deterministic and stochastic systems and models.

Table 5.1. Examples of Deterministic and Stochastic Systems and Models

System	Model	Example
Deterministic	Deterministic	Equations of motion in a physical system
Deterministic	Stochastic	Calculation of the area under a curve using Monte Carlo integration
Stochastic	Deterministic	Pseudo-random number generation
Stochastic	Stochastic	Simulation of activities at a toll bridge

The decision to implement a deterministic or stochastic model of a specific system is very difficult and subjective. Considerable knowledge of the system to be modelled is essential. There are two established principles relevant to this decision:

1. If a deterministic model of the system is available, it should always be used; stochastic models *should approximate* deterministic models of the same system in the limit.
2. If a stochastic model appears necessary, comparable simulations with differing models should be performed (see Table 5.1). As noted, the design

of stochastic models is very subjective, and a function of available knowledge of the system modelled.

GLOSSARY OF TERMS

Computer Simulation: A model of a proposed or existing system whose elements can be represented by arithmetic and logical processes that can be executed on a computer to predict the dynamic properties of the system in operation.

Deterministic (Process or Model): A process or model for which for every value of input the output can be determined in some reproducible fashion, as by means of algorithm.

Event: A condition of significance to a system or model.

Model: A representation of a system. A basic requirement of a model is that it should describe the system in sufficient detail for the behavior of the model to provide valid predictions of the behavior of the system.

Modelling: The ability to design a conceptual model that imitates the system under study at the required level of detail.

Monte Carlo: A term applied to techniques for obtaining approximate solutions to deterministic or stochastic problems.

Problem Time: The duration of a process.

Random Number Sequence: An unpredictable array (sequence) of numbers produced by change, and satisfying one or more of the tests of randomness; each number is essentially an independent item of information, and it cannot be predicted from its neighbor or from some underlying rule; the information embodied in a random series of numbers cannot be "compressed" or reduced to a more compact form.

Sampling: The method of deducing properties of a large set of elements by studying only a random subset.

Simulation: The technique of constructing and operating a model of a real system in order to study the behavior of that system during its design and/or without disrupting the environment of the real system.

Stochastic (Process or Model): A process or model that is random or in which the interrelationships among all components cannot be defined. In such a process or model, when sufficient observations have been made, it may be possible to determine the statistical basis or set of rules that govern the behavior of that system.

Subsystem: A component of the total system that can be treated either as a part of the total system or as an independent system.

System: A set of parts organized functionally to form a connected whole.

EXAMINATION OF DETERMINISTIC AND STOCHASTIC SYSTEMS AND MODELS

Table 5.1 gives examples of the possible combinations of deterministic and stochastic systems and models. Each of these combinations defines a unique application of simulation requiring the use of specific techniques. The following sections examine each of these combinations and techniques for implementing them in greater detail.

Deterministic System/Deterministic Model

A *deterministic* system/model is characterized by the fact that the relationships between all parameters of the system and model are all explicitly defined.

The simplest case of a deterministic system/model is one which can be expressed as an *algorithm*. In such models a well-defined relationship exists between input and output as embodied in the steps of an unambiguous algorithm.

Systems can also be deterministic without being explicitly algorithmic. Software design methodologies such as Yourdon/DeMarco depict software (usually on-line) systems in terms of deterministic models. A model of this type is defined by such properties as the movement of data within a system (depicted by DFDs), the relationships between system entities (depicted by ERDs) and the states of transitions the system encounters during operation (depicted by STDs).

The HIPO design methodology is based upon the explicit definition of the process that *converts* input into output. The logical model of all software systems thereby becomes one of a *black box* for input/output transformation.

Deterministic System/Stochastic Model: Sampling

Statistical sampling typically refers to methods of deducing properties of a large population of entities by examination of a smaller randomly selected subset. The role of statistical sampling in a simulation model is to generate transactions or events that drive that model. Such events may include the frequency of events, the duration of a single event, and so forth. This information is generated by statistically sampling the probability distribution that describes the anticipated frequency of these events. Statistical sampling is the primary stochastic element of simulation.

Pseudo-random number sequences play a crucial role in simulation models. They provide the means by which statistical sampling is accomplished. Consequently, the effectiveness of the sampling function of a model is dependent upon the characteristics of the source of random numbers.

EXAMPLE: Monte Carlo techniques can approximate the area under a curve (i.e., integration) by approximating the *probability* that random points lie above or below the curve. The ratio of these probabilities can in turn be used to calculate the integral to a predetermined level of accuracy. The system in this case is deterministic since integration is a well-defined process of the calculus. However, digital computers are incapable of performing primitive operations equivalent to the primitives of the calculus. Therefore, such processes may be accomplished only via numerical (digital, e.g., trapezoidal method) means or via stochastic means such as sampling.

The following program calculates

$$\int_0^4 x^2 \, dx$$

by sampling 10,000 random points in a rectangle enclosing the curve within the desired limits of integration.

```
Program Int(Output);
Var x, y, area : Real;
    i, count : Integer;
Begin
 count := 0;
 y := Random(5);
 for i := 1 to 10000 do
  Begin
   x := Random(0)*4.0;
   y := Random(0)*16.0;
   If y <= x*x then count := count + 1
  End;
 area := count/10000 * 64;
 WriteLn(' The value is ',area:10:5)
End.
```

However, if such a Monte Carlo technique is used to estimate an integral, the asymptotic orders of magnitude for the error in estimating integrals of well-behaved functions in k dimensions by sampling values at N points are applicable (Table 5.2).

From the table, it can be seen that a uniform distribution is superior to random sampling in one dimension, and is competitive with Monte Carlo in two dimensions. It can also be seen that quasi-random sequences are vastly superior to either uniform or random distributions in two or more dimensions.

Table 5.2. Asymptotic Orders of Magnitude For the Error in Estimating Integrals of Well-Behaved Functions in K Dimensions by Sampling Values at N Points.

Uniform distribution	$1/(N**(1/K))$
Random distribution	$SQRT((\log \log N)/N)$
Special low-discrepancy (Quasi-random) sequences	$((\log N)_K)/N$

Stochastic System/Deterministic Model

Pseudo-random number generation is an example of a stochastic system with a deterministic model in that by definition a random number sequence cannot be uniquely described by a closed model. Deterministic models provide sequences of numbers that are satisfactory when compared with the potential overhead costs of storing tables of random numbers. Pseudo-random number generation is discussed in Chapter 4.

Stochastic System/Stochastic Model

A typical multilane toll bridge (Figure 5.1) is an example of an extremely complex system involving the interaction of many poorly-defined subsystems (e.g., toll-booth availability, driver tolerance, and so forth). A simulation involving a stochastic system and model appears to be one of the most efficient means of studying the behavior of these subsystems. Relevant parameters in such a model may include

- Number of entry traffic lanes.
- Number of available toll booths.
- Toll-booth selection strategy of approaching motorists.
- Arrival rate of automobiles.
- Time to conduct toll-paying transactions.
- Reaction time of motorists to traffic movement.

Other parameters may be identified depending upon the desired complexity of the model.

The managers of such a bridge may desire the answers to questions such as the following in order to assure optimum bridge operation:

1. What percentage of the working day is each toll booth actually collecting a toll?

2. What is the maximum number of automobiles that will have to wait for service at each toll booth?
3. These automobiles must wait an average of how many minutes?

There may be several ways to obtain answers to these questions:

- Describe the system deterministically.
- Visit the bridge, make observations and calculate the required results.
- Duplicate the process on a computer (i.e., simulate the bridge, toll-booths, automobiles and times).

Management decisions resulting from the acquired information may result in

- The operation of additional toll-booths
- A program to minimize the toll collection time

Adjustment of the model to reflect such changes could provide a measure of their influence on the behavior of the system.

Simulation programs can be and often are as varied as the systems they model. There are, however, six common elements that occur repeatedly in simulation programs of stochastic models. These elements are

1. Movement.
2. The passage of time.
3. Statistical sampling.
4. Simulation of system facilities and storages.
5. Queues.
6. Accumulation of system statistics.

It is these elements, which are not primitives in algorithmic languages, that must be emulated with software techniques.

Movement.   Transactions are the units of traffic that move through the system simulated. They vary with the system itself. Operations upon transactions are called *events*.

Statistical Sampling.   Statistical sampling typically refers to methods of deducing properties of a large population of entities by examination of a smaller randomly selected subset. The role of statistical sampling in simulation models is to generate transactions or events that drive the models. Such events may include the frequency of events, the duration of a single event, and so forth. Such information is generated by a statistical sampling of the probability distribution describing the anticipated frequency of these events. Statistical sampling is the primary stochastic element of simulation.

The use of pseudo-random number sequences plays a crucial role in simulation models. It provides the means by which statistical sampling is accomplished. Consequently, the effectiveness of the sampling function of a model is dependent upon the characteristics of the source of random numbers.

Simulation of System Facilities and Storages. Transactions move from point to point through the system as they would in an actual situation. These points to which, or through which, a transaction must move, or that a transaction uses, are known as *facilities* and *storages*. A particular facility may be occupied by only a single transaction at a time. A storage, on the other hand, may be occupied by a number of transactions simultaneously, the limit usually being specified.

Queues. Because a particular facility may be occupied by only one transaction at a time, any attempt by another transaction to enter the facility forces it to stand in a waiting line, or queue. When a transaction leaves the facility, the first transaction in the queue will then be processed. (Transactions may be processed out of arrival sequence if they are assigned priorities.)

Most systems of any complexity involve *multiserver queues*. It is important to distinguish between a multiserver queue and several single-server queues. The requirements for a multiserver queue are that the next transaction to be "served" by the facility be handled by the next available "server," and that all servers are equally loaded. A simple example of a multi-server queue is that of a bank where a single line (queue) of customers is served by a number of tellers in turn. Each teller window in service can accommodate only a single customer/transaction.

Time. Time is the element by which progress of a transaction (and all transactions) through the system may be measured. The unit of time may be days, hours, minutes, or microseconds, whichever is appropriate. There is usually no connection between time expressed in the model and the time it takes to simulate the situation.

In system simulation, the behavior of the system with respect to time is usually an important factor. As a result, the model must include some mechanism to simulate the passage of time.

The passage of time is usually modelled continuously or discretely:

- *Continuous time*—in this model, the system "clock" moves continuously whether an event of relevance to the model occurs or not.
- *Discrete time*—in this model, the system clock advances only to those times at which events of relevance to the model are scheduled to occur.

Each of these time models includes the other with varying effectiveness. Selection of the appropriate time model depends on the system model in which it will be embedded.

Both time models are event/transaction-driven. Therefore all activities to be simulated in the system model occur in one of two time-dependent categories:

- *Current events*—this "collection" contains events/transactions that are "active" at the current clock count; the processing of current events is the fundamental description of the system model.
- *Future events*—this collection consists of transactions or events that are to occur at some future time; with each clock step, all events scheduled for the current time would move from future events to current events; a scheduling activity, concurrent with current events processing, would add transactions and events "created" at the current time.

Three of the important time factors are

- *Transit time*—the time taken by a transaction from starting point to termination in the system.
- *Facility time*—the time a transaction takes to be processed in a facility. Facility times are a function of the individual transaction and the individual facility through which it passes.
- *Queue time*—the time a transaction has to wait before entering a facility; Queue time depends upon the number of transactions waiting for the facility and the time required to process them through the facility. Queue time for any specific transaction is thus *cumulative*.

Accumulation of System Statistics. This function describes the mechanism created to accumulate vital statistics generated during the simulation. The results of this activity may be used for debugging the model and for system analysis.

This program output usually consists of the following:

1. Facility utilization statistics.
2. Queue occupancy statistics.
3. Tables of time distributions.
4. A measure of system throughput.

Facility utilization is defined most simply as the measure of how busy the servers to a facility are at an average time. Therefore the following would be valid calculations of facility utilization (FU):

$$FU = (\text{time spent working}/(\text{hours expended})$$

$$FU = \text{(capacity being used)} / \text{(maximum capacity)}$$

$$FU = \text{(number of arrivals)} * \text{(time of service)} / \text{(number of servers)}$$

Using Unique Data Structures in Simulation Programs.   Simulation programs are most often used to describe the activity of "real-life" systems. As a result, the relationships between data items in these programs should accurately reflect the relationships in the "real" systems. These descriptions often require the definition of unique data structures.

Chapter 3 describes a special FIFO data structure called the *priority queue*. Such a queue is quite useful in simulation programs for the generation of a *future events chain* and a *current events chain*. In these data structures, the ordering of transactions according to a associated value (such as a time) provides an accurate logical model of physical operations.

The following is a Pascal program that demonstrates a specialized application of a priority queue to accomplish the processing required by the event chain in a simulation program.

```
Program Pri(Output);
Type EvChain = ^List;
     List = Record
                  Time_Event : Integer;
                  Event_Type : Integer;
                  Link : EvChain
              End;
Var Top : EvChain;
    N,I,K,Clock : Integer;

Procedure ChAdd(VAR Q: EvChain; NewType:Integer;
NewTime:Integer);
  Var P : EvChain;
  Begin
    If Q = Nil Then
       Begin
         New(Q);
         Q^.Event_Type := NewType;
         Q^.Time_Event := NewTime;
         Q^.Link := Nil
       End
                 Else
                    If NewTime < Q^.Time_Event Then
                       Begin
                         New(P);
                         P^.Event_Type := NewType;
                         P^.Time_Event := NewTime;
```

```
                                P^.Link := Q;
                                Q := P
                            End
                                                Else

ChAdd(Q^.Link,NewType,NewTime)      )
   End;

 Procedure ChList(Q:EvChain);
    Var P : EvChain;
    Begin
      P := Q;
      While P <> Nil Do
        Begin
          Write(P^.Time_Event);
          Writeln;

Type Ptr = ^Element;
     Element = Record
                  ElementData:Integer;
                  Link:Ptr
                  End {Element Definition};

               * * * *

Procedure SeqSearch(ListPtr : Ptr);
Var X : Ptr;
    Large : Integer;
Begin
  Large := 0;
  X := ListPtr;
  While X <> Nil Do
                 Begin
                    If X^.ElementData > Large
                       Then Large := X^.ElementData;
                    X := X^.Link
                 End;
   WriteLn(Large)
End {SeqSearch Procedure};
        P := P^.Link
      End
   End;

Procedure ChDelete(VAR Q:EvChain);
Var Temp : EvChain;
Begin
  Temp := Q;
  Q := Q^.Link;
```

```
   Dispose(Temp)
End;

   Begin
     Top := Nil;
     For K:= 1 To 10 Do
       Begin
         Repeat I := Random(100) Until I > 0;
         N := Random(5);
         ChAdd(Top,N,I)
       End;
     For Clock := 1 To 100 Do
       While Top^.Time_Event = Clock Do
         Begin
           Writeln('Time = ',Clock,'  Type = ',Top^.Event_Type);
           ChDelete(Top)
         End
End.
```

Example: A Toll Bridge Model.   The following Pascal program simulates a
simplistic model of a toll bridge as described previously. A description of the
physical and logical models upon which the program is based follow the
program.

Program Bridge (Input.Output);

Const Period = 100;
    BoothCount = 4;

Type Ptr = ^Car;
    Car = Record
            CarNumber:1..Maxint;
            EntryTime:1..Maxint;
            ExitTime:0..Maxint;
            Link:Ptr
          End {Car Definition};

Var Clock:1..Period;
    Booth:Array[1..BoothCount,1..2] of Ptr;
    NewCar, OldCar:Ptr;
    Lane, LaneCount:Integer;
    I, J, K, Counter, Minimum, Choice:Integer;
    TollTime, ReactTime, TimeDiff, TotalTime:Integer;
    Init, Arrival, AvgWait:Real;

Procedure EnQueue (Var RearPtr, FrontPtr, NewPtr:Ptr);

```
Begin
   If FrontPtr = Nil Then FrontPtr := NewPtr;
   NewPtr^.Link := RearPtr;
   RearPtr := NewPtr
End {EnQueue Procedure};


Procedure DeQueue (Var RearPtr, FrontPtr, DataPtr: Ptr);
Var X: Ptr;
Begin
   If RearPtr = FrontPtr Then
                        If RearPtr = Nil Then DataPtr := Nil
                                          Else
                                             Begin
                                                DataPtr := FrontPtr:
                                                RearPtr := Nil;
                                                FrontPtr := Nil
                                             End
                     Else
                        Begin
                           X := RearPtr;
                           While X^.Link < > FrontPtr Do
                              X := X^.Link;
                           DataPtr := FrontPtr;
                           FrontPtr := X;
                           If FrontPtr = Nil Then RearPtr := Nil
                        End
End {DeQueue Procedure};


Procedure QueueCheck(ListPtr: Ptr; Var Entries: Integer);
Var X: Ptr;
Begin
   Entries := 0;
   X := ListPtr;
   While X < > Nil Do
      Begin
         Entries := Entries + 1;
         X := X^.Link
      End
End {QueueCheck Procedure};


Begin {Bridge Simulation}
   LaneCount := BoothCount Div 2;
   For I := 1 to BoothCount Do
      For J := 1 to 2 Do
         Booth[I,J] := Nil;
   Init := Random(5);
   Counter := 0;
   TotalTime := 0;
   ReadLn (Arrival);
   For Clock := 1 to Period Do
```

```
    Begin
      If Random(0) < = Arrival Then
          Begin
            New(NewCar);
            Counter : = Counter + 1;
            NewCar^.CarNumber : = Counter;
            NewCar^.ExitTime : = 0;
            Lane : = Trunc(Random(0)*LaneCount + 1); {What lane?}
            Minimum : = 0;
            K : = 0;
            For I : = 2*Lane−1 to 2*Lane+1 Do {What booth?}
            If ((I> =I) And (I< =BoothCount)) Then
              Begin
                QueueCheck(Booth[I,1],K);
                If K < = Minimum Then Begin
                                        Minimum : = K;
                                        Choice : = I
                                        End
            End;
            NewCar^.EntryTime : = Clock;
            EnQueue (Booth[Choice,1],Booth[Choice,2],NewCar)
          End;
  For I : = 1 to BoothCount Do
    Begin
      If Booth[I,2] < > Nil Then
        Begin
          If Booth[I,2]^.ExitTime = 0 Then
            Begin
              TollTime : = 4 + Trunc(Random(0)*4 + 1);
              ReactTime : = 3 + Trunc(Random(0)*4 + 1);
              Booth[I,2]^.ExitTime : = Clock + TollTime + ReactTime
            End;
          If Booth[I,2]^.ExitTime = Clock Then
            Begin
              TimeDiff : = Booth[I,2]^.ExitTime − Booth[I,2]^.EntryTime;
              TotalTime : = TotalTime + TimeDiff;
              DeQueue(Booth[I,1],Booth[I,2],OldCar);
              Dispose(OldCar)
            End
        End
    End
  End;
  AvgWait : = TotalTime/Counter;
  WriteLn(' For ',Counter:3,' Automobiles');
  WriteLn(' Average Wait/Automobile is ',AvgWait:10:3,' seconds')
End.
```

The physical system describes a bridge with an approach of 6 automobile lanes accommodated by a maximum of 12 toll booths. The logical model attempts to determine what the average waiting time for an automobile is when presented with a specific set of conditions/limitations.

The following physical constraints are defined:

- The rate of automobile arrival is defined in terms of the probability of arrival per each time increment simulated.
- The distribution of arriving automobiles is uniform across the 6 arrival lanes simulated.
- Each arrival lane will have access to 3 toll booths (except for the outermost lanes).
- The selection of a toll booth will be made according to minimum occupancy (i.e., the accessible toll booth with the smallest number of waiting automobiles will be chosen).
- Factors affecting delay time in a toll booth are

  * Number of automobiles.
  * Time of toll-collecting process per automobile.
  * Reaction time of each automobile driver to traffic flow at the toll booth.

The logical model for the simulation program is described as follows:

- Transaction (automobiles) are represented as records. Each record contains the following information:

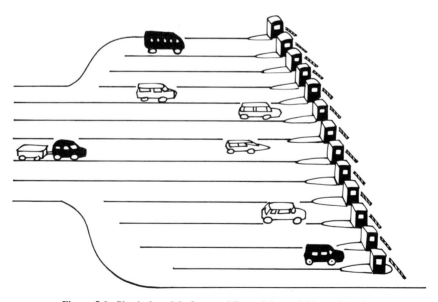

Figure 5.1. Physical model of automobiles arriving at bridge toll booth.

* An automobile identification number.
* The time at which that automobile enters a toll booth queue.
* The calculated time at which that automobile will leave the toll booth based on queue population, toll-collecting times and automobile driver reaction times.

• Each toll booth will be represented by a queue data structure whose elements are records representing transactions (automobiles).
• Events within the model are controlled by a discrete clock.

The operation of the program/model is then described:

1. The time period simulated is 2 hours (7200 seconds) set in the Const declaration for identifier Period.
2. Variable Arrival is input and represents the probability that an automobile will arrive in one of the 6 approach lanes each second of the simulation period.
3. Procedure *EnQueue* and Procedure *DeQueue* operate in the same manner described in Chapter 3.
4. Procedure *QueueCheck* determines the number of entries in a particular queue. This information is used in toll booth selection.
5. For each second in time simulated, the following processes occur:
   a. It is determined if an automobile arrives.
   b. If an automobile arrives:
      • It is assigned a number.
      • The lane in which it appears is randomly selected.
      • It is added to a toll booth queue according to queue selection criteria.
      • Its entry time in the toll booth queue is recorded.
   c. The toll booth queues are polled and the following operations performed:
      • If the calculated exit time for the automobile at the head of the queue is equal to the clock time, the time that automobile spends in the queue is calculated and added to an accumulator; The automobile is then covered from the queue. This operation is a variation on the concept of a *current events queue*.
      • If the automobile at the head of the queue does not have a calculated exit time, then it is calculated using the following empirical data:
         * The times for toll collection are uniformly distributed between 5 and 8 seconds.
         * The times for automobile driver reaction to traffic flow are uniformly distributed between 4 and 7 seconds.
   d. At the end of the time period simulated, the total time spent at toll booths divided by the total number of automobiles that exited a toll

booth will be equivalent to the average wait time of an automobile at a toll booth.

Table 5.3 gives an example of output data obtained from this simulation program.

Table 5.3. Results of Toll Bridge Simulation.

Probability of Arrival Each Second	Total Number of Automobiles	Average Wait Per Automobile (in seconds)
0.10	13	10.538
0.15	23	14.913
0.25	32	14.937

Shortcomings of Simulation.   The limitations of the toll bridge simulation program example are indicative of the general shortcomings that arise with the simulation of a stochastic system/stochastic model.

1. Development of a *good* simulation model is often expensive and time-consuming;
2. A simulation can appear to reflect accurately a *real world* situation when in truth it does not. Model design is the epitome of the *Garbage-In-Garbage Out* (*GIGO*) rule;
3. Simulation is imprecise, and it should be remembered that the degree of this imprecision is very difficult, if not impossible, to measure. Analysis of the sensitivity of the model to changing parameter values can only partially overcome this difficulty. It must be remembered that since a simulation is statistical in nature, that if the time period over which it is run is of sufficient length the output data should closely resemble, if not duplicate, the input data.

REFERENCES

1. Gordon, Geoffrey, *System Simulation*. Englewood Cliffs, NJ; Prentice-Hall, 1969.
2. Lewis, T. G., and Smith, B. J., *Computer Principles of Modeling and Simulation*. Boston, MA: Houghton Mifflin, 1979.
3. Szymankiewicz, J. Z. and Poole, T. G., *Using Simulation to Solve Problems*. By T. G. Poole, New York: McGraw-Hill, 1977.

4. Pritsker, A. Alan B., *The Gasp IV Simulation Language.* New York: Wiley, 1974.
5. Reitman, Julian, *Computer Simulation Applications: Discrete Event Simulation for Synthesis and Analysis of Complex Systems.* New York: Wiley, 1971.
6. Rubinstein, Reuven Y., *Simulation and the Monte Carlo Method.* New York: Wiley, 1981. (Wiley series in Probability and Mathematical Statistics).
7. Schoemaker, S., ed., *Computer Networks and Simulation.* Amsterdam: North-Holland, 1978.
8. Schriber, Thomas J., *Simulation Using GPSS.* New York, Wiley: 1974.
9. Shah, Manesh J. *Engineering Simulation Using Small Scientific Computers.* Englewood Cliffs, New Jersey: Prentice-Hall, 1976. (Prentice-Hall series in Automatic Computation).
10. Smith, Jon M., *Mathematical Modeling and Digital Simulation for Engineers and Scientists.* New York: Wiley, 1977.
11. Soucek, Branko, *Minicomputers in Data Processing and Simulation* New York: Wiley, 1972.

6

SURVEY OF GRAPHICS TECHNIQUES

"The computer has become a lens for the mind's eye. Never before has there been such a relationship between human and machine, each performing the function for which it is best suited. A human mind toys with concepts and forms, a computer races through millions of numbers, building pictures out of networks of interrelated coordinates."

Charles Barnett
'Computer Vision Can Show Us What the Mind Can Imagine,'
Smithsonian Magazine
June, 1981

The inclusion of graphics has become, in recent years, a factor of increasing importance to a software designer. The user public has become increasingly familar with systems that portray information graphically. As a result, this public has come to expect such facilities in specific software.

Advances in hardware technology have increased the pressure upon software designers to incorporate graphics techniques in their work. The availability of inexpensive display devices, inexpensive memory, fast processors, and laser printers has made graphics no longer the luxury it was in the past.

This chapter introduces the basic fundamentals of computer graphics. The techniques described do not produce impressive graphics by themselves, but instead are the foundation upon which more sophisticated graphics algorithms and techniques can be developed. These fundamentals may be classified into three categories: 1) the display of points, 2) the construction of lines, and the 3) manipulation of data.

GRAPHICS PRIMITIVES

To implement the graphics fundamentals (point display, line construction, and data manipulation) it is necessary to define a family of *graphics primitives*. These primitives represent the minimum set of software procedures required to define a graphics system. The following primitives are assumed for discussions in this chapter:

- *MoveTo(x, y)*—identifies and moves the graphics rendering device (i.e., beam, pen, etc.) to point in the display area with the coordinate values of *x* and *y*.
- *LineTo(x, y)*—draws a straight line from the current position of the graphics rendering device to a point in the display area with the coordinate values of *x* and *y*.
- *BitOn(x, y)*—instructs the graphics rendering device to place a point graphic at the point in the display area with the coordinate values of *x* and *y*. For raster devices, this primitive would be analogous to illuminating a specific picture element (*pixel*); for vector devices, this primitive would be synonymous to a PenDown operation.
- *BitOff(x, y)*—instructs the graphics rendering device *not* to place (or remove) a point graphic at the point in the display area with the coordinate values of *x* and *y*. For raster devices this primitive would be analogous to darkening a specific picture element (pixel); for vector devices this primitive would be synonymous to a PenUp operation.

Some of these primitives may appear to be redundant or inclusive of others, (e.g., LineTo in a raster system would certainly involve the use of BitOn). However, in other specific graphics applications, a distinction between them may be important (e.g., points may be used for applications other than drawing lines).

BITMAP GRAPHICS

Raster display differs from *line-drawing* (or vector) display chiefly in how displayed data are represented. A display file for a line-drawing display contains only information about about lines and characters to be drawn; the void areas of the display area are ignored. The raster scan display, however, controls the intensity of each dot (or pixel) in a rectangular matrix (or raster) of dots that covers the entire displayed area.

Bitmap graphics refers to the simplest form of a raster display, in which pixels are either on or off (illuminated or not illuminated, black or white). This bi-state allows the raster to be composed of only one value per pixel indicating its on/off state. 0's and 1's are usually used to represent these states. These values allow the raster to be expressed solely in terms of bit values, hence the term *bitmap*.

The flexibility of bitmap graphics allows the display of data in a geometrical form (graphs, lines, planes, etc.) as shown in Figure 6-1. Bitmaps may also be used to display nongeometrical data such as the example shown in Figure 6-2.

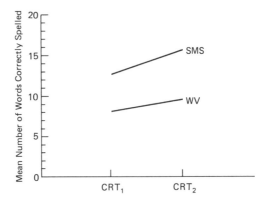

Figure 6-1. A vector graphics application.

Figure 6-2. A raster/bitmap graphics application.

All techniques in this chapter are described in terms of *raster* or *bitmap* graphics. The author believes this area of graphics to be of more general interest than *vector* graphics and supported more strongly by current technological advances.

GLOSSARY OF TERMS

Aliasing: A jagged or "stair-step" appearance of a graphically drawn line that is not vertical, horizontal, or at 45°. Aliasing is a function of the resolution of the display device (usually associated with raster devices) or the line-drawing algorithm (*also see* Jagging). Because of the sampling of image space at discrete points corresonding to pixels, techniques to alleviate this condition are referred to as *antialiasing* techniques.

Aspect Ratio: The ratio of one horizontal unit in the display area to one vertical unit in the display area;

Bit Manipulation: The facility or activity involved in reading and writing single bit values;

Bitmap: The representation of data for a raster scan display. Each picture element/pixel of the image is represented by (mapped into) an individual bit in computer memory, 1 denoting black and 0 denoted white (or vice versa). Such a bitmap is conveniently described as a two-dimensional array of bit values.

Bytemap: A two-dimensional array of byte values.

Clipping: A process by which portions or discrete elements of a graphical display are divided into visible and invisible portions. This process then allows the invisible portions to be discarded as necessary, removing those parts of display elements that lie outside of a given boundary.

Computer Graphics: The process of generating, manipulating, and displaying graphics (pictures) with the aid of a computer.

Interactive Computer Graphics: Computer graphics applications involving user control of image with an input device; characterized by a two-way communication between the computer and the user.

Display: A meaningful arrangement of output.

Dot Matrix: A grid or array in which marks (e.g., dots of light on a screen or inked impressions on paper) can be placed to construct graphic characters.

Graph: A two-dimensional representation of numeric values consisting, typically, of one or more lines, bars, or curves superimposed on a grid.

Histogram: A plot of the frequency of occurrence of discrete values.

Jagging: The condition in raster graphics in which curved and diagonal lines appear as "stair steps" with the distance between adjacent steps equal to the spacing of the display scan lines.

Passive Computer Graphics: Computer graphics applications involving no user/observer control over the image.

Pixel: Picture element.

Plot: To place graphic images on a display area.

Raster: A coordinate grid of addressable points containing all possible positions within a display area.

Resolution: The number of visibly distinct dots/picture units/pixels that can be displayed and used in graphics per unit linear measure of display.

Scaling: The application of a multiplicative factor to one or more display elements.

Shielding: Suppression of all or parts of display elements falling within a specified region. *Syn.*: Reverse Clipping.

Translation: The application of a constant displacement to the position of one or more display elements.

Windowing: The operation or facility involved in using "windows," or the act of placing a window around a particular portion of a display image.

Zooming: Progressively scaling the entire display image to give the visual impression of movement of all or part of a display group toward or away from an observer.

Display of Points

CONCEPT: To implement the BitOn/BitOff graphics primitive thereby enabling the identification of specific points within a graphics display

PROCESS: By definition, the display of data in a bitmap format necessitates the ability to deal with data at the *bit* level. Such data operations are typically restricted to low-level or assembler languages which are dependent on the host computer architecture.

However, such operations may be emulated if the data representation of higher level data abstractions is known. The following example demonstrates how BitOn can be implemented in Pascal.

EXAMPLE: In Pascal, bit manipulation is accomplished via *sets*. This is possible because the language represents set membership in terms of bit values within bit strings (i.e., bytes). These bit strings are ordered according to the ordinal values of the enumerated data type of the values that may compose the set. Therefore the presence of a value in a set is indicated by setting the bit in the appropriate bit string whose position corresponds to the ordinal value of the member.

Given this data model, a *bitmap* may be represented as a tabular arrangement of bit strings (or bit sets). BitOn is then accomplished by identifying the appropriate bit set within the bitmap and using the Pascal set operations to "turn on" the appropriate member of that set. This operation is demonstrated in the following Pascal procedure:

```
Type Bits = (bit7,bit6,bit5,bit4,bit3,bit2,bit1,bit0);
     BitSet = Set of Bits;
     Byte = Record
                 Entry : BitSet
            End;
     Line = Array[1..128] of Byte;
     Map = File of Line;

     *****

Var BitMap : Map;

Procedure BitOn(X,Y : Integer);
Var ByteRec : 1..128;
    BitRec : 0..7;
Begin
  ByteRec := Y Div 8 + 1;
  BitRec := Y Mod 8;
  Case BitRec of
     0 : BitMap^[ByteRec].Entry := [bit0];
     1 : BitMap^[ByteRec].Entry := [bit7];
     2 : BitMap^[ByteRec].Entry := [bit6];
     3 : BitMap^[ByteRec].Entry := [bit5];
     4 : BitMap^[ByteRec].Entry := [bit4];
     5 : BitMap^[ByteRec].Entry := [bit3];
     6 : BitMap^[ByteRec].Entry := [bit2];
     7 : BitMap^[ByteRec].Entry := [bit1];
  End {End Case}
End; {BitOn}
```

This procedure is designed to manipulate a bitmap, represented as a file, which has a resolution of 1024 bits in one direction (Y-axis) and indeterminate resolution in the other direction (X-axis). Each line of this file (bitmap) is composed of 128 bit sets (bytes). Each line of the bitmap is in *column-major form* (i.e., maps along the Y-coordinate axis).

This procedure does assume that the arguments X and Y are absolute bitmap addresses so some scaling based on display resolution may be required.

The manipulated file (bitmap) is global to this procedure and should be a random access file to permit updating of bits to occur.

Construction of Lines

CONCEPT: To implement the LineTo graphics primitive thereby enabling the drawing of straight lines within a graphics display

PROCESS: Line-drawing is perhaps the most "taken-for-granted" activity in computer graphics. Acceptable criteria for good computer-generated straight lines are that

- They should appear straight with minimal distortion or distraction.
- The end points should be well-defined.
- They should be of constant density unless otherwise desired.
- The quality of lines should be independent of their length, angular displacement, and other characteristics.
- The lines should be drawn or generated rapidly.

EXAMPLE: The following is a listing of three Pascal procedures that implement well-known line-drawing algorithms. The availability of a primitive BitOn is assumed

```
Procedure DDA (x1,y1,x2,y2 : Integer);
Var Length, i : Integer;
        x, y, DeltaX, DeltaY : Real;
Begin
  If Abs(y2−y1) > Abs(x2−x1) Then
                                    Length : = Abs(y2−y1)
                                Else
                                    Length : = Abs(x2−x1);
  DeltaX : = (x2−x1)/Length;
  DeltaY : = (y2−y1)/Length;
  x: = x1 + 0.5; y: = y1 + 0.5;
  For i : = 1 to Length Do
    Begin
      BitOn(Trunc(x), Trunc(y));
      x : = x + DeltaX;
      y : = y + DeltaY
    End
End {DDA};

Procedure Bresenham(x,y,xDif,yDif : Integer);
Var i : Integer;
    increment : Real;
Begin
  increment : = yDif/xDif − 0.5;
  For i : = 1 To xDif Do
    Begin
      BitOn(x,y);
      If increment > 0 Then
                            Begin
                              y : = y + 1;
                              increment : = increment − 1.0
                            End;
      x : = x + 1;
      increment : = increment + (yDif/xDif)
    End
End {Bresenham};

Procedure Bresenham2(x,y,xDif,yDif : Integer);
Var i, increment : Integer;
```

```
Begin
     increment := 2 * yDif − xDif;
     For i := 1 To xDif Do
        Begin
           BitOn(x,y);
           If increment > 0 Then
                                Begin
                                   y := y + 1;
                                   increment := increment + 2 * (xDif − yDif)
                                End
                             Else
                                increment := increment + 2 * yDif;
           x := x + 1
        End
End {Bresenham2};
```

Procedure DDA is an example of the implementation of one of a family of algorithms called *digital difference analyzers*. The concept of these algorithms is that, given the endpoints of a desired line segment, the rate of change of the coordinates with respect to one another may be calculated and used to define the intermediate points. If the definition of the procedure BitOn is the same as the one discussed earlier in this chapter, a scaling of the relative values of x and y into absolute bitmap coordinates based on the display resolution is necessary.

Procedure Bresenham is another example of a *digital difference analyzer* in which a line segment is defined in terms of one endpoint and the offsets from that endpoint of the other endpoint.

A weakness of this sequence of operations lies in the division step required to compute the initial value and increment. This division can be avoided, however, since the algorithm is unaffected if the increment is multiplied by a constant.

Procedure Bresenham2 illustrates how multiplication of the increment by 2 results in the elimination of any division operations.

Manipulation of Data

A major problem associated with the display of data in a bitmap format is the conformance of existing data to that format. In its most fundamental definition, bitmaps are only capable of graphics defined in two states (most typically black and white). Filtering existing data to accommodate these states may result in a loss of information otherwise afforded by the data. One of the techniques that addresses the problems associated with this type of data manipulation is *dithering*.

Dithering

CONCEPT: To produce continuous-tone images on a bilevel display by achieving the effect of continuous tone through the appropriate spatial density of bilevel states.

GIVEN: Assume a continuous-tone grey scale defined in terms of five allowable grey scales.

PROCESS: The input data *bytemap* is subdivided into 4 × 4 arrays representing each of the possible grey scales defined.

The output *bitmap* is also subdivided into 4 × 4 arrays, each element is which represents a bilevel state (1 = on, 0 = off).

Figure 6-3 illustrates how each of the five possible grey scales are represented as 4 × 4 arrays containing bilevel values. The average grey scale level (intensity) of each input 4 × 4 arrays of the bilevel forms of this figure.

EXAMPLE: Figure 6-4 illustrates how a 4 × 4 bytemap containing information expressed in five grey scales can be "dithered" using the definitions in Figure 6-3 into an equivalent bilevel (black and white) bytemap.

RESTRICTIONS: Since each 4 × 4 array of the original *bytemap* is represented by a single element of the dithered array, the original data was sampled at half

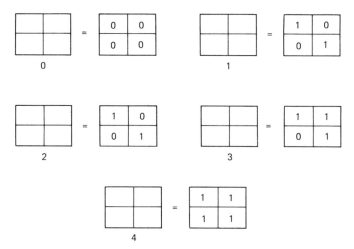

Figure 6-3. Definition of 5-level gray scale in terms of bilevel values.

with an input <u>bytemap</u> of:

average grey scales per 4 × 4 array yield:

The output bitmap becomes

The output display is therefore:

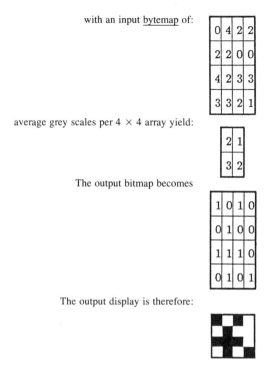

Figure 6-4. Dithering with average gray scale values.

resolution. Therefore the spatial fidelity of the original data is lost (see Figure 6-4).

To achieve consistent spatial fidelity requires that the output display has twice the resolution of the original data to be sampled. Averaging the grey-scale values is therefore not necessary (see Figure 6-5).

Thus an obvious restriction in this technique is that to retain the spatial fidelity of the original data requires four times the number of pixels (two times the resolution) in the output display than was present in the original data.

Ordered Dither

CONCEPT: To produce continuous-tone images on a bilevel display while retaining the spatial fidelity of the original image; The continuous-tone scale is defined in terms of an arbitrary number of intensity levels.

PROCESS: In ordered dither, each digitized picture element (pixel) of the input image is compared with an image position-dependent threshold intensity. If the

With the input bytemap of:

0	4	2	2
2	2	0	0
4	2	3	3
3	3	2	1

the output bitmap becomes:

0	0	1	1	1	0	1	0
0	0	1	1	0	1	0	1
1	0	1	0	0	0	0	0
0	1	0	1	0	0	0	0
1	1	1	0	1	1	1	1
1	1	0	1	0	1	0	1
1	1	1	1	1	0	1	0
0	1	0	1	0	1	0	0

yielding a display of:

Figure 6-5. Dithering with full spatial fidelity.

picture element (pixel) is greater than the threshold value corresponding to that element, the bilevel display is turned on at that point.

The threshold values are arranged in an array congruent with the input data array called the *dither matrix*. This dither matrix is "overlaid" on the input matrix to ascertain bilevel state levels.

Dither matrices are derived from the following iterative process:

$$D_2 = \begin{pmatrix} 0 & 2 \\ 3 & 1 \end{pmatrix}$$

$$D_n = \begin{pmatrix} 4D_{n/2} & 4D_{n/2} + 2V_{n/2} \\ 4D_{n/2} + 3V_{n/2} & 4D_{n/2} + V_{n/2} \end{pmatrix}$$

where

$$V_n = \begin{pmatrix} V_{n/2} & V_{n/2} \\ V_{n/2} & V_{n/2} \end{pmatrix}$$

$$V_2 = \begin{pmatrix} 1 & 1 \\ 1 & 1 \end{pmatrix}$$

n is the number of rows and columns in the square dither matrix. Therefore

$$D_4 = \begin{pmatrix} 4D_2 & 4D_2 + 2V_2 \\ 4D_2 + 3V_2 & 4D_2 + V_2 \end{pmatrix}$$

$$D_4 = \begin{pmatrix} 0 & 8 & 2 & 10 \\ 12 & 4 & 14 & 6 \\ 3 & 11 & 1 & 9 \\ 15 & 7 & 13 & 5 \end{pmatrix}$$

Likewise

$$D_8 = \begin{pmatrix} 4D_4 & 4D_4 + 2V_4 \\ 4D_4 + 3V_4 & 4D_4 + V_4 \end{pmatrix}$$

$$V_4 = \begin{pmatrix} V_2 & V_2 \\ V_2 & V_2 \end{pmatrix}$$

$$D_8 = \begin{pmatrix} 0 & 32 & 8 & 40 & 2 & 34 & 10 & 42 \\ 48 & 16 & 56 & 24 & 50 & 18 & 58 & 26 \\ 12 & 44 & 4 & 36 & 14 & 46 & 6 & 38 \\ 60 & 28 & 52 & 20 & 62 & 30 & 54 & 22 \\ 3 & 35 & 11 & 43 & 1 & 33 & 9 & 41 \\ 51 & 19 & 59 & 27 & 49 & 17 & 57 & 25 \\ 15 & 47 & 7 & 39 & 13 & 45 & 5 & 37 \\ 63 & 31 & 55 & 23 & 61 & 29 & 53 & 21 \end{pmatrix}$$

The dither matrices may be scaled so that the threshold values they contain accommodate the range of intensity values in the input array to be "dithered."

$$8 \cdot D_4 = \begin{pmatrix} 0 & 64 & 16 & 80 \\ 96 & 32 & 112 & 48 \\ 24 & 88 & 8 & 72 \\ 120 & 56 & 104 & 40 \end{pmatrix}$$

EXAMPLE: Given: the following input *bytemap* as an 8 × 8 array with an intensity range of data of 8 bits (256 possible levels).

$$I_8 = \begin{pmatrix} 8 & 47 & 41 & 46 & 63 & 94 & 201 & 256 \\ 13 & 22 & 39 & 35 & 42 & 77 & 194 & 128 \\ 0 & 6 & 23 & 76 & 97 & 186 & 163 & 152 \\ 0 & 9 & 28 & 79 & 91 & 242 & 163 & 97 \\ 1 & 9 & 26 & 73 & 92 & 211 & 141 & 123 \\ 3 & 11 & 47 & 92 & 102 & 227 & 132 & 97 \\ 5 & 13 & 12 & 96 & 107 & 247 & 169 & 87 \\ 7 & 15 & 19 & 69 & 94 & 199 & 174 & 43 \end{pmatrix}$$

If D_8 is scaled by a factor of four, the threshold values in the dither matrix will be consistent with the intensity ranges of the input array (I_8).

$$4 \cdot D_8 = \begin{pmatrix} 0 & 128 & 32 & 160 & 8 & 136 & 40 & 168 \\ 192 & 64 & 224 & 96 & 200 & 72 & 232 & 104 \\ 48 & 176 & 16 & 144 & 56 & 184 & 24 & 152 \\ 240 & 112 & 208 & 80 & 248 & 120 & 216 & 88 \\ 12 & 140 & 44 & 172 & 4 & 132 & 36 & 164 \\ 204 & 76 & 236 & 108 & 196 & 68 & 228 & 100 \\ 60 & 188 & 28 & 156 & 52 & 180 & 20 & 148 \\ 252 & 124 & 220 & 92 & 244 & 116 & 212 & 84 \end{pmatrix}$$

Comparing each element value of the input *bytemap* (I_8) with the threshold value given in the corresponding element of $4 \cdot D_8$ yields the following output *bitmap* O_8:

$$O_8 = \begin{pmatrix} 1 & 0 & 1 & 0 & 1 & 0 & 1 & 1 \\ 0 & 0 & 0 & 0 & 0 & 1 & 0 & 1 \\ 0 & 0 & 1 & 0 & 1 & 1 & 1 & 1 \\ 0 & 0 & 0 & 0 & 0 & 1 & 0 & 1 \\ 0 & 0 & 0 & 0 & 1 & 1 & 1 & 0 \\ 0 & 0 & 0 & 0 & 0 & 1 & 0 & 0 \\ 0 & 0 & 0 & 0 & 1 & 1 & 1 & 0 \\ 0 & 0 & 0 & 0 & 0 & 1 & 0 & 0 \end{pmatrix}$$

I_8 could have likewise been subdivided into 4 × 4 arrays, each of which is dithered using $16 \cdot D_4$ to yield the same result.

Graphic Orientation

Another major topic in the manipulation of data for graphic presentation involves *orientation*. Unlike dithering, these techniques address the issues of how the data is to be displayed with respect to the display area. The result is the definition of techniques that allow the *rotation*, *scaling*, and *translation* of data.

Two-Dimensional Point Rotation

CONCEPT: To accomplish the rotation of a point or family of points clockwise about the origin through a prescribed angle.

PROCESS: The trigonometric formulas for the rotation of point (x, y) into point (x_1, y_1) clockwise about $(0, 0)$ through angle θ are

$$x_1 = x \cos \theta + y \sin \theta$$
$$y_1 = -x \sin \theta + y \cos \theta$$

These formulae may be expressed parametrically as:

$$\begin{pmatrix} x_1 \\ y_1 \end{pmatrix} = \begin{pmatrix} \cos \theta & \sin \theta \\ -\sin \theta & \cos \theta \end{pmatrix} \begin{pmatrix} x \\ y \end{pmatrix}$$

where $\begin{pmatrix} \cos \theta & \sin \theta \\ -\sin \theta & \cos \theta \end{pmatrix}$ is defined as the two-dimensional *rotational matrix* **R**.

Two-Dimensional Coordinate Scaling

CONCEPT: To accomplish the scaling of coordinates by a constant factor about the origin of the defined coordinate system.

PROCESS: Scaling individual coordinate values can be described by the following formulas:

$$x_1 = F_x \cdot x$$

$$y_1 = F_y \cdot y$$

These formulas may be expressed parametrically as:

$$\begin{pmatrix} x_1 \\ y_1 \end{pmatrix} = \begin{pmatrix} F_x & 0 \\ 0 & F_y \end{pmatrix} \begin{pmatrix} x \\ y \end{pmatrix}$$

where $\begin{pmatrix} F_x & 0 \\ 0 & F_y \end{pmatrix}$ is the two-dimensional *scaling matrix* **S**.

F_x is defined as the scaling factor for the x-coordinate.

F_y is defined as the scaling factor for the y-coordinate.

Scaling has the effect of causing a point or family of points to expand or contract about the origin. If $F_x = F_y$ then this expansion or contraction occurs uniformly along both coordinates.

The scaling matrix $\begin{pmatrix} -1 & 0 \\ 0 & 1 \end{pmatrix}$ has the effect of defining the mirror image of the point or family of points scaled.

Two-Dimensional Point Translation

CONCEPT: To accomplish the translation of a point or family of points within their defined coordinate system

PROCESS: Translating individual coordinate values can be described by the following formulas:

$x_1 = x + x_T$ where x_T = *translation offset in x-direction*

$y_1 = y + y_T$ where y_T = *translation offset in y-direction*

These formulas may be expressed parametrically as

$$\begin{pmatrix} x_1 \\ y_1 \end{pmatrix} = \begin{pmatrix} 1 & 0 & x_T \\ 0 & 1 & y_T \end{pmatrix} \begin{pmatrix} x \\ y \\ 1 \end{pmatrix}$$

where $\begin{pmatrix} 1 & 0 & x_T \\ 0 & 1 & y_T \end{pmatrix}$ is defined as the two-dimensional *translation matrix* **T**.

Combined Transformations

CONCEPT: To accomplish a combination of two or more transformations (rotation, scaling and translation) on a point or family of points within their defined coordinate system.

PROCESS: In order to define a combination of two-dimensional transformations in terms of the appropriate transformation matrices, each of these matrices must be redefined as 3×3 matrices.

Therefore,

$$\text{the rotation matrix, } \mathbf{R} = \begin{pmatrix} \cos \theta & \sin \theta & 0 \\ -\sin \theta & \cos \theta & 0 \\ 0 & 0 & 1 \end{pmatrix}$$

$$\text{the scaling matrix, } \mathbf{S} = \begin{pmatrix} F_x & 0 & 0 \\ 0 & F_y & 0 \\ 0 & 0 & 1 \end{pmatrix}$$

and

$$\text{the translation matrix, } \mathbf{T} = \begin{pmatrix} 1 & 0 & x_T \\ 0 & 1 & y_T \\ 0 & 0 & 1 \end{pmatrix}$$

Therefore, a generalized transformation may be expressed as

$$\begin{pmatrix} x_1 \\ y_1 \\ 1 \end{pmatrix} = \mathbf{M} \cdot \begin{pmatrix} x \\ y \\ 1 \end{pmatrix}$$

where $\mathbf{M}$ is defined as the product of any number of $\mathbf{R}$, $\mathbf{S}$, and/or $\mathbf{T}$ matrices.

Combinations of the $\mathbf{R}$, $\mathbf{S}$ and $\mathbf{T}$ matrices may be used to define special purpose transformation matrices.

EXAMPLE:

$$\mathbf{S \cdot T} = \begin{pmatrix} F_x & 0 & 0 \\ 0 & F_y & 0 \\ 0 & 0 & 1 \end{pmatrix} \cdot \begin{pmatrix} 1 & 0 & x_T \\ 0 & 1 & y_T \\ 0 & 0 & 1 \end{pmatrix}$$

$$\mathbf{S \cdot T} = \begin{pmatrix} F_x & 0 & F_x x_T \\ 0 & F_y & F_y y_T \\ 0 & 0 & 1 \end{pmatrix}$$

Since matrix multiplication is generally not commutative,

$$\mathbf{S \cdot T \neq T \cdot S}$$

$$\mathbf{T \cdot S} = \begin{pmatrix} 1 & 0 & x_T \\ 0 & 1 & y_T \\ 0 & 0 & 1 \end{pmatrix} \cdot \begin{pmatrix} F_x & 0 & 0 \\ 0 & F_y & 0 \\ 0 & 0 & 1 \end{pmatrix}$$

$$\mathbf{T \cdot S} = \begin{pmatrix} F_x & 0 & x_T \\ 0 & F_y & y_T \\ 0 & 0 & 1 \end{pmatrix}$$

USE OF DATA STRUCTURES IN GRAPHICS

A wide variety of algorithms have been developed for use in computer graphics. An important aspect of any of these algorithms involves their use of data structures.

Of concern in the development of a data structure to support computer graphics operations are

- The structural relationship of the graphical elements.
- Space (storage) considerations.
- Fast access to the graphical data.

Techniques described for *bitmap graphics* have assumed, for simplicity, the storage of graphical data in an array data structure. This structure is convenient in that it simulates the tabular form of the pixels that compose a bitmap. The array as a *direct-access* data structure guarantees fast access to the individual data items. Both of these attributes of arrays are compromised when the space requirements for bitmap data are considered. For graphic displays of any size and resolution, the bitmap arrays required can become extremely large.

Processing Cones

CONCEPT: To define an alternative data structure to the array in the description of bitmap graphics.

PROCESS: The *processing cone* or *pyramid* is a hierarchical representation of a graphical image organized into layers, with each successive layer representing a finer resolution. Such a cone, in that it is hierarchical, can be represented by a *tree data structure*.

The root of this tree structure represents the entire graphical image. This root has four children, each of which represent one of the subimages obtained by dividing the image into four quadrants. If this is a *grey-level* image, the value of each of the four children is the average value of the grey levels in its respective quadrant.

Similarly, each node of the tree that is not a leaf has four children representing four subimages of the image represented by the node. Such a tree is perfectly balanced owing to the uniform subdivision of respective images. At the lowest hierarchical level, the leaves of the tree actual represent the pixels composing the bitmap.

Because of the relationships between nodes (elements) of a tree, this data structure can be extremely effective in operations affecting limited portions of the graphical display (e.g., edge finding, clipping, texture analysis).

REFERENCES

1. Angell, Ian O., *A Practical Introduction to Computer Graphics.* New York: Wiley, 1982. (Contains FORTRAN examples).
2. Artwick, Bruce A., *Applied Concepts in Microcomputer Graphics.* Englewood Cliffs: NJ, Prentice-Hall, 1984.
3. Artwick, Bruce, A., *Microcomputer Displays, Graphics and Animation.* Englewood Cliffs: NJ, Prentice-Hall, 1985.
4. Booth, Kellogg S. *Computer Graphics: Tutorial.* New York, IEEE, 1979. (Initially presented at Compcon79, held Feb. 26–Mar. 1, 1979).
5. Chasen, Sylvan H., *Geometric Principles and Procedures for Computer Graphic Applications.* Englewood Cliffs, NJ: Prentice-Hall, 1978.
6. Encarnacao, Jose Luis and Schlechtendahl, E. G., *Computer Aided Design: Fundamentals and System Architectures.* Berlin: Springer-Verlag, 1983. (Symbolic computation, computer graphics).
7. Foley, James D. and Van Dam, Andries, *Fundamentals of Interactive Computer Graphics.* Reading, MA: Addison-Wesley, 1983. (Contains Pascal examples; related to CORE and GKS standards.)

8. Freeman, Herbert, *Interactive Computer Graphics: Tutorial and Selected Readings.* New York: IEEE, 1980.

9. Giloi, Wolfgang K., *Interactive Computer Graphics: Data Structure, Algorithms, Languages.* Englewood Cliffs, NJ: Prentice-Hall, 1978.

10. Greenberg, D., et al., *The Computer Image: Applications of Computer Graphics.* Reading, MA: Addison-Wesley, 1982.

11. Harrington, S., *Computer Graphics: A Programming Approach.* New York: McGraw-Hill, 1983.

12. Katzen, H., *Microcomputer Graphics and Programming Techniques.* New York: Van Nostrand-Reinhold, 1982.

13. *Computer Graphics: Theory and Applications: Proceedings, InterGraphics '83*, Tokyo, Japan, Apr. 11–14, 1983. Tosiyasu L. Kunii, ed., Tokyo: Springer-Verlag, 1983.

14. Myers, R. E., *Microcomputer Graphics.* Reading, MA: Addison-Wesley, 1982.

15. Newman, William M., and Sproull, Robert F., *Principles of Interactive Computer Graphics,* 2nd ed. New York: McGraw-Hill, 1979.

16. Rogers, D. F., and Harris, J. A., *Mathematical Elements for Computer Graphics,* New York: McGraw-Hill, 1976. (Good beginning book; particularly good for algorithms and examples involving geometric figures.)

17. Ryan, Daniel L., *Computer Aided Graphics and Design*, 2nd, rev. and expand. ed. New York: Dekker, 1985. (Mechanical Engineering, 38.)

18. Scott, J., *Introduction to Interactive Computer Graphics.* New York: Wiley, 1982.

19. Waite, Mitchell, *Computer Graphics Primer.* Indianapolis: Sams, 1979.

20. Shapiro, Linda G., "Data Structures in Picture Processing," *SIGGRAPH '78 Proceedings, 12,* 3, (Aug. 1978).

21. Waite, Mitchell, and Morgan, Christopher L., *Graphics Primer for the IBM PC.* Berkeley, CA: Osborne/McGraw-Hill, 1983.

22. Walker, B. S., Gurd, J. R., and Drawneek, E. A., *Interactive Computer Graphics.* New York: Crane Russak, 1975. (Computer Systems Engineering Series.)

7

HUMAN FACTORS

"The attitudes of the designer *is that the best way to deal with the user is simply to take more care in considering the user—all the system designer needs is to be given the time to do so. The designer is, after all, human and has the intuitions to predict what will be easy for the user. It is mostly common sense, anyway, isn't it? The limitation of this approach is obvious: The designer's intuitions do not necessarily match the user's. The designer, relying on an egocentric 'folk philosophy' has no way to gauge his intuitions; and intuitions about complex psychological behavior (even about one's own behavior) can be remarkably deceptive."*

Thomas P. Moran
Xerox Corporation

Designing computer-user interfaces *for* users has become an increasingly important issue because of the widespread applications of computers and a rapidly expanding technology (i.e., complexity). This man-machine interface is an applications area too easily overlooked by software designers.

The techniques discussed in this chapter should more accurately be viewed as *guidelines* or *sets of design rules* that have been found through research to provide an optimal human interface environment to a computing system. Although some of these guidelines may be presented as algorithms, they should not be interpreted in that manner. Research-based guidelines should be followed as *general principles*, tempered by the cautions that complex sets of circumstances alter individual cases, and guidelines strictly applied can conflict.

For teachers, students, human factors practitioners, or researchers, these guidelines can serve as a starting point for the development and application of expert knowledge.

For managers responsible for user interface software design, these guidelines may provide a means to make the design process more efficient.

For systems, analysts can use such guidelines to establish design requirements.

Software designers/programmers can consult these guidelines to derive the specific design rules appropriate for a particular system application. Such translation from general guidelines to specific rules will focus attention on critical user interface design questions early in the design process.

A study of computer human factors is deeply rooted in the sciences of psychology and education, often involving principles not specifically associated with the interaction between humans and computers. The specific areas addressed in this chapter include

- Cognitive human factors.
- Temporal human factors.
- Affective human factors.

Most of the techniques discussed are actually interdisciplinary and deal with issues in more than one of these areas. For this reason, a discussion of specific techniques and guidelines occurs at the end of this chapter. All of the techniques discussed can be implemented within software design to varying levels of satisfaction. Implementation-dependent features in software and hardware are often available that complement and enhance the application of these techniques.

GLOSSARY OF TERMS

Affective/Emotional: Describes user's feelings about interaction.

Cognitive: How the user acquires and uses knowledge necessary for proper operation.

Conversational: A mode of operation of a computer system in which a sequence of alternating entries and responses between a user and the system takes place in a manner similar to a dialog between two persons. *Syn.*: interactive; real-time

Cursor: A marker (dot of light) that appears on a video screen to indicate the position the next activity (input or output) will occur. The marker might be an underline that is stable or blinks, or the marker may be a rectangle that contains a letter in reverse video, either static or blinking.

Cursor Key: A key that, when pressed, causes the cursor to move in a designated direction. Arrows engraved on the keys indicate direction of cursor movement: up, down, right, left or home (top left corner of screen).

Default: A system-provided value or option that is used in processing when no alternative has been specified.

Diagnostic: A computer message pertaining to the detection and isolation of a malfunction or mistake. *Syn.*: error message.

Dialog: The interchange between a computer program and a user of that program.

Documentation: The management of documents, which may include identification, acquisition, processing, storing and distribution.

Ergonomics: The science or practice of ascertaining the needs of people and reflecting those needs in the design of equipment and workspaces.

Error Condition: A condition in which a computer operation cannot continue because of an error detected by hardware or software.

Exception Routine: A routine to which control is passed in order to deal with some abnormal condition that occurs during processing.

Function Key: A key on a console or terminal keyboard that controls an operation.

Highlight: To change the appearance of the display of part of an image on a CRT.

Immediate Memory: The concepts or ideas of which people are conscious at an immediate point of time. Information retrieval is closely related to the level of attention or attention span of an individual; immediate memory is often not distinguished from short-term memory.

Initialize: To establish prescribed starting conditions prior to a processing procedure.

Interval: A separating time between successive events.

Inverse Video: On the screen of a CRT, a display in which the background is light and the display elements dark.

Log Off: To terminate a computer session.

Log On: The begin a computer session.

Long-term Memory: The concepts or ideas that can be considered permanent memory. Information must usually be placed consciously in long-term memory by means of repetition, mnemonic association, or conscious effort.

Menu: A displayed list of items or services available with identifiers by which they may be selected.

Mnemonic: A set of letters that represents the activity performed by a command. It suggests these actions so that the user/programmer can more easily recall the meaning of the command.

Options: Indicators of optional activities available in the operation of a function.

Parameter: An argument (value) used in the operation of a function, usually indicating the required entities necessary for function operation.

Prompt: A symbol represented on an output display that indicates the operating system or a program is ready to accept input.

Protected Field: On a display device, a data field whose values cannot be assigned, modified, or deleted by a user.

Response: A reply or action taken following a request or the receipt of a message.

Response Time: The elapsed time between the end of an inquiry or demand on a computer system and the beginning of the response.

Running Time: The elapsed time taken for the execution of a target program. *Syn.*: run duration.

Sensorimotor: Perception and motor skills.

Short Term Memory: The concepts or ideas which people are conscious of or can be recalled to consciousness quickly; In general, the contents of short term memory usually have few associations with ideas or concepts in permanent memory. *Syn.*: Post-Distractional Memory.

Temporal: Deals with the role of time in a user's interaction.

Time-Out: An interrupt condition that occurs at the expiration of a designated time for an event occurrence, without the event having occurred.

Tracing Routine: A routine that provides a historical record of specified events in the execution of a computer program.

Unavailable Time: From the point of view of the user, the time duration during which a functional unit cannot be used.

Unprotected Field: On a display device, a data field whose values can be assigned, modified or deleted by a user.

Window: A portion of display characterized differently from the rest of the display (screen). A window may show values of magnified size or from a different area of memory.

COGNITIVE HUMAN FACTORS

A study of *cognitive human factors* deals primarily with the following questions and the techniques which attempts to address them:

1. How does a computer user learn and acquire information?
2. What user learning styles can be addressed in the design of computer systems and programs?
3. What is the role of memory in the human/computer interface?

Learning

Andragogy is defined as the study of adult learning. Research into this field has led to the development of a series of principles that are applicable to a wide variety of situations:

- The learner's self-concept moves from one of being a dependent personality toward one of being a self-directed human being.
- The learner accumulates a growing reservoir of experience that becomes an increasing resource for learning.
- The learner's readiness to learn becomes oriented more to the developmental tasks of their social and professional roles.

- The learner's time perspective changes from one of postponed application of knowledge to immediacy of application. Accordingly, his or her orientation toward learning shifts from one of subject-centeredness to one of problem-centeredness.

As a result of these principles, the following consequences of adult learning have been recognized:

- adults are themselves a rich resource for their own learning and the learning of others.
- adults possess finite and somewhat restricted capability to learn and recall information for which they have no built-in associations.
- adults have a large number of fixed habits and patterns of thought, which require them to question carefully each new idea they acquire.

Learning styles refer to the methods and techniques with which individuals acquire knowledge. Most individuals exhibit a natural preference of learning styles—visual, auditory, kinesthetic and/or multisensory. In that the designer of an interactive system cannot possibly anticipate the appropriate learning style of all possible users, then the appropriate method of presentation should be chosen based upon the content of the material presented. If the content is a representation of procedural knowledge, sequences, or descriptions of tasks, *serial* presentation can be the most suitable. If the material contains spatial content, then some *spatial* representation (like a map or menu) can be more effective.

A learning style common to most individuals is one which is *experience-oriented*. This style is significant in the design of a human/computer interface in that a large portion of the learning a computer user experiences while using a program or system is directed toward the use of that system. It is important that users become familiar with the operations of the system (at the user level) and with the interface that they must understand in order to use the system effectively.

If they are to benefit from the advantages of experience-oriented learning, software techniques for cognitive human factors should

- Tap the experience of the user.
- Encourage active participation and ego involvement in the learning and operation processes.
- Illustrate broad generalizations with actual experiences.
- Present learning experiences which allow the learner to plan—or even rehearse—how they are going to apply the new information in continued or repetitive use.

Memory

The role and capacity of user memory in the design of interactive programs and systems is critical. Users of such systems are constantly being bombarded with information in the form of data, inquiries, and messages they must analyze and act upon. If the designer of a system (i.e., the author of those inquiries, messages, and so forth) fails to appreciate the effects of memory on the human/computer interface, then the success of that system is limited.

Studies of the psychology of memory in man include both *short-term* and *long-term* memories.

Short-term memory refers to the facts, concepts, or ideas of which people are conscious or which they can recall to consciousness quickly. In experiments, short-term memory is sometimes referred to as *post-distractional* memory because subjects can become distracted and forget if their attention is not focused on the contents of that memory.

The studies of psychologist George Miller indicates that the number of "chunks" of information that a person can retain in short-term memory is 7 ± 2. This is basically information that is "free-form" (i.e., with which the person cannot make an association or form a mnemonic). Additional studies indicate that a more typical limit to short-term memory is *two* or *three* items.

Long-term memory is dependent upon efficient short-term memory. Long-term memories are not created immediately after the acquisition of a new item of information. The memory of "new" information is "held" in short-term memory. The more permanent long-term memory appears to occur gradually over periods of many hours, days, or weeks.

To the user of a computer system, information about that system is easier to recall if the entities (or their names) are familiar (i.e., they have an association with other knowledge stored in long-term memory or an association with other items in short-term memory). It is for this reason that programs should use familiar mnemonics and meaningful keywords and variable names.

The *organization* or *grouping* of information of importance to a program user often determines the ability of that user to recall any of the information after either a short or long period of time. When such groups contain too many "chunks" of information for short-term memory, the user is forced to re-read. Such organization is of importance in the design of program menus, parameter lists, and so forth.

TEMPORAL HUMAN FACTORS

The role of time in cognitive human factors has a limited definition in the descriptions of short- and long-term memories. The presentation of data in an interactive system affects the functioning of these memories in the cognitive processes of a user. If that presentation does not address the mechanics of those processes, time-consuming activity, such as re-reading, often results.

Temporal human factors deal primarily with the role of time in the user's *interaction* (i.e., dialog) with the computer system. Notions of interactivity, appropriate response times, boredom, and the perception of long durations and of action selection times are treated in this field. As with the analysis of the role of memory, temporal human factors are sometimes difficult to separate from cognitive human factors.

A major consideration in temporal human factors is the ability of an interactive system/program to capture the *attention* of its user and perform its operations within a time period consistent with the *attention span* of that user.

Attention can be defined as "the focusing of perception leading to heightened awareness of a limited range of stimuli." The designer of an interactive system needs to be aware that a variety of stimuli may be competing for the attention of the system user. Research has shown that among competing stimulus patterns the advantage rests with the ones of greatest size, strongest intensity, most frequent repetition, and the most vivid because of contour, contrast, or color.

Attention span is the time period during which a particular stimulus has the attention of an individual. This time period can actually be the result of a series of related stimuli in that the attention-getting qualities of stimuli depend in part upon (1) other stimuli the individual has lately experienced, and (2) that which an individual perceives depending partially on what he or she expects.

Software techniques designed to address user attention span should be concerned with:

- What stimuli are likely to be competing for the attention of the system user?
- How can the periods of user inactivity (i.e., when they are not interacting with the system) be affected?
- What are realistic user expectations regarding system operations?

System processing time can be thought of as divided into time periods composed of *response times*. These are time periods required to complete specific tasks (or subtasks) that are often under the control of the system user. Techniques that affect the processing time (or efficiency) of these tasks (or subtasks) then contribute to the consideration of temporal human factors (some of these techniques are discussed in Chapter 8, Program Attributes).

It is important that these response times fit within the attention spans of the system users. If this is not possible, the system should provide *reinforcing stimuli* in an attempt to prolong the attention span. Such stimuli reinforcers (e.g., messages, blips, beeps, etc.) must be used carefully so that they do not lose their effectiveness.

Two time periods to be weighed against a user's attention span are: 1) the elapsed time between a user input and a program or system response; 2) the elapsed time between consecutive program or system responses. The degree to which these two time periods preserve a user's continuity of thought and conform to a user's expectation of response time can positively affect user convenience and efficiency. Likewise, the degree to which elapsed time or the volume of output matches the availability of information and the user's requirement for information can have positive or negative effects.

The major external stimulus competing with an interactive system for the attention of its user is *the perception of the passage of time*. Crucial to note is that the user measures the passage of time by "wall clock" or "real" time rather than in the sense of artificial "computer" time (e.g., CPU seconds, number of instructions, input/output). Time intervals appear short (usually on the order of 1–10 seconds) when they are most easily reproduced by the user. For this reason, users often judge system response times in terms of their own reaction times.

Boring, unfamiliar, and passive activities accentuate the passage of time. Long intervals (usually on the order of 10 seconds to 10 minutes) are affected and perceived by such factors as

- Previous or recent experience.
- User expectations.
- Value considerations (e.g., "My time is too valuable to wait for this!").
- Irregular time intervals.

Of these items, user expectations is the most likely to be affected by system design. It is a clearly understood "fact" that users will want ever shorter execution and response times until the operation appears to be executed instantaneously. Studies indicate that an action appears instantaneous to humans if it takes <0.2 seconds.

User expectation is closely related to experience. Quite simply, this means that the time to complete an operation using a computer system should not be longer than the time required by another, presumably simpler, means. A computer user's expectations may also be based upon that user's experience and exposure to other or similar computer systems. When considering the time required to perform a familar task (e.g., running a program, accessing data, etc.), few users would consider the differences in system environments (hardware, software, operating systems) or capabilities that contribute to differences in the task completion time. For example, experienced microcomputer users would judge the response time of a mainframe system by microcomputer standards and vice versa. Therefore, a generalized judgement as to "how long an operation *should* take" is quite misleading.

Software techniques that address temporal human factors issues can realistically be expected only to deal with, not compensate for, the effects of time on an interactive system user.

AFFECTIVE HUMAN FACTORS

Affective or *emotional* human factors attempts to quantify the system user's feelings about the system/user interaction. Comments from users concerning hostility, frustration, intimidation, stress, friendliness, approachability, and so forth, speak to the content of this area.

In his description of the design of the Etude interactive editor system, Michael Hammer[1] describes the new user "anxiety factor;"

> Frequently a long period of acclimatization must elapse before an operator is sufficiently expert with a system to feel truly comfortable with it. In the interim, the user's feelings are akin to those associated with walking a tightrope while wearing a blindfold. Because of the obscure nature of the interface that he is forced to employ, the operator cannot fully anticipate the consequences of the actions he performs. This leads to feelings of tension and uncertainty. Moreover, the user develops a fear of committing an unrecoverable error, and thereby becomes overly timid and cautious in his dealings with the system.

Perhaps one of the most overused and misunderstood contributions of the computer age to the English vocabulary is the term *user-friendly*. Interpretation of this term appears to imply that an implementation would incorporate a consideration of affective human factors.

A user-friendly system usually incorporates extensive use of system to user messages. Such messages are designed to guide a novice user through the computer/user interface at the lowest level. These messages are typically written in a way to personify the system and in an amicable and helpful tone.

User-friendly systems are also often characterized by their higher level of flexibility in such areas as their tolerance of user errors and an expanded vocabulary and allowable abbreviations for commands.

While the concepts of user-friendliness are quite valid, it is unfortunate that their implementation is often taken to extremes. Research supports the fact that users feel *threatened* by systems which attempt to emulate human behavior. Also the usefulness of such systems is short-lived; as users gain more experience and confidence, the features of a user-friendly system can become hindrances or annoyances that contribute to the ineffectiveness of the user.

As demonstrated in the description of the "anxiety factor," the key to an understanding of affective human factors is an understanding of those aspects of the computer/human interface that *create* or *contribute to human stress.*

Stress can be defined as "any stimulus that disturbs or interferes with the normal equilibrium of an individual." In most cases, stress hinges on a person's internal beliefs about the situation current facing them. Therefore, to a user involved in a computer dialog, the computer/human interface can be a potential source of stress.

Psychologists agree that one major cause of stress is due to the lack of adequate internal models or analogies. System users are likely to feel such stress if

- They have little or no experience with interactive computer systems.
- They encounter unexpected situations or circumstances.
- They have inadequate knowledge of a situation which may be interpreted as a state of overwhelming complexity.

It is also well known that stress causes more stress in that of the perception of an emotion alters the overall psychological evaluation of a situation.

There are numerous software design techniques that can be employed in the computer/human interface to deal with conditions of user stress. Some of these techniques are interdisciplinary and address causes of stress that are related to cognitive and/or temporal processes. Examples of these include the availability of help information to the user and techniques to facilitate ease-of-learning.

Techniques that define a "user-friendly" interface also can be used to reduce user stress if they are used carefully and appropriately. A "natural" interface easily addresses questions of complexity and user insecurity.

There are several stress-reducing guidelines which can be fundamental aspects of the design of any human/computer interface:

- The user must always feel in control of the interaction. This can be accomplished by offering the user a variety of options for controlling (and even terminating) the process.
- The user should always be aware of the state of a process. Status messages or other devices keep a user informed and thereby provide an indication of their level of control. A good example for the case of video systems is that the screen should *never* be blank.
- The user should always feel that the system is a tool to accomplish a task, not that the user is a tool to operate the system.
- System messages, responses, and so forth, should not insult the intelligence of the user. Great care should be taken in the organization, writing, and display of all messages that define the dialog.

A SURVEY OF TECHNIQUES AND GUIDELINES

Menu-Driven Programs

CONCEPT: To identify guidelines for the construction of menus for use in menu-driven programs.

FACTORS INVOLVED: Cognitive, affective.

PROCESS: Menu-driven programs have come to typify human factors design in interactive programs. Menus can demonstrate in a serial, spatial, and hierarchical manner the capabilities of a program or system.

The concept of menus supports a program design incorporating independent modularization of functions in that the selection of a specific menu item may initiate that procedure.

Human factors research into the optimal development of menu layouts has led to the following guidelines:

1. Menu data should be arranged in logical groups—sequentially, functionally, or by importance.
   a. For a group consisting of up to seven entries, the most probable entries should be at the top of the group in order to minimize the time spent reading the menu.
   b. For a group of any size where no obvious frequency of use pattern can be predicted, alphabetic order by entry identifier should be used.
   c. Each group should have a standardized organization of the information it includes.
2. The text paragraphs that compose a menu should, optimally, be separated by at least one blank line.
3. When points are enumerated within a menu, each point should begin on a new line.

The selection of a menu entry by a program user is a kinesthetic process that emphasizes the spatial organization of the menu. For that reason, entries are more likely to be selected should, optimally, appear in the more accessible area (i.e., the top) of the menu.

For full-screen display systems, menus can often be created in the context of a screen editor. Such a system allows a user access to all points of the screen and thereby can make a menu selection simply by using some input device (typically, the cursor) to point to the desired selection.

Non-full-screen systems are typically limited to providing menus in the form of an extended input prompt offering the user a choice of various program paths available at that time. The following Pascal program fragment demonstrates the use of a menu of this type.

EXAMPLE:

```
                      Demonstration Program
                         Menu System

1. Run Demonstration Program
2. Exit Demonstration Program
3. Help for Demonstration Program
4. Run Demonstration Program With Sample Data

Enter Menu Option by Number
  * * * *
ReadLn(Choice);
If ((N >= 1) And (N <=4 )) Then
   Case Choice Of
       1:Run;
       2:Exit;
       3:Help;
       4:RunDemo
   End; {Case}
                      Else Error;
```

The menu itself can be formatted with a simple sequence of WriteLn statements. The If and Case statements serve to invoke the Run, Exit, Help, RunDemo, or Error procedures respectively, depending upon the resultant value of the variable Choice.

In a menu of this type, there may be a programmer tendency to present multiple columns of entries, presumably in the interest of either reducing display space or increasing the amount of information presented within a fixed space. But multiple columns tend to increase the density of information in each line, which may confuse a user and disrupt the prioritization of entries within the menu.

Multiple columns are justified only if the display speed (characters/second) is an issue.

OTHER CONSIDERATIONS: *Information overload* results when there are too many entries on a menu at one time. In such circumstances, the user may have difficulty selecting an entry (especially if ambiguity exists in the entry description) due to a flood of information.

A technique for dealing with a problem of menu overloading is to create a *hierarchy of menus*. A menu in such a system contains one or more entries that are themselves menus at a lower hierarchical level. Such *submenus* provide more detail regarding a menu entry at a higher hierarchical level.

As user expertise increases, the need for an explicitly displayed menu may decrease. In such cases, the full menu display could be suppressed and replaced by an abbreviated prompt. Similarly, program code could include default values for the menu selection variable, enabling the program user to bypass the menu altogether when repetitive use of the program involves the same menu selections (i.e., normal execution of the program).

Program Help

CONCEPT: To identify techniques for including within a program accessible information regarding its use.

FACTORS INVOLVED: Cognitive, affective.

PROCESS: Perhaps the most critical human factors issue in the design of a system/program is *documentation*. The availability of descriptive, well-written documentation in the form of manuals, reference cards, and so forth, is a *necessity* to support users of a system of any complexity.

Often overlooked as a part of documentation is providing a user with *on-line* or *in-line* documentation in the form of *program help*. Such documentation includes as a functional part of the program itself brief descriptions of program features and criteria of interest to a program user. Program help, however, is not a substitute for more comprehensive documentation, but instead complements it.

Some operating systems support separate help systems that afford the designer of a program/system the capability to isolate program help from the functional parts of the program itself. While such a system has many advantages, it can present a maintenance problem when program modifications are made in that the program maintainer must remember to make appropriate changes to the help file. *In-line* program help (i.e., help information that is a part of the actual program it supports), addresses this problem in that it minimizes the number of separate files affected by a modification. In-line program help also supports a popular design philosophy suggesting that the best time to write documentation is either *before* programming coding (i.e., during the design phase), or *during* program coding, when the processes involved are fresh in the programmer's mind.

Program help is best implemented in such a way that the program user has access to help at *any* time during program execution. In this way, a user can obtain help information at the point in time when it is most needed. Unfortunately, such an implementation of help is usually possible only on *interrupt-driven* systems and systems which allow 'graceful' escapes during execution. Such systems could then implement program help via function keys, control keys or restart-like commands.

The most general implementation of program help is its incorporation in a separate, addressable program help module. This module could then be invoked by the user as one of the command level options available in the program (such as from a program menu).

It is important that program help be terse, informative and address those areas of program use that are the most likely to generate questions. The following program features should always be available in program help:

- *Program description*—a short description of what the program does, but not how it operates.
- *Format*—the command level format used within the program. It is important that the user of a program understand the precise syntax of any commands that can be issued during program execution; such syntax can be presented in an unambiguous fashion such as Backus-Naur Form (BNF) or syntax diagrams.
- *Parameters*—a description of any program parameters under the control of the user. If any program parameters are optional, a complete description of all default values should be given.
- *Options*—a description of any program options under the control of the user. If any program options are optional, a complete description of all default values should be given.
- *Errors*—a complete description of any error or diagnostic messages that may result *from the program* (not the operating system) during program execution.
- *Miscellaneous*—any usage notes or examples the user of the program would find helpful.

EXAMPLE: The following Pascal procedure operates as an in-line program help module for a hypothetical system named BLATZ. This procedure may be invoked from the program menu of BLATZ or from any other allowable program module of BLATZ. The argument of this procedure indicates the specific area of help information desired at the time it is invoked.

```
Procedure Help (N : Integer);
Begin
   Case N of
     1: Begin
          WriteLn('*****Description*****');
          WriteLn('BLATZ performs the BLITZ or BLOTZ operation on');
          WriteLn('two program files.')
        End;
     2: Begin
          WriteLn('*****Format*****');
          WriteLn('BLITZ file1 file2 : option1 ');
          WriteLn('or');
          WriteLn('BLOTZ file1 file2 : option1 ')
        End;
```

```
3: Begin
      WriteLn('*****Parameters*****');
      WriteLn('file1 — input file');
      WriteLn;
      WriteLn('file2 — output file');
      WriteLn;
      WriteLn('no default parameters are permitted')
   End;
4: Begin
      WriteLn('*****Options*****');
      WriteLn('TRACE');
      WriteLn('              outputs trace of program');
      WriteLn('              to screen');
      WriteLn;
      WriteLn('NOTRACE');
      WriteLn('           — suppresses trace of program');
      WriteLn('              to screen');
      WriteLn;
      WriteLn('NOTRACE is default option')
   End;
5: Begin
      WriteLn('*****Errors*****');
      WriteLn('No Input File');
      WriteLn('      — file specified as first');
      WriteLn('          parameter does not exist.')
   End;
6: Begin
      WriteLn('*****Miscellaneous*****');
      WriteLn('None')
   End;
   Otherwise : WriteLn('Illegal Help Parameter')
   End
End;
```

OTHER CONSIDERATIONS: It may be desirable to design program help modules such that multiple informational areas are provided with a single invocation, or call (e.g., Description and Format, or All).

If at all possible within the constraints of the system, help information is best displayed at relevant points during program execution. For example, when a user is expected to provide a system command, information regarding the required syntax of such commands is at its highest value to the user.

Sample Program Runs

CONCEPT: To identify techniques for providing to a progam user an example of the program's operation

FACTORS INVOLVED: Cognitive, affective.

PROCESS: Sample program runs support the well-established cognitive approach of *teaching by example*. Research supports the belief that many users benefit more from a realistic sample implementation of a program/system than from any other cognitive approach. Sample programs are an established part of large training systems generally implemented as tutorial programs.

The goal of a sample program should be to provide a user or potential user with a *realistic simulation* of a full *production program*. Such a simulation should indicate of *normal* and *abnormal* production program behavior.

Datasets defined during the test phase of a program provide an excellent basis for sample programs. Selection from such datasets should provide a sequence of scenarios of *typical* production program operation.

The following techniques can be used in the design of sample programs:

- Interactive inputs are replaced by inputs from datasets and used in the following manner:
    * Interactive input prompts present in the *production* program remain in the sample program;
    * As dataset values are assigned values that are normally entered interactively, the sample program provides information regarding format, datatype, default values, and so forth, wherever appropriate; this information is displayed in a manner such that the user is aware that the information is part of the sample program only;
- All production program output operations are duplicated in the sample program.

Sample programs should be designed to operated independently of and not interfere with the production system. If actual data files are used, care should be taken to insure that the sample programs are incapable of corrupting data.

Appropriate *garbage collection* procedures should be employed in the design of sample programs. No extraneous files should remain upon the completion of a sample program. Likewise, the computing environment (default values, etc.) should be either unaffected by the sample program or returned to its state prior to the execution of the sample program.

Program Messages

CONCEPT: To provide guidelines for the composition of messages from the program to the user

FACTORS INVOLVED: Cognitive, affective.

PROCESS: The concept of *user-friendly* programs has threatened to dilute the significance of many other considerations in the human factors design of interactive programs. The program attribute of *friendliness* is most often associated with the quantity and quality of the messages which the program provides to its users. The design of program messages (usually for input prompt and error indication) is of utmost importance and deserves the careful attention of the programmer/analyst.

The research of Engel and Granda of IBM indicates that in the design of messages, no attempts at humor or punishment should be made. It is their belief that most "people are still threatened by an anthropomorphic machine, and until the optimal 'personality' of a computer can be derived, messages should be kept strictly factual and informative."

Similar beliefs taken to the extreme or the lack of attention spent on messages by program designers is possibly the reason "message" has often come to mean a terse one-liner that a user is *not* expected to understand without an explanation.

Careful design of program messages should include the following two considerations:

- The application of psychology in the design of messages.
- The setting of human goals for messages.

Psychology.   Cognitive and affective psychology are important to the design of program messages. Messages are perhaps the strongest element reflecting the rapport between a program and a user. Research has emphasized the importance of the following psychological factors:

- The choice of vocabulary in a message not only affects the user's understanding of the message but also the user's attitude toward the program.
- A message that results from a user's action must relate specifically to that action.
- When a message contains too many *chunks* of information for short-term memory, the user is forced to reread the message. Rereading can be avoided by
  * Writing messages in terms of the familiar and providing the user with a basis of memory association.
- The user should have control over the messages received. Such control can be provided in a program by
  * Allowing the user to turn messages *on* and *off*.
  * Allowing the user to define the complexity or quantity of information within a message.
  * Allowing the user to assign program defaults in lieu of a message.

Human Goals.   The importance of human goals is perhaps the most obvious consideration in the design of error messages. Programs via their error messages should indicate a tolerance of *user* errors and define the steps being taken by the program in an attempt to cope with those errors.

An example of this involves the design of an error routine to replace simple error messages. Gilb and Weinberg (see chapter References) describe such a routine that is driven by a series of messages and responses between the program and the user. This example supports the belief that programs should *correct* user errors for which the corrections are *safe* and high probable. The algorithm for accomplishing this follows.

1. If the error is due to probable cause, then correct that cause, inform the user, and proceed with the modification.
2. If the cause is questionable, then explain the situation to the user, and request whether the program should continue execution.
3. If the cause is unusable, explain to the user the reason execution must cease.

The application of such a system could be quite effective in the reduction for error messages for misspellings, typing errors, and the like.

Text and Data Presentation

CONCEPT: To provide guidelines for the presentation of text and data from the program to the user

FACTORS INVOLVED: Cognitive, Affective.

PROCESS: Engel, Granda, and Teitelbaum of IBM (see chapter References) have done considerable research concerning the optimal display of data for interactive systems. The guidelines which have resulted from their work are applicable to a generalized discussion of all program output which is interpreted by a user, including

- Prose/text.
- Prompts.
- Messages.
- Instructions.
- Data field entry names (including menu fields).
- Output data.

The following is a synopsis of recommended guidelines for the display of data:

1. Accept a standard for use of letter case. As a rule, all prose/text should be output in mixed case. Mixed case improves the readability of infor-

mation and assists memory. Reserve upper case for headers and emphasis. Use emphasis itself sparingly to maintain its effect.

2. Display data in units that can be remembered. Presenting data with the likelihood that its rereading will not be necessary can be accomplished with proper organization. Strings of five or more digits and/or alphanumeric characters (not comprising a word) should be displayed in groups of three to four at a time (where no natural split or no predefined break occurs) with a blank character between them. As with mixed case, such organization addresses the capacity of short-term memory.

3. Organize data for ease of scanning and reading. Data fields should be presented, if possible, in an order and/or format which is recognizable to the user. Vertically aligned lists with left justification are the most easily scanned for text and other alphanumeric formats. Right justification is more effective for numeric data. Subclassifications of such lists can be accomplished with indentation.

4. Organize the items within a list carefully. Menu and other list items should be numbered starting with one, not zero (in counting, people start with one; in measuring, they start with zero). Numbers should be used only for the listing of selectable items. Alphabetic characters or 'bullets' may be used in prose/text. Numeric lists should use decimal alignment.

5. Pay close attention to the use of words and sentences. Words should be chosen and sentences composed in such a way that additional reading or interpretive processes are not required. Use complete words, not word contractions or shorter forms of words, so that users are more likely to understand the sense of a message. Abbreviations, mnemonics, and acronyms should not use punctuation. Avoid unnecessary punctuation and minimize hyphenation.

Processing Status Information

CONCEPT: To provide guidelines for providing processing status information to the user during program execution.

FACTORS INVOLVED: Temporal, Affective.

PROCESS: A programmer/analyst defining large, complex operations in interactive programs that require extended processing time should always consider the effect of that time on the user of those programs. Extended periods of time during which there are no interactive operations can lead to user anxiety. Potential problems that may arise from this anxiety (e.g., program interrupts) can be addressed by incorporating within the program design a mechanism or mechanisms for providing the user with processing status information.

Techniques to indicate program status are most easily associated with

- The counting of operations.
- The passage of time. The ability to incorporate a mechanism measuring either of these entities and reporting status to the program user is typically a trivial operation.

EXAMPLE 1:   The following Pascal procedure copies records from one file to another. After each 500 records are copied from the input file, a status message is sent to the user of the program. This message keeps the user informed of the procedure's progress and assured that the copy operation is proceeding without interruption.

```
Procedure Copy;
    Var Count : Integer;
    Begin
      Reset(InFile);
      Rewrite(OutFile);
      Count := 0;
      While Not EOF(Infile) Do
          Begin
              OutFile^ := InFile^;
              Count := Count + 1;
              If (Count Mod 500) = 0 Then WriteLn(Count,' Records Read');
              Put(OutFile);
              Get(InFile)
          End
    End;
```

EXAMPLE 2:   Most program or operating system libraries contain a program-callable function that accesses the system clock. The availability of such function allows the generation of time-based processing status information.

In the following Pascal program fragment, the clock function is named RunTime( ).

```
While (---) Do
      Begin
          . . . .
          T := RunTime();
          . . . .
          Time := RunTime() - T;
          . . . .
      End;
```

The incorporation of such operations around time-intensive program segments can generate processing time information. Such information may be relayed to the program user in the form of a message or *time blip*.

REFERENCES

1. Barmack, J., and Sinako, H., *Human Factors Problems in Computer Generated Graphic Displays*. Institute for Defense Analysis Study. Vol. 5, 234, 1966.
2. Bennett, Edward, *Human Factors in Technology*, Edward Bennett, et al., New York: McGraw-Hill, 1963.
3. Brooks, F. P., *The Mythical Man-Month*. Reading, MA: Addison-Wesley, 1979.
4. Card, Stuart K., Moran, Thomas P., and Newell, Alan, *The Psychology of Human-Computer Interaction*. Hillsdale, NJ, Lawrence Erlbaum Associates, 1983.
5. Dean, M. *How a Computer Should Talk to People*, IBM Systems Journal, Volume 21, No. 4, 1982.
6. Dreyfuss, Henry *The Measure of Man: human factors in design*. N.Y., Whitney Library of Design.
7. Engel, S., and Granda, R., *Guidelines for Man/Display Interfaces*. Poughkeepsie, NY: IBM Technical Report TR00.2720, Dec. 19, 1975.
8. Gilb, T., and Weinberg, G. M., *Humanized Input*. Cambridge, MA: Winthrop, 1977.
9. Grimes, Jack D., *A Cognitive View of User Interfaces*, Beaverton, OR: Tektronix, 1980.
10. Hendricks, Daniel E., et al., *Human Engineering Guidelines for Management Information Systems*, 1983. Available from Director, U.S. Army Human Engineering Laboratory, ATTN: DRXHE-CSS (MIS Guidelines), Aberdeen Proving Ground, MD 21005.
11. Martin, J., *Design of Man-Computer Dialogues*. Englewood Cliffs, NJ: Prentice-Hall, 1973.
12. McCormick, Ernest J., and Sanders, Mark S., *Human Factors in Engineering and Design*, 5th ed. New York: McGraw-Hill, 1982.
13. Mehlmann, Marilyn, *When People Use Computers: An Approach to Using an Interface*. Englewood Cliffs, NJ, Prentice-Hall, 1981.
14. Miller, George A., "Information and Memory," *Scientific American*, Aug. 1956.
15. Miller, George A. "The Magical Number Seven, Plus or Minus Two: Some Limits on Our Capacity for Processing Information," *Psychological Review 62*, 2, 81–97 Mar. 1956.
16. Morland, D. Verne, "Human Factors Guidelines for Terminal Interface Design," *Communications of the ACM 26*, 7, (July 1983).
17. Ramsey, H. R., and Atwood, M. E., *Human Factors in Computer Systems: A Review of the Literature*. Englewood, CO: Science Applications, 1979. Rubinstein, Richard; Hersh, Harry; and Ledgard, Henry, *The Human Factor—Designing Computer Systems for People*. Burlington, MA: Digital Press, 1984.
18. Ramsey, H. R., Atwood, M. E., and Kirshbaum, P. J., *A Critically Annotated Bibliography of the Literature on Human Factors in Computer Systems*. (AD A058 081). Englewood, CO: Science Applications, 1978.
19. Shneiderman, Ben, *Software Psychology: Human Factors in Computer and Information Systems* (Winthrop Computer Systems series). Cambridge, MA, Winthrop, 1980.
20. Smith, Sidney L., and Mosier, Jane N., *Design Guidelines for User–System Interface Software*. Mitre Publ. No. ESD-TR-84-190 MTR-9420 (1984). Available from Sidney L. Smith, The Mitre Corporation, Burlington Road, Bedford, MA 07130.
21. Weinberg, G. M., *The Psychology of Computer Programming*. Auerbach, 1971.
22. Woodson, Wesley E., *Human Factors Design Handbook: Information and Guidelines for the Design of Systems, Facilities, Equipment*. New York: McGraw-Hill, 1981.

NOTE

[1] Hammer, Michael et al., *Etude: An Integrated Document Processing System*. Proceedings of the 1981 Office Automation Conference, AFIPS, March 1981.

8

PROGRAM ATTRIBUTES

"Look beneath the surface; let not the several quality of a thing nor its worth escape thee."

Marcus Aurelius,
[A.D. 121–180]
Meditations. VI, 3

The noun *Attribute* is defined as "an inherent quality, a characteristic, often hidden or accidental." Software design methodologies help identify the algorithms that define *how a process is accomplished* and the data structures that define *the organization of the data upon which the process is accomplished.*

Neither of these definitions establishes any criteria for how well the pieces "fit together." Too often a *running program* is viewed as being synonymous with a *successful program.* This chapter identifies techniques for determining or measuring the hidden qualities, the attributes of programs.

Donald Knuth is "convinced that all compilers written from now on should be designed to provide all programmers with feedback indicating what parts of their programs are costing the most; indeed this feedback should be supplied automatically unless it is specifically turned off." (Computing Surveys, *6*, 268 (1974))

The specific program attributes discussed in this chapter are performance/efficiency, complexity, and sizing. These particular attributes were chosen because of their general interest and because they are somewhat system-independent.

GLOSSARY OF TERMS

Complexity: Within a program or algorithm, a measure of the logical inter-relationships.

Cyclomatic Complexity: A complexity measure of a program (or algorithm) based upon its representation as a program graph and the calculation of the cyclomatic number of that graph.

Cyclomatic Number: A measure of the connectivity of a graph defined by

$$V(G) = e(G) - v(G) + n(G)$$

where $e(G)$, $v(G)$ and $n(G)$ are the number of edges, vertices, and components, respectively, of a graph G.

Debug: With respect to a program or other software, to detect, locate and correct errors.

Efficiency: In a computer program or algorithm, a measure of how well available resources are used and how well interaction occurs between input and output;

Optimization: The improvement of a system or process to the point it is neither time- nor cost-effective to seek further improvement. The term is often applied to the rewriting and testing or programs to improve their running speed.

Order of Magnitude: A measure of the proportionality of behavior between two quantities.

Program Discriminations: The fine distinctions that must be made by a programmer, both consciously and subconsciously, in writing a program.

Program Graph: The representation of a computer program as a directed graph each vertex represents a program statement or block of program statements and each edge corresponds to the transition between the statements represented by the vertices at the endpoints of that edge.

Sizing: The determination of the storage requirements of a program.

Strongly Connected Graph: A graph in which a path of edges connects any pair of arbitrary distinct vertices.

PROGRAM PERFORMANCE/EFFICIENCY

After correctness, the next most basic issue in the study of algorithms and programs is that of *efficiency.* Efficiency is typically expressed as a function of algorithm or program complexity or it is measured in terms of functions that either directly or indirectly relate to the resource requirements necessary for implementation. These requirements, usually time and memory are most often examined as to their behavior with varying quantities of input data.

Program performance and efficiency can be achieved by working at several levels:

* Algorithms and data structures.
* Algorithm tuning.
* Data structure reorganization.
* Program code tuning.

The techniques discussed in this section address a number of these issues.

Order of Magnitude—"Big O"

CONCEPT: To provide a quantitative measure of the running time (efficiency) of an algorithm in terms of the size of its input. Such a measure would allow a machine-independent comparison of algorithms.

PROCESS: In the analysis of an algorithm it is usually possible to derive the function that relates key operations of the algorithm to the size of the input and thereby identifies its asymptotic rate of growth. Within this function may be identified the dominant factors (terms) that most greatly influence the function as the quantity of input increases. The effect of additional terms in the function often becomes insignificant when compared to the behavior of the dominant terms.

It may then be said that the growth of this function is on the "order" of that dominant term. The "Big O" notation is used to express this relation.

For example, if $F = 40N + 24$ defines the relationship between a number of key operations (F) in the algorithm and the number of input datum (N), then the function F is order N or $F = O(N)$. This is obvious from the fact that the value of F is dominated by the term $40N$ as N increases and the addition of the constant 24 has decreasing influence.

The rigorous definition associated with the "Big O" notation states:

If F and G are two functions, then $F = O(G)$ if and only if there are two constants, A and B such that

$$F \leq AG + B$$

In the previous example, the selection of $A = 40$ and $B = 24$ indeed indicates that $F = O(N)$.

"Big O" notation has several advantages in that it eliminates the distracting clutter of constants and slow-growing terms in the functions, making it easier to compare their overall performance.

The following identities may be used to further quantify the "Big O" of a function:

- $F(N) = O(F(N))$
- $c \times O(F(N)) = O(F(N))$ (where c is a constant)
- $O(F(N)) + O(F(N)) = O(F(N))$
- $O(O(F(N))) = O(F(N))$
- $O(F(N)) \times O(G(N)) = O(F(N) \times G(N))$
- $O(F(N) \times G(N)) = F(N) \times O(G(N))$

It must be emphasized that these relationships are *identities* and not *equalities*. The expressions on the left of the "=" may be replaced by the expression on the right but *not* vice versa.

In the example, the second identity demonstrates why the coefficient of the dominant term is not applicable. Using this identity

$$F = 40 \times O(N) = O(N)$$

It must be remembered that the order of magnitude ("Big O") of an algorithm is a measure of the *asymptotic* performance of the algorithm, as the size of the input increases. It is possible, for small inputs, that an algorithm of higher order actually can be more efficient than one of lower order. There is a tendency, for instance, to assume that an algorithm with running time of order N^2 is better than one with running time of order N^3. Indeed, that assumption is correct for large values of N, but in some practical situations, the latter *may* have a better performance for small values of N.

An algorithm is said to be *polynomial-bounded* if its running time is bounded by a function of order N^k, where N is the input size and k is some constant. Accordingly, an algorithm is regarded as being relatively *fast* or *efficient* if it is polynomial-bounded, and *inefficient* otherwise. Therefore, a problem is said to be *easy* if some polynomial-bounded algorithm has been found to solve it.

Associating polynomial-boundedness with computational efficiency is theoretically justified in that, above a certain input size, a polynomial-bounded algorithm will always have a smaller running time than a non-polynomial-bounded algorithm. Of course, for very small input sizes, the non-polynomial algorithm could have a better performance.

Writing for Optimization

CONCEPT: To identify programming sequences that complement the compiler optimization of programs

PROCESS: Program efficiency is particularly important at the compilation and execution stages.

Sophisticated language compilers often include an *optimization* step in which recognized poor code sequences are replaced by better ones that avoid obvious inefficiencies. Sequences that may be optimized usually include those recognized by the compiler author(s) as resulting in poor code generation impacting program performance and efficiency.

Compilers that produce efficient code tend to be large and slow because of the processing required to optimize the resulting object code.

Although a compiler can optimize a program, the programmer can usually optimize better or at least aid in the optimization. The process of writing programs that recognize common sequences susceptible to optimization may aid in increasing program efficiency even if an optimizing compiler is not used.

For example, with structured programming techniques, the efficiency of an optimizing compiler can be further improved. This is due to simplified program flow (fewer GOTOs), which results in reduced program analysis by the optimizing compiler.

The optimizing techniques discussed here do not eliminate the need for an optimizing compiler since machine-dependent optimizing can seldom be anticipated or controlled at the source code level. Also, even the best optimized source program will be improved by an optimizing compiler.

Using Arrays Efficiently

CONCEPT: To aid in the optimization of a program by identifying techniques that use arrayed variables efficiently

PROCESS: All compilers must allocate storage space for arrays in either *row-major form* or *column-major form.** The knowledge of which scheme is used by the compiler a program is being written for can increase the ability of that compiler to produce optimized code. For example, Pascal compilers use row-major storage while FORTRAN compilers use column-major storage.

The following recommendations are based on a knowledge of compiler techniques and generally represent minimal additional effort on the part of a programmer to implement.

1. Minimize the number of subscripts. This, by definition, decreases complexity by simplifying the addressing of array values.
2. Eliminate variably dimensioned arrays. When a subroutine parameter is an array with variable dimensions, several overhead calculations must typically be performed on each entry to the subroutine. Further, additional indexing computations are required when such an array is subscripted.
3. Use arrays with identical dimension specifications. It helps, when different arrays are being subscripted, if all of the arrays have the same *shape*. A subscript computed for one array can then serve to subscript the others. Therefore, consider expanding some smaller arrays to match the shape of the other arrays with which they are involved.
4. Use arrays with identical element specifications. When different arrays are being subscripted, it helps if all of the arrays have not only the same shape but also the same element length.
5. Let the opposite subscript of the allocation scheme vary fastest. If the compiler used allocates arrays in row-major form, then let the column subscript vary fastest in nested loop situations. Proceed similarly with

---

*Row-major form or column-major form are discussed in Chapter 3.

arrays allocated in column-major form. This practice can optimize the calculations performed by the subscript transformation function.

6. Develop a strategy for dealing with sparse arrays. In some situations, it may be worthwhile considering other available data structures.

Optimizing Loops and Control

CONCEPT: To aid in the optimization of a program by identifying techniques associated with statement repetition.

PROCESS: Most programs of any complexity involve repetition and looping. Likewise, no other logical sequence can so dramatically affect the number of times program statements are executed. Therefore, any optimization of a looping process is a benefit with each repetition.

1. Avoid loops that have a variable as an increment. Loops can be either ascending or descending depending upon whether the increment is positive or negative. When the compiler can determine the sign of the increment during compilation, it can usually generate very efficient code. When the compiler cannot determine the sign of increment, then it cannot tell whether the loop limit variable is an upper bound or a lower bound and therefore cannot tell whether to generate a compare against an upper limit or a compare against a lower limit. Consequently, the compiler may generate both compares. Therefore, the sign of the increment is tested on each pass through the loop and a branch made to the appropriate compare.

2. Protect the loop index variable. While this recommendation may not aid in optimization, a problem lies in the fact that many compilers do not recognize alterations in the loop index variables. As a result, undesirable and/or unpredictable operations can occur when the loop index varies.

3. Consider writing critical loops explicitly. Critical loops may be optimized if the repeated operations are defined with explicit language statements for initialization, incrementing, and testing rather than with a specific language repetition statement.

4. Complicated subscript calculations within a loop should be avoided. Such calculations should occur only once.

Minimizing Dependence in Programs

CONCEPT: To aid in the optimization of a program by minimizing the dependencies between variables used in that program.

PROCESS: The fewer dependencies that exist between variables and statements in a program allow an optimizing compiler to *move statements around* during the optimization process in order to produce the most efficient compiled code possible.

A *use-definition chain* is used to represent scalar dependencies that exist within a program by identifying a range of statements dependent upon a particular value of a variable. For example, the following program fragment may represent the endpoints of a sequence of statements forming a use-definition chain for the variable I. Accurate completion of the processes represented by this chain may depend on the constancy of I.

```
A(I)      =
          .
          .
          .
B(I)  = A(J)  + 3
```

Such *variable dependence* may be accentuated by the presence of loops and may result in *program statement dependence*.

In the following BASIC program fragment, statement S_2 *depends upon* statement S_1 if

1. S_2 can be executed after S_1.
2. On some executions, S_2 uses as input a value that has been computed by a previous execution of S_1.

```
       For I=1 To 50
S₁     A(I) =
           .
           .
           .
S₂     B(I) = A(I-1) + 3
       Next I
```

Nested loops often create a situation of *layered dependence* in which a dependence is *carried* by the loop whose iteration gives rise to the dependence. For example, in the following program fragment

```
       For I = 1 to N
       For J = 1 to M
       A(I,J+1) = B(I,J) + C
       X(I,J) = X(I,J)/A(I,J)
       B(I+1,J) = A(I,J+1)*D
       Next J
       Next I
```

there exists a layered dependence that is *carried* between the I and J loops.

This dependency can be seen by assigning N the value 3, and M the value 2, and "unrolling" the loops for several iterations:

```
A(1,2) = B(1,1)+C
X(1,1) = X(1,1)/A(1,1)
B(2,1) = A(1,2)*D
A(1,3) = B(1,2)+C
X(1,2) = X(1,2)/A(1,2)
B(2,2) = A(1,3)*D
A(2,2) = B(2,1)+C
X(2,1) = X(2,1)/A(2,1)
B(3,1) = A(2,2)*D
```

In this sequence, the use definition chain defined by the calculation of B(2,1) and its use can be seen to span its use can be seen to span an iteration of the outermost (index I) loop (I goes from 1 to 2). This condition creates the layered dependence.

A useful mechanism for visualizing the dependencies within a loop is to consider that if the separate iterations of that loop *can be executed in parallel* then the loop *carries no dependence*.

Removing Dependencies. There are three useful techniques for removing dependencies within program loops: (1) loop interchange, (2) loop distribution, and (3) alignment.

The effect of loop interchange with the previous program fragment example yields

```
For J = 1 to M
For I = 1 to N
A(I,J+1) = B(I,J) + C
X(I,J) = X(I,J)/A(I,J)
B(I+1,J) = A(I,J+1)*D
Next I
Next J
```

The effect of this interchange is to isolate the dependence between the two loops. This can be seen if M is assigned the value 2, N is assigned the value 3, and the first several iterations of the loops are "unrolled."

```
A(1,2) = B(1,1)+C
X(1,1) = X(1,1)/A(1,1)
B(2,1) = A(1,2)*D
A(2,2) = B(2,1)+C
X(2,1) = X(2,1)/A(2,1)
B(3,1) = A(2,2)*D
```

In this example, the use definition chain resulting from the calculation of B(2,1) and its use is shortened from the previous example and is confined to the inner-most (index I) loop. Therefore, there still exists a carried dependence due to the use-definition chain on the array B that exists in the I loop, but there is no longer a layered dependence.

The loop distribution technique is equivalent to inserting an explicit synchronization point in order to remove a carried dependence.

Application of this technique to the previous program fragment example yields

```
For J = 1 to M
For I = 1 to N
A(I,J+1) = B(I,J) + C
B(I+1,J) = A(I,J+1)*D
Next I
Next J
***Synchronization Point***
For J = 1 to M
For I = 1 to N
X(I,J) = X(I,J)/A(I,J)
Next I
Next J
```

The alignment technique involves rewriting the loops and shifting in order to make the dependence move into a single iteration:

```
For J = 1 to M+1
For I = 1 to N
If J >= 2 Then A(I,J) = B(I,J-1) + C
If J <= M Then X(I,J) = X(I,J)/A(I,J)
If J >= 2 Then B(I+1,J-1) = A(I,J)*D
Next I
Next J
```

Examination of this fragment indicates that each iteration can now be executed in parallel.

Writing Expressions for Optimization

CONCEPT: To aid in the optimization of a program by careful organization of program statements, expressions and use of variables

PROCESS: A substantial part of the optimization step in compilation involves the movement of code in an attempt to make operations more efficient and minimize processes. By its nature, this process attempts to ''second-guess'' the programmer's intentions. The results of this process may lead to circumstances that are undesirable and maybe even undetectable. As a result, when writing expressions the programmer needs to consider the underlying methods by which those expressions will be evaluated by the compiler:

1. Initialize variables at compile time. Default values of variable or data types should not be assumed.
2. Recognize the speed of arithmetic operations:
   - Fastest: $+ \; -$
   - $\times$
   - $\div$
   - Slowest: ** (exponentiation)
3. Avoid mixed data types. If allowed, they invariably lead to additional processing.
4. Insure that duplicate computations can be recognized. When several components of a computation are duplicates, then insure that the compiler is permitted to optimize them. For languages that evaluate expressions left-to-right, optimization may be accomplished by moving all duplicates to the left end of the expression or grouping them within parentheses.
5. Insure that constant computations can be recognized. When several components of a computation are constant (as in a loop), then insure that the compiler is permitted to optimize them. This can be accomplished as with duplicate computations.
6. Factor expressions and eliminate scaling computations. Factoring can save a lot of computation as well as insure that duplicate computations can be recognized.
7. Do not introduce artificial intermediate temporaries. Do not assign intermediate calculations to temporary variables unnecessarily. While such variables may improve the form of an expression visually, they typically do not aid in its evaluation. Additional variables also force to compiler to search for dependencies with other variables.
8. Use scalars, not arrays, as accumulators. Using scalars reduces the array addressing overhead.
9. Consider changing operators. Change subtractions into addition wherever possible because addition, being commutative, is optimizes better than subtraction. Likewise, multiplication is preferable to division.

PROGRAM COMPLEXITY

Logical Complexity, Cyclomatic Complexity

CONCEPT: To measure the complexity of a program by computing the number of linearly independent paths through the corresponding program graph. This number is considered to be an indication of the *logical* complexity of the program which the graph depicts.

PROCESS: The definition of a *program graph* is that each node corresponds to a block of code where flow is sequential and each edge corresponds to a transition between nodes. Program graphs do not reflect the logical process in that same manner as a *flow chart*.

The *cyclomatic complexity* (C) of a program graph (G) is defined as the number of linearly independent paths through a program graph that according to graph theory can be calculated by

$$C(G) = e - n + n_s + n_t$$

where,

e = the number of graph edges.
n = the number of nodes.
n_s = the number of entry nodes.
n_t = the number of exit nodes.

For a single-entry/single-exit program ($n_s = n_t = 1$),

$$C(G) = e - n + 2$$

Graphs are *strongly connected* if there is a path that joins any pair of distinct vertices. This property insures that each node can be reached from the entry node and each node can reach the exit node.

Additional properties of cyclomatic complexity are that

- $C(G) \geq 1$.
- $C(G)$ is the maximum number of linearly independent/non-redundant paths in G.
- Inserting or deleting functional statements in G does not affect $C(G)$.
- G has one path if and only if $C(G) = 1$.
- Inserting a new edge in G increases $C(G)$ by 1.
- $C(G)$ depends only on the decision structure of G.

Therefore, any process that minimizes $C(G)$ of a program graph also minimizes the complexity of the program to which that graph corresponds.

While extremely useful in a testing procedure and in the preparation of test data, a cyclomatic measure has well-known limitations:

1. It is exclusively a measure of logical complexity and includes no information on data structures and data flow.
2. The cyclomatic complexity of a sequence of any length remains constant and thereby does not reflect any added complexity as a function of the number of nodes.
3. Complex logical operations may be hidden within nodes that control branching; such nodes should be expanded into simple predicates in order to obtain an accurate complexity measure. This expansion is demonstrated in Example 2, on page 184.
4. Calculations indicate that the complexity of decision and repetition structures are equivalent; this does not typically correspond to experience.

EXAMPLE 1: COMPLEXITY OF UNSTRUCTURED AND STRUCTURED PROCESSES
Calculation of cyclomatic complexity of the basic four control structures defined by the Structure Theorem is shown in Figure 8.1.

Likewise, unstructured program graphs (non-single-entry/single-exit) may be categorized as containing two or more of the control structures with corresponding cyclomatic complexities shown in Figures 8.2 and 8.3.

These calculations substantiate an assertion that *structured* programs utilizing the basic four control structures are less complex than unstructured ones.

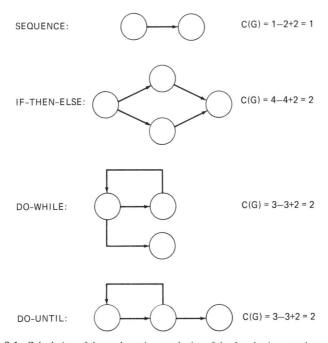

SEQUENCE: $C(G) = 1-2+2 = 1$

IF-THEN-ELSE: $C(G) = 4-4+2 = 2$

DO-WHILE: $C(G) = 3-3+2 = 2$

DO-UNTIL: $C(G) = 3-3+2 = 2$

Figure 8-1. Calculation of the cyclomatic complexity of the four basic control structures.

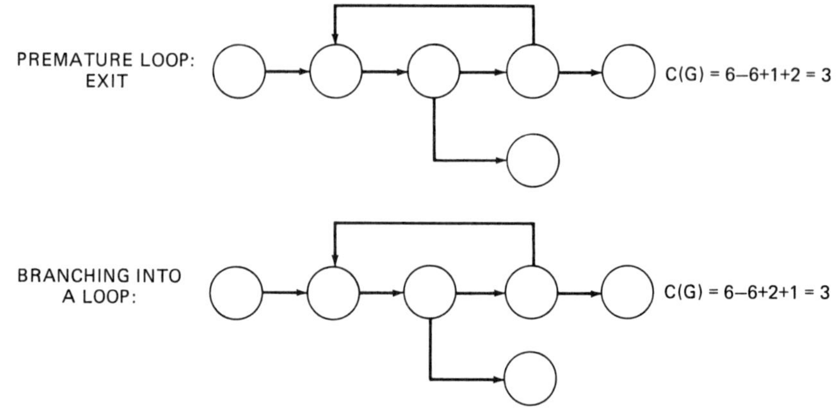

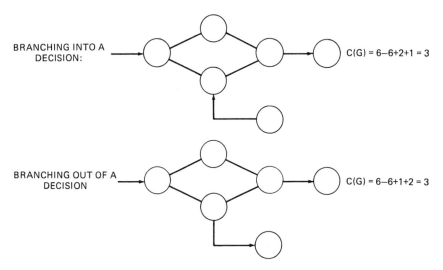

Figure 8-2. Calculation of the cyclomatic complexity of unstructured forms of repetition.

Figure 8-3. Calculation of the cyclomatic complexity of unstructured forms of decision.

EXAMPLE 2: HIDDEN COMPLEXITY IN BOOLEAN PREDICATES   It is easy to conceal the logical complexity of a program graph is any of the nodes contain decision processes involving logical conjunction or disjunction.

The flowchart and program graph shown n Figure 8.4 include the use of an AND operator (conjunction) in an If-Then-Else control structure. These diagrams may be interpreted as indicating that the cyclomatic complexity is unaffected by the AND operator and $C(G) = 2$.

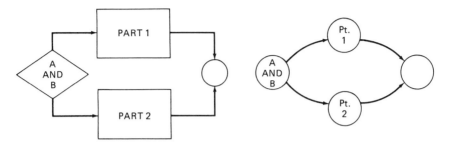

Figure 8-4. Hidden cyclomatic complexity in use of logical conjuction.

However, the hidden complexity of this operation can be observed by expanding the flowchart and program graph as shown in Figure 8.5. This expansion indicates that the actual $C(G) = 3$.

The diagrams shown in Figures 8.6 and 8.7 demonstrate the hidden cyclomatic complexity in processes involving *Inclusive* and *Exclusive* OR (logical disjunction).

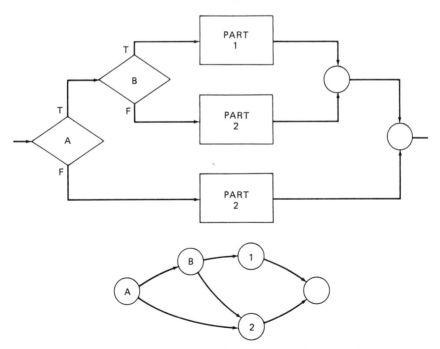

Figure 8-5. Actual cyclomatic complexity in use of logical conjunction.

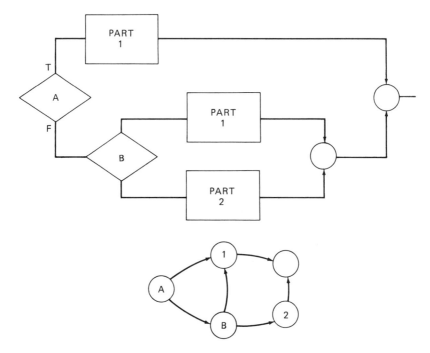

Figure 8-6. Actual cyclomatic complexity in use of logical inclusive disjunction (IOR). (Condition is true if either or both predicates are true).

Cyclomatic Complexity and Program Testing. One technique for testing programs is to identify a set of test data that will exercise all program execution paths in a complete fashion. This technique defines the concept of *path analysis*.

The cyclomatic complexity of a program can be useful in the determination of test paths within a program. Hidden cyclomatic complexity can also be used to illustrate the *coupling* of complex errors to simple errors.

Complexity Measured by Programming Effort—Software Science

CONCEPT: To measure the complexity of a program by empirically calculating a measure of the effort required by knowledgeable programmer to write the program in a high-level programming language.

PROCESS: Program complexity might be described as the mental effort required to understand a program. The more complex the program, the more mental effort required to understand it and the greater the chance for errors when writing or modifying the program. The more lines of code in a program increases the

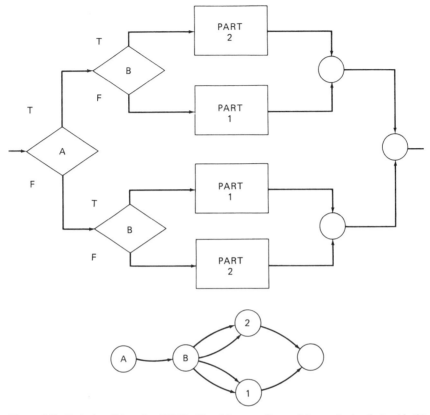

Figure 8-7. Exclusive disjunction (XOR). (Condition true if one of the predicates (but not both) is true.)

chances of introducing an error both in the original coding and in any future maintenance or modification.

Methods of quantifying programming effort were proposed by Halstead (chapter References) along with a number of other invariant laws similar to those of the natural or physical sciences with which algorithms may be characterized. Thus, a number of measures were hypothesized and tested in an effort to quantify the relationships that apparently govern the implementation of algorithms. To this end, four basic measures were defined:

n_1 = the number of unique or distinct operators appearing in a program.
n_2 = the number of unique or distinct operands appearing in a program.
N_1 = total usage of all of the operators appearing in a program.
N_2 = total usage of all of the operands appearing in a program.

   With the above, other measurable properties of a program can be derived including volume, program and language levels, time required to write a program, and purity. Of the measures that can be derived from the foregoing, the one perhaps most revealing is termed *effort* (E), or the number of mental discriminations needed by a concentrating programmer to write a program. This effort increases as program volume (or the size of a program in bits) increases and decreases as program level (or the ratio of the smallest program volume to actual volume) increases resulting in the following equation:

$$E = V/L = \{ n_1 N_2 (N_1 + N_2) \log_2 (n_1 + n_2) \} / 2 n_2$$

This measure, E, captures the overall notion of program complexity.

EXAMPLE: The following demonstrates the increasing complexity in the development of a series of Pascal program statements using Halstead's software sciences.

(a)

```
Begin
    X := 25;
End.
```

   An analysis of this program yields:

n_1	n_2	N_1	N_2
Begin Compound Statement (Begin)	X	1	1 Assignment
Assignment ($:=$)		1	
End Simple Statement (;)		1	
End Compound Statement (End)		1	
End Program (.)		1	
Total = 5	Total = 1	Total = 5	Total = 1

yielding,

$$E = 15 \log_2 (6) \approx 38.8$$

(b)

```
Begin
    X := 25 * X;
End.
```

An analysis of this program yields:

n_1	n_2	N_1	N_2
Begin Compound Statement (Begin)	X	1	1 Assignment
Assignment (: =)		1	1 Multiply
Multiplication (*)		1	
End Simple Statement (;)		1	
End Compound Statement (End)		1	
End Program (.)		1	
Total = 6	Total = 1	Total = 6	Total = 2

yielding,

$$E = 48 \log_2 (7) \approx 134.8$$

(c)

```
Begin
    X := 1;
    X := 25 * X;
End.
```

An analysis of this program yields:

n_1	n_2	N_1	N_2
Being Compound Statement (Begin)	X	1	2 Assignment
Assignment (: =)		2	1 Multiply
Multiplication (*)		1	
End Simple Statement (;)		2	
End Compound Statement (End)		1	
End Program (.)		1	
Total = 6	Total = 1	Total = 8	Total = 3

yielding,

$$E = 99 \log_2 (7) \approx 277.9$$

Interpretation of Halstead's metrics is empirical. In the three sample programs, this technique suggests that program (c) requires almost nine times as many *mental discriminations* on the part of the programmer as program (a).

PROGRAM SIZING

Another important program attribute involves the *size* or *storage utilization* of all data used in and by a program. It is characteristic of most computers that programs and data are stored in the same memory, with the distinction between the two being recognized only by the operating system. Therefore, in order to calculate the quantity of memory required to run a program, *both* the size of the program and its data must be considered.

It is typical of most language compilers that the size of the executable form of a program is directly proportional to the size of the source form (uncompiled). Therefore, the quantity of memory required by a program is usually not subject to change during the program's execution.

However, it is easy to understand that the memory requirements of an executing program are quite subject to change as a result of declarations occurring in that program.

The storage required for data is determined by two factors:

• The storage required by each data type (*static* space requirements).
• The number of unique values of each data type that exist simultaneously (*dynamic* space requirements).

Static Space Requirements

CONCEPT: To define a technique for calculating the static space requirements of a program.

PROCESS: The static space requirements of a program are based upon three implementation-dependent characteristics of the system in which the program is to execute:

• The quantity of storage required for each *primitive* data type (integer, real, character, logical, complex, etc.)
• The number of elements of composing a *structured* data type (array, record, etc.) composed of primitive or structured data types.
• The quantity of memory overhead required by each structured data type.

EXAMPLE: Consider the space requirements of the procedures defined to implement a linked list.

```
Type  Ptr = ^Element;
      Element = Record
                    ElementData:Array[1..N] of Integer;
                    Link:Ptr
                End;
```

```
Var  Head, Temp : Ptr;
     Data : Element;
     Number : Integer;
```

The storage requirements of each primitive data type represented are denoted $S_{integer}$ and S_{ptr} respectively. The overhead storage requirements for the structured data types are denoted S_{record} and S_{array}.

Expansion of each user-defined data type into respective primitive data types leads to a calculation of their respective storage requirements, as shown in Table 8-1.

Table 8-1. Analysis of Storage Requirements for Implementation of a Singly Linked List of Integer Values.

Type	Storage Requirements
Ptr	S_{ptr}
Element	$N \times S_{integer} + S_{array} + S_{ptr} + S_{record}$

The variable declaration part of this program (Var) allocates space for two static variables of type Ptr, one static variable of type Element, and one static variable of type Integer, leading to a total static space requirement for data of

$$(N + 1)S_{integer} + 3S_{ptr} + S_{array} + S_{record}$$

This equation does make the assumption that a Type declaration requires no storage.

For the sake of example, let the following storage requirements for the primitive data types and structures be assumed:

$$S_{integer} = 1; \ S_{ptr} = 1; \ S_{array} = 3; \ S_{record} = 0.$$

With these values, the static space requirements of this program is

$$N + 7$$

Such requirements are often expressed in order of magnitude (''Big-O'') form and yields in this case $O(N)$, a result that is not very surprising.

Dynamic Space Requirements

CONCEPT: To define a technique for calculating the dynamic space requirements of a program.

PROCESS: The dynamic space requirements of a program are not as easily quantified as are the static space requirements. Since a declaration of dynamic values does not occur, an estimate of space requirements must be based upon the operations in a program that result in the dynamic allocation of storage. The three most common of these operations are:

- Variable scoping (local and global variables).
- Recursion.
- Dynamic variables and data structures.

In programming languages such as Pascal, which allow restricted variable scopes, the storage required for variables declared in a scope is no longer required when program control leaves that scope. Consequently, storage used when that scope is active is reused for other purposes when the scope is inactive. As a result, the space requirement of a program utilizing restricted scope is the maximum amount of space in use (i.e., scopes active) at one time, not the sum of the space requirements for all declarations. While a scope is active, calculation of storage requirements for its local values is accomplished in the same way as for static storage requirements.

Recursion represents the extreme case of variable scoping. By definition, recursion permits multiple "copies" of the same scope to be active simultaneously. As a result, the dynamic storage requirements of a recursive procedure depends upon the requirements of a single scope of that procedure and the depth of recursion (the number of times a recursive invocation occurs).

For programs that use dynamic variables and/or dynamic data structures, the calculation of storage requirements becomes more complex. Allocation of storage for such variables usually results from a procedural call executed from a program (in Pascal, the predefined procedure NEW). The storage requirements of a program may be reduced by calls to a complementary procedure which deallocates space (in Pascal, the predefined procedure DISPOSE). As a result, the number of dynamic variables and elements in dynamic data structures are constantly subject to change during the execution of a program. Estimates of the storage required by such variables may be calculated by monitoring the difference between the number of allocation calls and deallocation calls of each dynamic type and the static storage definition of that type. For example, in a program using a linked list data structure, the difference between the number of allocation calls for storage of the data type that composes the elements of that list and the number of deallocation calls for the same type provides some estimate of the number of elements contained in data structures of that type.

REFERENCES

1. Halstead, M. H., *Elements of Software Science*. New York: Elsevier North Holland, 1977.
2. McCabe, T., "A Complexity Measure," *IEEE Transactions on Software Engineering*, SE-2, 6, (Dec. 1976), pp. 308–320.
3. Mills, Harlan, "Mathematical Foundations for Structured Programming," Gaithersburg, MD: IBM (FSC 72-6012) 1972.
4. Shneiderman, Ben, *Software Psychology: Human Factors in Computer and Information Systems* (Winthrop Computer Systems series). Cambridge, MA: Winthrop, 1980.
5. Van Tassel, Dennie, *Program Style, Design, Efficiency, Debugging, and Testing.* Englewood Cliffs, NJ: Prentice-Hall, 1978.

9

GAMING TECHNIQUES

"When we write programs that 'learn,' it turns out that we do and they don't."

Alan J. Perlis
Yale University
"Epigrams on Programming"
ACM SIGPLANNOTICES (Sept. 1982)

The association between computing and game-playing has existed since the early days of computers. Games can be an excellent introduction to computing in general and programming in particular. By their very nature, most games are designed to appeal to a range of senses, as well as to the intellect. The conventional idea of a computer program that accepts data, massages it in some way, and produces some form of output is perfectly acceptable for most applications where the volume of data, speed, and accuracy are the driving forces. But with the challenge and sensory stimulation lacking, most of these programs would make dreadfully boring games.

The goal of this chapter is to provide a survey of disciplines involved in computer game-playing. By studying computer games, programmers can learn new strategies and problem-solving techniques that can be applied to large, complex problems.

Eric Berne defines a game as "an ongoing series of complementary ulterior transactions progressing to a well-defined, predictable, outcome."* This definition sounds remarkably like the description of an algorithm or a *deterministic* model.

Descriptively, a game is a recurring set of transactions, often repetitions, superficially plausible, with a concealed motivation. In this sense, game-playing by computer can be accomplished by designing a computer simulation of the set of transactions (the model) that define the game to be played.

---

*Berne, Eric, "Games People Play," Grove Press, Inc., New York, 1964, page 48.

Consequently, computer games, puzzles, and so forth, can be classified in the same manner as simulations of systems of other types and often incorporate the general techniques of system simulation.

GLOSSARY OF TERMS

Adjacency Matrix: An array whose values represent the relationships between elements of a corresponding data structure, i.e., define the adjacency relationships between elements of a data structure;

Artificial Intelligence: The study of nonliving devices that solve problems for which they are not *explicitly* programmed. They must adapt to the natural logic of an individual task in some way and be capable of handling a variety of similar situations.

Backtracking: The process of returning to a previous point of choice and choosing again.

Game: An amusement or sport involving competition under a specific set of rules. The competition may be against oneself or against the laws of chance.

Heuristic Process: A routine by which the computer attacks a problem not by a direct algorithmic procedure, but by a trial-and-error approach frequently involving the act of learning. The approach usually seems reasonable but is probably not always optimum.

Heuristic Programs: Computer programs that contain as much information as the programmer can provide concerning the specifics of the problem to be solved, together with some logical rules for optimizing the chance of success at intermediate points in the computation. Therefore, heuristic program writing is an attempt to endow a computer with the information an intelligent human would use in approaching and solving a particular problem.

Learning: The ability of a program to retain pointers defining access paths within a data structure and to reject those combinations that define unsuccessful paths while accepting those that will be followed in a subsequent trial.

Lookahead: The process of evaluating a decision that includes an examination of the effects of alternate choices including future decisions.

Pattern Recognition: The recognition of shapes or other patterns by a machine system.

Puzzle: A problem that has a baffling quality or great intricacy, which one must exercise substantial mental ingenuity and thought to solve.

DETERMINISTIC GAMES AND PUZZLES

A strong distinction between a *game* and a *puzzle* can be made based on the *determinism* of each. Most puzzles are assumed to be somewhat deterministic with well-defined methods of solution while games are more *stochastic* employing the elements of chance, strategy and skill.

In some circumstances, games that appear to be stochastic are, in fact, deterministic in that they have a specific underlying rule which guarantees success.

The following two algorithms are examples of deterministic models. The first illustrates an algorithmic solution to a puzzle. The second shows an algorithmic *strategy* to a game which could easily be interpreted as stochastic.

EXAMPLE 1: A "magic square M of order n" is an n array M of numbers with the property that the numbers in each row, each column and both 'diagonals' add up to the same 'magic number' Mag(M).

De la Loubere* has found a method of generating magic squares of order n (where n is an odd number). Given two integers i, j with $1 \le i$ and $j \le n$ the following algorithm will determine the element of the magic square M in row i and column j (i.e., $M_{i,j}$).

1. Let $b = j - i + ((n - 1)/2)$ and let $c = 2j - i$.
2. If $b \ge n$ then let $b = b - n$ and go to step 4.
3. If $b < 0$ then let $b = b + n$.
4. If $c > n$ then let $c = c - n$ and go to step 6.
5. If $c \le 0$ then let $c = c + n$.
6. Let $M_{i,j} = bn + c$ and Stop.

EXAMPLE 2: A variation of the game of *Nim* is played with an arbitrary number of objects arranged in three piles. These piles can be conveniently represented as a triple of numbers (n_1, n_2, n_3).

The game is played by two persons who move in turns. Each move consists of removing one or move objects from one of the three piles. A player *wins* by removing all remaining objects (i.e., manage to remove the last of the total number of objects and attain the situation $(0, 0, 0)$).

A situation (n_1, n_2, n_3) reached by a player is called "winning" if it guarantees success at that point in the game if followed by subsequent "winning" moves by that player. An opponent cannot create a winning situation from a winning situation given the rules of play. Therefore, the knowledge of what constitutes a winning situation and how one can be achieved is of critical importance to a player of the game.

It is known that a player can determine for the game of Nim whether a situation (n_1, n_2, n_3) is winning or not by using the following algorithm:

---

*Maurer, H. A. and M. R. Williams, "A Collection of Programming Problems and Techniques," Englewood Cliffs, NJ: Prentice-Hall, 1972, p. 46.

1. Represent n_1, n_2, n_3 in binary form as $b_2b_2b_3$, $c_1c_2c_3$, $d_1d_2d_3$ respectively.
2. Define variables r_1, r_2, r_3 with the relation $r_n = b_n + c_n + d_n$.
3. If r_1, r_2 and r_3 are all even, then (n_1, n_2, n_3) is a 'winning' situation; otherwise it is not.

GAMES AND DATA STRUCTURES

The role of data structures is the design of game-playing programs can be extremely widespread. Choice of appropriate structures can affect program performance to an important extent in interactive applications. Stochastic games can use data structures in any of the various applications common to simulation models.

Two additional applications for data structures are in the areas of logical element relationships and heuristics. The following example demonstrates how the concept of *odd-shaped* arrays can be used in the definition of a board game that utilizes a hexagonal game board. This example demonstrates the use of data structures in the representation of unusual element relationships. Odd-shaped arrays are discussed in greater detail in Chapter 3.

HEXAGONAL GAME BOARD   The relationship between elements in a hexagonal grid is characterized by each element being adjacent to (sharing an edge with) six other elements, except at the perimeter of the grid. In addition, the distances between the "center" of each grid element and the center of each adjacent element are equal.

The relationships between elements in a hexagonal grid may be expressed in terms of a non-Cartesian coordinate system (see Figure 9.1).

The scale of the x and y axes is expressed in units equal to the distance between the centerpoints of grid elements. Therefore, the elements adjacent to $(0, 0)$ (numbered 1 to 6 in the above illustration) can be identified using the coordinates in Table 9.1.

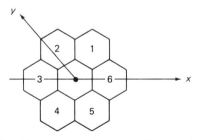

Figure 9-1. Representation of an array of hexagonal elements.

Table 9-1. Coordinate Relationships Between Elements of a Hexagonal Array.

Adjacent Element	Coordinates
1	$(x+1, y+1)$
2	$(x, y+1)$
3	$(x-1, y)$
4	$(x-1, y-1)$
5	$(x, y-1)$
6	$(x+1, y)$

Similarly, adjacent elements of any element of the grid may be identified in terms of offset values to the coordinates of that element as in (Table 9.2).

These offsets accessed in a 6×2 array provide information regarding the logical relationship of elements within a hexagonal grid.

In a Pascal program segment, this "adjacency" matrix may be initialized as follows:

```
Type Adjacency = Array[1..6,1..2] of -1..1;
Var Offset : Adjacency;
..........
Offset[1,1] := 1;
Offset[1,2] := 1;
Offset[2,1] := 0;
Offset[2,2] := 1;
  etc.
```

Table 9-2. Coordinate Relationships of a Hexagonal Array Expressed In Terms of Offset Values.

Adjacent Element	Δx	Δy
1	+1	+1
2	0	+1
3	-1	0
4	-1	-1
5	0	-1
6	+1	0

The following Pascal function returns the Boolean value TRUE if the two elements identified in its parameter list are adjacent:

```
Function Compare (x1,y1,x2,y2:Integer):Boolean;
   Var  x,y : Integer;
   Begin
      Compare := FALSE;
      x := ABS(x1-x2);
      y := ABS(y1-y2);
      If  ((x+y) ≠ 0) Or (x ≤ 1) Or (y ≤ 1)
          Then Compare := TRUE
   End;
```

When given element (x_1, y_1), the following Pascal procedure returns in (x_2, y_2) the Nth adjacent element to (x_1, y_1) identified in the "adjacency" matrix.

```
Procedure Next ( x1,y1,N:Integer;  Offset:Adjacency;
                     Var x2,y2:Integer);
Begin
    x2 := x1 + Adjacency[N,1];
    y2 := y1 + Adjacency[N,2]
    End;
```

STOCHASTIC GAMES—HEURISTICS

As with the case of stochastic system simulation, some games are of such complexity that a closed definition as with an algorithm is either impractical or impossible. Therefore the transactions that occur in such games are described best in a stochastic model.

The stochastic nature of such games can often be attributed not only to the elements of *chance* but also to the ambiguous qualities of *strategy* and *skill*. Successful computer games must be able to demonstrate these qualities as well as the capacity to learn during either the course of a single game or a sequence of games. In order to accomplish these ends, game-playing programs often incorporate the features of *heuristic programming* and techniques more often associated with studies in *artificial intelligence*.

The following techniques described how elements of skill, logic, and strategy can be simulated in the context of game-playing or puzzle-solving computer programs.

Evaluating Game Trees

CONCEPT: To determine the path of greatest potential success in a game whose moves (states) are defined as the nodes of a game tree.

PROCESS: A *game tree* is a data structure commonly used by game-playing programs like chess and checkers. In a game tree, each node represents a position in a game. The children of any node represent positions resulting from the various possible moves. Thus, the root node represents a position in which the first player must move; the children of this node are positions in which the opposing player may move, and so forth.

In order to choose which of the possible moves to take, an evaluation mechanism is needed to select from the possible next positions. One possible mechanism is the selection of a *static evaluation function*. This function evaluates a game move in terms of external parameters. For a board game, this function may calculate a value computed from patterns formed by the game pieces.

One common evaluation mechanism is the *min-max* strategy. This strategy is defined as follows:

- Since the first player wants to choose the best possible next move, it is reasonable to assign to any node representing a position that player faces the value of the best of its children (i.e., the *maximum* of the values of nodes immediately below it.
- Since the second player wants to choose the best possible move, he or she wants to pick that move giving the *worst* position to the first player. Hence, it is reasonable to assign to any position faced by the second layer the *minimum* of the values of the nodes immediately below it.

Many game-playing programs do not store the game tree explicitly, it being too large. Instead, they provide routines which

- Compute a list of legal moves for a given position.
- Compute a new position, given a starting position and a move.
- Determine whether a position is a leaf of the tree for which a value can be computed (i.e., node evaluated) immediately.

EXAMPLE: Consider the familiar game of tic-tac-toe. Assume that X makes the first move. Nodes will be evaluated by an evaluation function, F, where at a node, F equals the number of complete rows, columns, or diagonals that are still open to X minus the number of complete rows, columns, or diagonals that are still open to O. If a node is a win for X, $F = +\infty$. If a node is a win for O, $E = -\infty$.

Thus if a node presents 6 winning possibilities for X and 4 winning possibilities for O, then F at that node is $6 - 4 = 2$. With symmetries simplifying the situation, the decision tree for the first two moves of a tic-tac-toe game is shown in Figure 9.2(a).

Each node of move 1 is now assigned the minimum F function value of move 2 that can be made from the particular move 1 node. The node of move 1 that has the maximum F function is the best move, as shown in Figure 9.2(b).

The value of a node is the minimum of all values of nodes descending from it, and can be evaluated at any stage of the game where X is about to move, as in Figure 9.2(c).

Note, in Figure 9.2(c), that at the nodes that lead to an O win, it is not necessary to evaluate any other paths. As soon as a value of $-\infty$ is found, no path with a smaller F function can be found. This is the basis of the $\alpha - \beta$ procedure, which is similar to the min-max method. The difference is that nodes are generated and evaluated at the same time and a particular node is ignored as soon as its backed-up value becomes unfavorable to a predecessor.

For optimum performance, game-playing programs are a compromise between depth and the breadth of planning ahead. The success of a game-playing program is also determined by the choice of a proper F function for evaluating the value of paths through nodes.

Pattern Matching

CONCEPT: To define a pattern-matching mechanism whereby a program can recognize specific patterns or characters.

PROCESS: The recognition of characters and/or patterns is a common "intelligent" feature of game-playing and artificial intelligence programs. There are several ways in which a pattern can be scanned and converted into a machine representation. The result is usually a projection of the pattern image onto a grid. This grid can be stored in bitmap form or more simply as discrete values placed in grid boxes represented by an array.

The least complicated system for identifying a pattern or character is *template matching*. A series of standard or frequent grid patterns is stored in the computer's memory. For example, the digit 2 viewed as Figure 9.3(a) can be defined as in Figure 9.3(b). The input pattern image is matched against the prestored template images, and the comparison with the minimum number of mismatches is taken to be the character recognized. More sophisticated systems analyze the strokes and shape of the image and use statistical comparison schemes to decide which pattern the digitized image represents.

Files of standard templates are useful for character recognition and for the recognition of finite sets of other patterns. For example, in the game of tic-tac-

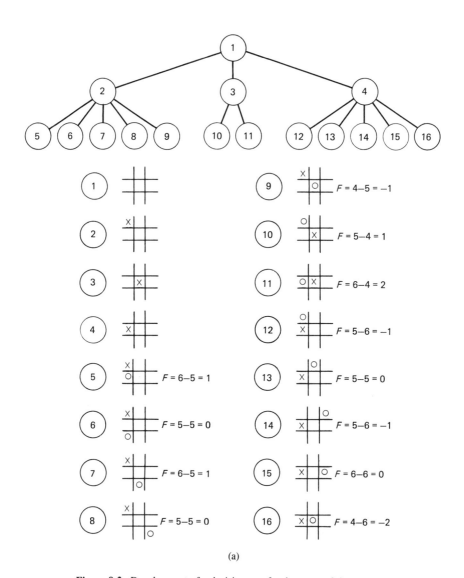

(a)

Figure 9-2. Development of a decision tree for the game of tic-tac-toe.

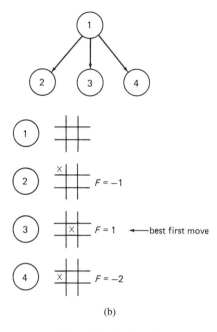

(b)

Figure 9-2. *Continued.*

toe, the number of board configurations, also including mirror images, is small enough that the template technique may be desirable as a means of communicating moves. This can be especially useful in systems that support input devices allowing a move to be specified by means other than a specification of the Cartesian coordinates (x and y) on the game board or display area.

Storage of patterns, rather than specific recognition, is often desired with specific circumstances. Sequences of patterns can indicate a progression of events such as the move sequence during the course of a game. Such sequences and their impact upon the final result (i.e., outcome of the game) can be used to build descriptive *game trees*.

A possible technique for building such a storage can be accomplished using a *push-down stack* as a memory device. Sequences of patterns, represented as vectors in row-major or column-major form, are then pushed onto the stack as the actions they represent occur. Traversal of the stack then presents a reverse chronological history of the sequence of patterns. Comparisons of adjacent patterns (i.e., moves) is easily accomplished by defining criteria for comparison of their vector representations.

Backtracking

CONCEPT: To define a technique that simulates a strategy of backtracking.

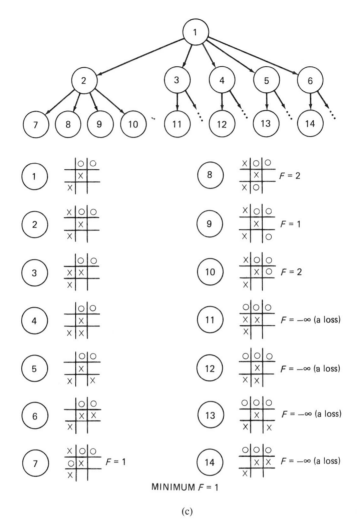

(c)

Figure 9-2. *Continued.*

PROCESS: *Backtracking* is defined as "returning over the same course or route; withdrawing." Therefore, any nondeterministic process involving "trial and error" is likely to require a strategy to accomplish backtracking.

A push-down stack is a useful tool in games and simulations involving a strategy of backtracking, the process of returning to a previous point of choice and choosing again. This process is also quite common to the area of artificial intelligence.

(a)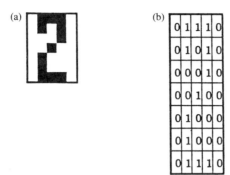

(b)

0	1	1	1	0
0	1	0	1	0
0	0	0	1	0
0	0	1	0	0
0	1	0	0	0
0	1	0	0	0
0	1	1	1	0

Figure 9-3. Example of character identification by template matching.

EXAMPLE: Navigation through a maze is a familar problem that utilizes a backtracking strategy. A two-dimensional array may be used as a physical model of a maze. Elements of the array that contain the value 0 are considered to be unobstructed and therefore part of a potential path through the maze. Elements containing the value 1 are obstructed and therefore represent a barrier around which a path must be found. (See Figure 9.4(a)). which represents the maze in Figure 9.4(b).

A restriction of this model is that movement through it may occur only horizontally or vertically, never diagonally. The current position of the traveller through the maze is indicated by the array coordinates (subscripts).

With this model definition, a possible path through the above maze from point (2,4) to point (6,2) is shown in Figure 9.5.

The logical model for this maze-tracing problem should enable the traveller to find a path through the maze (if one exists) and remember it. The stochastic nature of this model would indicate that any path found may only be one of a set of possible paths. Therefore, the model may yield a different path on other occasions.

(a)

0	0	0	0	0	0
0	0	0	1	0	0
0	1	1	1	0	0
0	0	1	0	1	0
0	1	1	1	1	0
0	1	0	0	1	0

(b)

Figure 9-4. The representation of a maze using an array.

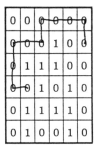

Figure 9-5. A path through the maze of Figure 9.4.

The array elements that describe a path may be stored in a push-down stack (the stack operates as the traveller's memory). Therefore, the final configuration of this stack will describe a successful path if one exists through the maze.

It is also necessary to describe a strategy that allows the traveller to test movement through the maze (take a step and evaluate that step).

Given the two-dimensional array characteristics of the physical model, there are only four possible moves from a location that is not in the first row or column. Starting from the border rows and columns, gives less than four. If the border rows and columns in the physical model always contain 1's (there are obstructions along the borders), then there will always be four possible moves from any meaningful location within the maze.

The possible moves from any location can be described using an *adjacency matrix*. This matrix can be described as shown in Table 9.3.

The values of this matrix represent the subscript offsets which define each of the four *neighbors* of any location within the maze.

Of the four possible moves from a location, at least one of the moves may represent a *backtrack*—the (prior) location from whence the traveler came. It is therefore logical the traveller should attempt all steps that are *not* backtracks in

**Table 9-3. Adjacency Matrix Defining
Relationships Between Elements of
Maze Array.**

Adjacent Element	Δx	Δy
1	-1	0
2	0	$+1$
3	$+1$	0
4	0	-1

order to make progress through the maze. If no step other than the backtrack is possible, then the current location should be erased because it represents a dead end.

```
Program Navigate (Input, Output);

Type Ptr = ^Element;
     Element = Record
                   X,Y : Integer;
                   Link : Ptr
               End;
     Table1 = Array[1..8,1..8] of Integer;
     Table2 = Array[1..4,1..2] of -1..1;

Var Maze : Table1;
    Adjacent : Table2;
    Flag, Next : 0..5;
    Path, Step : Ptr;
    XStart, XCurr, XEnd : Integer;
    YStart, YCurr, YEnd : Integer;
    I, J : 1..8;
    Goal : Boolean;


Procedure Push(Var ListPtr, NewPtr : Ptr);
Begin
  NewPtr^.Link := ListPtr;
  ListPtr := NewPtr
End {Push Procedure};


Procedure Pop(Var ListPtr, PopPtr : Ptr);
Begin
  If ListPtr < > Nil Then
                       Begin
                         PopPtr := ListPtr;
                         ListPtr := ListPtr^.Link
                       End
End {Pop Procedure};


Procedure Traverse(ListPtr : Ptr);
Var X : Ptr;
Begin
  X := ListPtr;
  While X < > Nil Do
                     Begin
                       WriteLn(X^.X, X^.Y);
                       X := X^.Link
                     End
End {Traverse Procedure};
```

```
Procedure Select(Point:Ptr;Moves:Table2;Next:Integer;Var X,Y:Integer);
   Begin
      X := Point^.X + Moves[Next,1];
      Y := Point^.Y + Moves[Next,2]
   End;

Procedure Check(Z:Table1;Point:PtrX,Y:Integer;Var Flag:Integer);
   Begin
      If Z[X,Y] = 0 Then
         If (Point^.Link = Nil) Then Flag := 2
                  Else
                      If (Point^.Link^.X = X) And (Point^.Link^.Y = Y)
                      Then Flag :=1
                      Else Flag := 2
   End;
Begin {Navigate Program}
   {Adjacency Matrix}
   Adjacent[1,1] := -1; Adjacent[1,2] := 0;
   Adjacent[2,1] := 0; Adjacent[2,2] := 1;
   Adjacent[3,1] := 1; Adjacent[3,2] := 0;
   Adjacent[4,1] := 0; Adjacent[4,2] := -1;
   {Maze Matrix}
   Maze[1,1] := 1; Maze[1,2] := 1; Maze[1,3] := 1; Maze[1,4] := 1;
   Maze[1,5] := 1; Maze[1,6] := 1; Maze[1,7] := 1; Maze[1,8] := 1;
   Maze[2,1] := 1; Maze[2,2] := 0; Maze[2,3] := 0; Maze[2,4] := 0;
   Maze[2,5] := 0; Maze[2,6] := 0; Maze[2,7] := 0; Maze[2,8] := 1;
   Maze[3,1] := 1; Maze[3,2] := 0; Maze[3,3] := 0; Maze[3,4] := 0;
   Maze[3,5] := 1; Maze[3,6] := 0; Maze[3,7] := 0; Maze[3,8] := 1;
   Maze[4,1] := 1; Maze[4,2] := 0; Maze[4,3] := 1; Maze[4,4] := 1;
   Maze[4,5] := 1; Maze[4,6] := 0; Maze[4,7] := 0; Maze[4,8] := 1;
   Maze[5,1] := 1; Maze[5,2] := 0; Maze[5,3] := 0; Maze[5,4] := 1;
   Maze[5,5] := 0; Maze[5,6] := 1; Maze[5,7] := 0; Maze[5,8] := 1;
   Maze[6,1] := 1; Maze[6,2] := 0; Maze[6,3] := 1; Maze[6,4] := 1;
   Maze[6,5] := 1; Maze[6,6] := 1; Maze[6,7] := 0; Maze[6,8] := 1;
   Maze[7,1] := 1; Maze[7,2] := 0; Maze[7,3] := 1; Maze[7,4] := 0;
   Maze[7,5] := 0; Maze[7,6] := 1; Maze[7,7] := 0; Maze[7,8] := 1;
   Maze[8,1] := 1; Maze[8,2] := 1; Maze[8,3] := 1; Maze[8,4] := 1;
   Maze[8,5] := 1; Maze[8,6] := 1; Maze[8,7] := 1; Maze[8,8] := 1;
   For I := 1 to 8 Do
       Begin
         For J := 1 to 8 Do
             Write(Maze[I,J]:1);
         Writeln
       End;
   ReadLn(XStart,YStart);
   ReadLn(XEnd,YEnd);
   Path := Nil;
   Goal := True;
   New(Step);
   Step^.X := XStart;
   Step^.Y := YStart;
```

```
    Push(Path,Step);
    XCurr : = XStart;
    YCurr : = YStart;
    While Goal Do
        Begin
          Flag : = 0;
          Next : = 1;
          While Next < =4 Do
              Begin
                  Select(Path,Adjacent,Next,XCurr,YCurr);
                  Check(Maze,Path,XCurr,YCurr,Flag);
                  If Flag = 2 Then Next : = 5
                                Else Next : = Next + 1
              End;
          Case Flag of
              0: WriteLn(' No Path');
              1: Begin
                    Maze[Path^.X,Path^.Y] : = 1;
                    Pop(Path,Step);
                    Dispose(Step)
                  End;
              2: Begin
                    New(Step);
                    Step^.X : = XCurr;
                    Step^.Y : = YCurr;
                    Push(Path,Step)
                  End
              End {Case};
          If Flag = 0 Then Goal : = False;
          If Path^.X = XEnd Then If Path^.Y = YEnd Then Goal : = False
      End; {Path Search}
  If Flag < > 0 Then Traverse(Path);
End. {Navigate Program}
```

Push is the generalized procedure for adding an element to a push-down stack. Since in this program a stack is used to "remember" moves, the value of the element *pushed* on the stack is a set of coordinates that defines the location of a move. These coordinates are added to the stack whenever a move is considered.

Pop is the generalized procedure for removing an element from a push-down stack. In this program, coordinates are removed from the stack if it is realized that they represent a backtrack.

Traverse is the generalized procedure for stack traversal. A traversal of the stack at the termination of the program provides a description of the successful or unsuccessful path through the maze.

Select locates a step in one of the four directions from the position indicated by the top of the stack. The parameters of this procedure include the stack pointer, the adjacency matrix that is used to define possible moves, and an integer between 1 and 4 that indicates which of the four neighboring locations will be the next move. The four possible moves are evaluated in a clockwise fashion. This procedure returns the coordinates of the next move to be attempted.

Check checks the stack to determine if the next move is a backtrack or a forward move. This information is contained in the variable Flag.

REFERENCES

1. Gardner, Martin, *The Unexpected Hanging*. New York: Simon & Schuster, 1968.
2. Hofstadter, Douglas R., *Metamagical Themas: Questing for the Essence of Mind and Pattern*. New York: Basic Books, Inc., 1985.
3. Spencer, Donald, *Game Playing with Computers*. Rochelle Park, NJ: Hayden Book Co., 1975.
4. Vajda, S., *The Theory of Games and Linear Programming*. London: Methuen, 1956.

10

SEARCHING

"Attempt the end, and never stand to doubt;
Nothing's so hard, but search will find it out."

Robert Herrick,
[1591–1674]
Search and Find

One of the world's foremost computer scientists, Donald Knuth, has said that "virtually every important aspect of programming arises somewhere in the context of sorting or searching." Certainly the two disciplines are hopelessly intertwined. All search techniques of any complexity (excluding the linear, sequential methods) are useless operating upon a collection of items that has been previously sorted.

This chapter provides a survey of techniques and applications for writing search routines.

GLOSSARY OF TERMS

Binary Search: A *dichotomizing* search in which, at each step of the search, the set of items is partitioned into two equal parts, with some appropriate action being taken in the case of an odd number of items.

Chaining Search: A search in which each item contains means for locating the next item to be considered in the search.

Fibonacci Search: A *dichotomizing* search in which the number of items in the set is equal to a Fibonacci number or is assured to be equal to the next higher Fibonacci number, and then at each step in the search the set of items is partitioned with the Fibonacci Series.

File: A sequence of records.

Key: That attribute of a given record which results from the evaluation of a certain function applied to that record.

Merge: To combine two or more sorted collections of items into a single sorted collection.

Pointer Value: An integer value associated with each position in a file.

Record: A unit of information; its contents cannot be altered.

Search Cycle: The part of a search that is repeated for each item, normally consisting of locating the item and performing a comparison.

SURVEY OF SEARCHING TECHNIQUES

Linear or Sequential Searches

The simplest method of searching is the *linear* or *sequential* search. It is also the only searching technique which effective for searching an *unsorted* collection of items.

DESCRIPTION: The algorithm searches a file of M records, looking for a given key K. K is assumed to be present in the file. The file is represented as an array F with positions denoted F_i where $1 \leq i \leq M$. Each position may either be empty (i.e., does not contain a value) or occupied (i.e., contains a value). The key of record F_i is denoted by $K[F_i]$.

ALGORITHM: 1. Assign i the value of 1;
2. If $K[F_i] = K$ then stop (record has been located)
3. Increment i; Go to step 2;

EXAMPLE The implementation of the sequential search algorithm is easily implemented for searching a collection of items represented by an array. *It is also quite unnecessary* in that numerous techniques have defined for sorting arrays.

Singly linked lists, defined as stacks or queues, represent data structures for which a linear search is the most effective.

The following Pascal procedure demonstrates a linear search of a stack in order to locate the key of the greatest value. It can be readily seen that the search is actually a minor modification of the generalized stack traversal procedure.

```
Type Ptr = ^Element;
     Element = Record
                   ElementData:Integer;
                   Link:Ptr
               End {Element Definition};
```

```
            ****
```

```
Procedure SeqSearch(ListPtr:Ptr);
Var X:Ptr;
    Large:Integer;
```

```
Begin
  Large : = 0;
  X : = ListPtr;
  While X < > Nil Do
              Being
                 If X^.ElementData > Large
                    Then Large : = X^.ElementData;
                 X := X^.Link
              End;
  WriteLn(Large)
End {SeqSearch Procedure};
```

Dichotomizing Searches

Dichotomizing search techniques are based upon a fundamental strategy of *divide and conquer*. This strategy is implemented by *partitioning* the collection of items to be searched into two parts, determining which of the two parts the key being sought should belong in and limiting continued searching to that part. This partitioning results in the definition of subsets of the original collection and leads to the isolation of the item sought in a somewhat recursive manner.

The differences in dichotomizing search techniques lies primarily in the partitioning scheme adopted. All dichotomizing searches are only effective on collections of items which are already sorted according to the sought key. The choice of a partitioning scheme may therefore lie in some knowledge of the distribution of keys as sorted within the set.

The Binary Search.   Perhaps the most well-known, dichotomizing technique is the binary search. The concepts of this technique have diverse applications ranging from a search of a collection of discrete items to the isolation of the roots of a continuous function.

The fundamental concept of a binary search is that given an ordered (i.e., sorted) collection of items, a search for an item with a particular key may be conducted as follows:

1. Partition the given item set into two subsets.
2. Determine which subset may contain the item with the desired key based upon a comparison of that key with the known ordering of the set.
3. Continue the similar partitioning of the subsets until individual items remain. If the lowest level subset (single item) has the desired key, then the search is successful; otherwise an item containing that key is not present in the original collection.

The popularity of the binary search is due in great part to its simplicity. Equal partitioning is also an effective strategy based upon the assumption that the sorted keys are uniformly distributed.

The binary search algorithm is independent of the data structure that defines the item collection organization. The selection of an appropriate data structure can facilitate the partitioning and efficiency of a particular application of a binary search.

Binary Search of a Static Data Structure — Array

DESCRIPTION: Array partitioning in order to perform a binary search of the array elements is accomplished in a straightforward manner by calculating the array subscripts that form the boundaries of the partitioned subset.

The algorithm searches a file of M records, looking for a given key K that is known to be present in the file. The file is represented as an array F with positions denoted F_i where $1 \le i \le M$. Each position may either be empty (not contain a value) or occupied (contain a value). Two additional variables, L and R, are defined to represent the left and right boundaries of a partitioned subset. The key of record F_i is denoted by $K[F_i]$.

ALGORITHM:

1. Assign L the value of 1 and assign R the value of M;
2. Assign i the value of the integer result of $(L + R)/2$;
3. If $K[F_i] = K$ then stop (record has been located);
4. If $K < K[F_i]$ then assign R the value of $i - 1$; go to step 2.
5. Assign L the value of $i + 1$; go to step 2.

Binary Search Trees

DESCRIPTION: A *binary search tree* is designed to be searched via a binary search. By definition, in these trees, all nodes in the left subtrees have key values less than the root node of that left subtree. Likewise, all nodes in right subtrees have key values that are greater than the root node of that right subtree. Therefore, the selection of a subtree based upon the key value of a node that is the root value of that subtree serves to partition the set of values contained in the nodes of the complete tree.

A binary search using a binary search tree has obvious advantages over a similar search using an array:

• The number of items in the collection to be searched is not restrained by the array size.
• Since the binary tree is designed to accommodate a search, the partitioning phase of the algorithm is automatic, requiring no calculations.

ALGORITHM: This algorithm searches a file of M records, looking for a given key K that may be present in the file. The file is represented as a binary search tree with the tree root pointer designated T and positions (nodes) designated R. The key of record R is denoted by $K[R]$. T initially points to the entire tree. R initially is the root node of the entire tree.

1. If T points to nil then stop (the search is unsuccessful);
2. If $K = K[R]$ then go to step 5; If $K < K[R]$ then go to step 3; If $K > K[R]$ then go to step 4;
3. Set T to the left subtree of R. If T points to nil (the left link is null) then go to step 6, else go to step 2;
4. Set T to the right subtree of R. If T points to nil (the right link is null) then go to step 6, else go to step 2;
5. Stop (the record has been located—a successful search).
6. Stop (the record is not present—an unsuccessful search).

EXAMPLE: The following Pascal function demonstrates the use of a binary search tree:

```
Type TreePtr = ^TreeNode;
     TreeNode = Record
                    Info : Some Data Type;
                    LeftLink, RightLink : TreePtr
                End;

     *****

Function BinSearch(T:TreePtr; B: Some Data Type):TreePtr;
   Var P : TreePtr;
       Found : Boolean;
   Begin
     P := T;
     Found := False;
     While (P < >Nil) And (Found < >True) Do
   Begin
     If B=P^.Info Then Begin
                         Found := True;
                         BinSearch := P
                       End;
     If B<P^.Info Then P:=P^.LeftLink
                  Else P:=P^.RightLink
   End
End; {BinSearch}
```

This function returns a pointer to the node of a binary search tree with a desired key. The tree is defined by means of the tree root pointer (variable T). Parameter B contains the key value for which the tree is to be searched.

Threaded Binary Search Trees

DESCRIPTION: A right threaded tree is a binary tree, containing M keys, plus the addition of a special infinity node and $M + 1$ threads. If a node of the tree has no left subtree, then it has a left thread pointing to itself. If a node has no right subtree, then it has a right thread pointing to its immediate successor in symmetric order. If a node has no such successor, then its right thread points to the infinity node.

ALGORITHM: This algorithm searches a file of M records, looking for a given key K that may be present in the file. The file is represented as a threaded binary search tree with tree root pointer designated T and positions (nodes) designated R. The key of record R is denoted by $K[R]$. T initially points to the entire tree. R is initially the root node of the entire tree. The node to which a left thread points is denoted by LT, and the node to which a right thread points is denoted by RT.

1. If T points to nil then stop (the search is unsuccessful);
2. If $K \le K[R]$ then go to step 3; If $K > K[R]$ then go to step 4;
3. Set T to the left subtree of R. If T points to nil (the left link is a thread) then go to step 5, else go to step 2;
4. Set T to the right subtree of R. If T points to nil (the right link is a thread) then go to step 6, else go to step 2;
5. If $K = K[LT]$ then go to step 7, else go to step 8;
6. If $K = K[RT]$ then go to step 7, else go to step 8;
7. Stop (the record has been located—a successful search).
8. Stop (the record is not present—an unsuccessful search).

Hashing

Hashing algorithms are a certain type of search procedure applicable to files of records. The goal of hashing is to organize records in such a manner that

1. Records having a given key K (if present in the file) can be quickly located.
2. Additional records may be added to the file in a straightforward manner.

Each entry in the file of records is either *empty*, or it contains a record, i.e, it is *full*. Such files may be searched for a record with a particular key by examining sequentially all entries of the file. Similarly, a new record can be inserted into the file by searching for an empty position in that file into which the record may be placed. The nature of such sequential searches to accomplish location or insertion is that they are directly related to the size of the file being manipulated.

The concept of hashing is to identify a transformation **H** on the key K which optimizes the location within a file where the record containing key K may be found. For example, if the file contains M entries or positions, numbered 0, 1, 2, ... $M - 1$, then **H** maps all keys into the set $\{0, 1, 2, ... M - 1\}$. The transformation **H** is called a *hash function*.

If $\mathbf{H}(K) = S$ then it is said that key K hashes into position S. Probabilistically, several keys may hash to the same position. In an attempt to insert a new key K into the file, it may be found that position $H(K)$ of the file is already occupied by another record. In that event, it is necessary to define a mechanism by which the remaining file may be searched until an empty position is located. Examination of a file that encounters a full entry is called a *collision*. The mechanism for resolving collisions is called a *collision resolution strategy*. The worst case in such a strategy must involve the resolution of an attempt to insert a record into an already full file, a situation known as an *overflow*. The strategy of an attempt to locate a record of a particular key will follow the same path of the *collision resolution strategy* in a complementary manner.

For the sake of example it will be assumed that the collision resolution strategy will be to examine each file position exactly once prior to a return to the original location designated by the hash function. The particular path followed during a search may depend on the key K and the state of the file at the time. It is also assumed that the hash function selects each of the file entries with equal probability. This assumption will have the effect of randomly scattering the keys throughout the file.

Therefore, the technique of hashing can be described with two steps:

1. The construction or determination of a hash function **H** capable of mapping all possible keys into the set $\{0, 1, 2, ... M - 1\}$ so that each set member is chosen with approximately equal probability.
2. The formulation of an efficient collision resolution strategy.

Selection of a Hash Function

CONCEPT: To determine the criteria for selecting a hash function that best complements hashing algorithms

PROCESS: The fundamental goal in the selection of a hash function is to minimize the number of collisions that occur with the use of that function. This goal can be accomplished with a function which selects values that are

- Distributed uniformly over the range of possible key positions.
- As random as possible and do not depend on any arrangement of keys or key values.

These criteria are quite similar to the criteria defined in the selection of a pseudo-random number generator to produce a sequence of uniformly distributed numbers. With this model, the range of values assumed by keys is comparable to the range of values produced by such a generator. It is likewise desirable that the sequence length of the generator approximately equals the number of items being searched.

Consequently, any suitable method for pseudo-random number generation should be adaptable for use as a hash function of a particular kind. As a result, the satisfactory statistical properties of the *multiplicative congruential methods* provide easily implementable hash functions suitable for many applications.

Therefore, a hash function of the form

$$\mathbf{H}(k) = \text{Ord}(k) \text{ MOD } N$$

could be defined given a collection of N items addressable with the integers $0..N - 1$, and the existence of ordinal function (Ord) that maps the range of values of the item keys in a unique way on the set of positive integers.

Since, like the pseudo-random number generators, the values of $\text{Ord}(k)$ and N very closely affect the statistical properties of the function, it may be desirable to alter *artificially* the number of items in the collection (N) and the range of values of the keys (range of $\text{Ord}(k)$) in order to improve the performance of the hash function and thereby decrease the probability of collisions.

Hashing Algorithms. Most of the common hashing algorithms are well documented and analyzed in references such as Knuth and Sedgewick. The following is simply a summarization of some of these algorithms.

Linear Probing

DESCRIPTION: The algorithm searches a file of M records, looking for a given key K. If K is not in the file and the file is not full, K is inserted. The file is represented as an array F with positions denoted F_i where $0 \le i < M$. Each position may either be empty (does not contain a value) or occupied (contains a value). An additional variable N is defined to count the number of positions within F that are occupied. Therefore, N is incremented by 1 each time a record is added to the file.

This algorithm makes use of a hash function $\mathbf{H}(K)$ and it uses a linear probing sequence to address the file.

ALGORITHM:

1. Assign i the value of $\mathbf{H}(K)$; $0 \le i < M$.

2. If the key of $F_i = K$ then stop (record has been located), else if F_i is empty, go to step 4;
3. Decrement the value of i by 1; If $i < 0$ Then Assign i the value of $i + M$; go to step 2;
4. (The search was unsuccessful.) If $N = M - 1$ the algorithm terminates with overflow. (This algorithm considers the file to be full when $N = M - 1$ not when $N = M$.) Otherwise increment N by 1, mark F_i occupied, and assign the key of F_i the value K;

Open Addressing With Double Hashing

DESCRIPTION: This algorithm is almost identical to the linear probing algorithm except that it probes the file utilizing two hash functions $H_1(K)$ and $H_2(K)$. As previously $H_1(K)$ yields a value in the range 0 to $M - 1$ inclusive; however, $H2(K)$ must yield a value in the range 1 to $M - 1$ that is *relatively prime* to M. For example, if M is prime, then $H_2(K)$ can be any value between 1 and $M - 1$ inclusive; or if $M = 2^P$, then $H_2(K)$ can be any *odd* value between 1 and $2^P - 1$. The probe sequences in this case are arithmetic progressions.

ALGORITHM:

1. Assign i the value of $H_1(K)$.
2. If F_i is empty, go to step 6; otherwise if the key of the record at position $i = K$ then stop (successful location of K).
3. Assign C the value of $H_2(K)$.
4. Assign i the value of $i - C$; if $i < 0$ then assign i the value $i + M$.
5. If F_i is empty, go to step 6, otherwise if the key of the record at position $i = K$ then stop (successful location of K); otherwise go to step 4.
6. If $N = M - 1$, the algorithm terminates with overflow, otherwise, increment N by 1, mark F_i occupied and set the key of the record at position i equal to K.

The main difference between the linear probing algorithm and the open addressing with double hashing algorithm is that in the latter the decrement distance C can itself depend on the key K.

Bucket Search

DESCRIPTION: In nonopen addressing methods, the probe path of a key K depends on the previous history of the file. This is usually accomplished by storing in each record and addition *link* field that can be a pointer to another entry of the file. The probe path of a key is then determined by hashing to a location S and then following the links from that location. If an empty entry or null link is encountered at this location, then it is evident that the record being sought is not in the file. Such hash algorithms are called *chained*.

With the bucket search algorithm, it is assumed that M list-heads HEAD$_i$, $0 \leq i \leq M - 1$ are present each pointing to (a possibly empty) list of records. Each record has an additional link field that can be a pointer to another record or have the value NIL. The lists of the algorithm are kept disjoint. If a new record has $\mathbf{H}(K) = S$, then this record is added to the end of the list pointed to by HEAD$_S$. It is also assumed that an operation $X \leq$ AVAIL that makes X point to a block of memory where the new record can be stored is also present.

ALGORITHM:

1. Assign i the value of $\mathbf{H}(K)$
2. If HEAD$_i$ = NIL then let $j \leq$ AV AIL, assign HEAD$_i$ the value of j, and go to step 5 else assign i the value of HEAD$_i$.
3. If $K =$ KEY$_i$ then stop.
4. If LINK$_i \neq$ NIL then assign i the value of LINK$_i$ and go to step 3, otherwise let $j \leq$ AV AIL and assign LINK$_i$ the value of j.
5. Assign KEY$_j$ the value of K and LINK$_j$ the value NIL.

Chaining With Coalescing Lists

DESCRIPTION: This algorithm searches an M-element table, looking for a given key K. If K is not in the table and the table is not full, then K is inserted.

The elements of the table are denoted by TABLE$_i$, for $0 \leq i \leq M$; and they are of two distinguishable types, and *occupied*. An occupied element contains a key field KEY$_i$, a link field LINK$_i$, and possibly other fields.

ALGORITHM:

1. Assign i the value of $\mathbf{H}(K) + 1$; (now $1 \leq i \leq M$).
2. If TABLE$_i$ is empty, go to step 6.
3. If $K =$ KEY$_i$ then stop (K located).
4. If LINK$_i \neq$ NIL then assign i the value of LINK$_i$ and go to step 3.
5. Decrease R one or more times until finding a value such that TABLE$_R$ is empty; if $R = 0$, then the algorithm terminates with overflow, otherwise assign LINK$_i$ the value of R and assign i the value of R.
6. Mark TABLE$_i$ as an occupied node with KEY$_i$ having the value K and LINK$_i$ having the value NIL.

Chained methods require more storage because of the link fields, but as the analyses in the Knuth reference show, they usually outperform open addressing techniques with respect to the number of probes for given M and N.

COMPARING SEARCHING TECHNIQUES

Table 10.1 presents a summary of order of magnitude comparisons of the searching algorithms discussed in this chapter.

**Table 10-1. Comparison of the
Performance of Selected
Searching Algorithms.**

Search	Order of Magnitude
Linear	$O(N/2)$
Binary	$O(log_2 N)$
Hash	$O(1)$

REFERENCES

1. Knuth, Donald E., Vol. 3 in *The Art of Computer Programming*, by Donald E. Knuth. Sorting and Searching. Reading, MA: Addison-Wesley, 1973.
2. Sedgewick, Robert, *Algorithms*. Reading, MA: Addison-Wesley, 1983.

11

SORTING

"Before him will be gathered all the nations and he will separate them one from another as the shepherd separates the sheep from the goats."

Matthew 25:32

In his classic, *The Art of Computer Programming*, Donald Knuth wrote, "Computer manufacturers estimate that over 25 percent of the running time on their computers is currently spent on sorting, when all their computers are taken in account. There are many installations in which sorting uses more than half of the computing time."

That estimate was made in 1973, before the advent of personal computers and of such specialized software applications as computer spreadsheets and fourth-generation database management systems. Some experts speculate that a current estimate of computer utilization involving the sorting of data may more accurately approach 90 percent.

It is now common practice for computer manufacturers to supply a "sort" package as part of their standard software. Such packages are typically invoked as commands to the operating system and are operable only upon files. Commercial software libraries typically contain "sorters" that may be called directly from COBOL, FORTRAN, PL/1, BASIC and other high-level language programs.

Many commercial "sorters" are tape-oriented or disk-oriented and are

- Highly implementation-dependent.
- Designed to accommodate 'large' sorts.

To sort a small number of items, such as a table consisting of a few hundred entries or less, a programmer may find it more convenient to write his or her own sorting routines. This chapter is *not* intended to be a comprehensive survey of sorting techniques. It is intended, however, to summarize operations common to sorting methods and to examine several of the more well-known

222

algorithms. For a thorough treatment of sorting, the works of D. E. Knuth are highly recommended.

GLOSSARY OF TERMS

Astable: Not stable.

Bubble Sort: An exchange sort in which the sequence of examination of pairs of items is reversed whenever an exchange is made. *Syn.*: sifting sort.

Exchange Sort: Based on the principle of comparing and exchanging pairs of items repetitively within the sequence until all items are sorted.

External Sort: A sorting technique that involves the use of external memory due to the size of the item set to be sorted; using in conjunction with merge techniques.

File: A sequence of records.

In-place Sorting: Sorting methods that actively sort a collection of data within its existing data structure; a consequence of this method is that the original data configuration (unsorted) is not retained.

Insertion Sort: Considers in each step only the one next item of the unsorted sequence and all items of the partially sorted sequence at that time.

Key: That attribute of a given record that results from the evaluation of a certain function applied to that record.

Oscillating Sort: A merge sort in which the sorts and merges are performed alternately to form one sorted set.

Out-of-place Sorting: Sorting methods that sort a collection of data external to its existing data structure. The original data configuration (unsorted) is not disturbed.

Partition: To divide into parts.

Pointer Value: An integer value associated with each position in a file.

Record: A unit of information; its contents cannot be altered.

Repeated Selection Sort: A selection sort in which the set of items is divided into subsets, and one item that fits specified criteria from each subset is selected to form a second-level subset. A selection sort is applied to this second-level subset; the selected item in this second level subset is appended to the sorted set and is replaced by the next eligible item in the original subset, and the process is repeated until all items are in the sorted set.

Selection Sort: Repetitively selects items with the maximum or minimum sorting characteristics from steadily decreasing subsets of the original unsorted collection. Items selected are placed sequentially in a subset of the original collection in order to build a sorted collection.

Sort Pass: The phase of a sort-merge program that consists of reading a set of unsorted data items, ordering them, and placing the ordered set in or on some location/data structure/device.

Sorting: The process of arranging a collection of items into a certain order (ascending, descending, alphabetic, etc.). The purpose of sorting is to facilitate the later search for members of a sorted set.

Stable Transformation: A permutation of a file that preserves the relative order of those records with equal keys, e.g., a stable sort.

Tournament Sort: A repeated selection sort in which each subset consists of no more than two items.

SURVEY OF SORTING TECHNIQUES

Sorting techniques can be classified into three principal categories according to their underlying method: insertion, selection, or exchange.

Insertion

The basis of all *insertion sorts* lies in the concept of *straight insertion*. This concept can be described as follows:

Given a collection of items, designated $F_1, F_2, \ldots F_M$; The characteristic of each of these items, upon which they will be sorted (i.e., the key), is designated K; therefore for the collection to be sorted, $K[F_1] \leq K[F_2] \leq \ldots \leq K[F_M]$ for an *ascending sort*, or $K[F_1] \geq K[F_2] \geq \ldots \geq K[F_M]$ for a *descending sort*.

Therefore, given $i < j \leq M$ and that $F_1, F_2, \ldots F_{j-1}$ have been arranged such that the K relationship (as shown above) for the type of sort desired over the range of $K[F_1]$ to $K[F_{j-1}]$ is true, then continuing sorting can be shown inductively.

For example, consider the next unsorted element F_j. $K[F_j]$ will be compared with $K[F_{j-1}]$, $K[F_{j-2}]$, and so forth, until its proper position in the K relationship is true. In this example, that position will be between $K[F_i]$ and $K[F_{i+1}]$. Therefore, F_j should be *inserted* between items F_i and F_{i+1}. Items F_{i+1}, F_{i+2}, $\ldots F_{j-1}$ must be shifted in order to provide room for the inserted item.

Selection

In the June 1984 issue of *Scientific American*, A. K. Dewdney describes a SAG, the Spaghetti Analog Gadget. In this device, lengths of uncooked spaghetti are used as analogs for numbers. To sort the numbers in decreasing order, the spaghetti bundle is held vertically and brought down sharply on a table top. Then the longest spaghetti is removed from the bundle. Continued selection of the longest spaghetti produces the desired decreasing sequence of numbers. SAG demonstrates the analog equivalent of the *selection sort*.

The basis of all selection sorts lies in the concept of *straight selection*, described as follows:

Given a collection of items, designated F_i, F_2, ... F_M, the characteristics of each of these items, upon which they will be sorted (the key), is designated K. Therefore for the collection to be sorted, $K[F_1] \leq K[F_2] \leq \ldots \leq K[F_M]$ for an *ascending sort*, or $K[F_1] \geq K[F_2] \geq \ldots \geq K[F_M]$ for an *descending sort*.

In essence, it can be seen that sorting is accomplished by the repetitive selection of the item with the minimum key from steadily shrinking subsets of the original collection.

This description of the item set before and after sorting is identical to that of the insertion sort. However, the description of the insertion sort implies that items will originate from a source external to the final set and that sorting will be accomplished by insertion into that set.

Selection sorts are accomplished *in place*. This means that the sort is accomplished by manipulating the items of the set within the confines of the set. There is, therefore, no time at which different configurations of the set in various stages of "sortedness" coexist.

The basic algorithm from *straight selection* is as follows:

1. Perform steps 2 and 3 for $j = M, M - 1, \ldots 2$.
2. Search through the items $K[F_j]$, $K[F_{j-1}]$, ... $K[F_1]$ and find the maximum value (for ascending sort) or minimal value (for descending sort). For the sake of example, let this be $K[F_i]$.
3. Interchange F_i and F_j; At this point, F_j ... F_M are in their permanent positions within the set.

In another form, straight selection becomes

```
Algorithm SelectionSort;
Begin
  For i := 1 to M Do
    Begin
      Min := i;
      For j := i+1 To M Do
        If F[j] < F[Min] Then Min := j;
      Swap(F[i], F[Min])
    End
End;
```

According to Robert Sedgewick, the selection sort algorithm is preferable when the files to be sorted have large records and small keys and it is necessary to perform file rearrangement rather than simply a manipulation of array indices.

Exchange

The fundamental concept common to the family of "exchange sorts" is that by exchanging out-of-order items, a sorted collection of items can be attained. To determine if an exchange is necessary, it is necessary to compare item key values. The primary differences between the techniques classified as *exchange sorts* lie in the relationship between the methods by which items are compared and by which items are exchanged. All exchange sorts are *in-place* sorters.

Bubble Sorts Bubble sorts are based upon the premise that sorting can be guaranteed by maximizing the number of comparisons (and necessary exchanges) between the items in the collection to be sorted. The term "bubble sort" stems from the characteristic that items tend to "float" until their appropriate sorted position can be determined.

The bubble sort has as a characteristic feature the use of only two array indices that determine the items being compared. There is no checking of indices except against the total number of items being sorted.

ALGORITHM 1: In the simplest implementation of the bubble sort, all possible pairs of items are compared exactly once.

The algorithm sorts a file of M records according to key K. The file is represented as an array F with positions denoted F_i where $1 \leq i \leq M$. The key of record F_i is denoted by $K[F_i]$. An additional variable j is defined to identify the second of the pair of records compared at any one time. The value of j is also defined $1 \leq j \leq M$. Upon completion, F is defined to be in *ascending order* by key K.

The algorithm is defined as follows:

1. Assign i the value 1;
2. Assign j the value 1;
3. If $K[F_i]$ is greater than $K[F_j]$ then exchange the values of F_i and F_j.
4. Increment the value of j; if $j \leq M$ then go to step 3.
5. Increment the value of i; if $i \leq M$ then go to step 2.
6. Stop (the file is sorted).

ALGORITHM 2: Another implementation of the bubble sort attempts to minimize the number of comparisons and exchanges, accomplished by comparing only adjacent items in the file and terminating the sort when it becomes evident that the file is sorted.

As before, the algorithm sorts a file of M records according to key K. The file is represented as an array F with positions denoted F_i where $1 \leq i \leq M$. The key of record F_i is denoted by $K[F_i]$. An additional variable c is defined to count the number of exchanges that occur with each pass through the file.

Since only adjacent records are compared, an additional variable to denote an index is not required. Upon completion, F is defined to be in *ascending order* by key K.

The algorithm is defined as follows:

1. Assign c the value of 0 and i the value of 1.
2. If $K[F_i]$ is greater than $K[F_{i+1}]$ then exchange the values of F_i and F_{i+1}; increment the value of c.
3. If $i < M - 1$ then increment i; go to step 2.
4. If $c \neq 0$ then go to step 1.
5. Stop (the file is sorted).

EXAMPLE   The following Pascal procedure demonstrates an application of the *brute force* bubble sort algorithm for sorting a 10-element array of real values:

Type Ary = Array[1..10] of Real;

****

```
Procedure BubbleSort (Var A : Ary; N : Integer);
    Var I, J : Integer;
        Temp : Real;
    Begin
      For I: = 1 to N Do
        For J: = I+1 to N Do
          If A[I] > A[J] Then
                        Begin
                        Temp : =A[I];
                        A[I] : = A[J];
                        A[J] : = Temp
                        End
    End;
```

Shell Sort.   An unfortunate characteristics of the "bubble sorts" is that although records move rapidly toward their correct final position in one direction, they move quite slowly in the other direction. This can be seen in the optimum case of the bubble sort where on each compare-and-exchange pass, the record with the largest key that is out of order moves to its final position. But other records move by much smaller amounts, often only one position per pass and sometimes in the wrong direction.

One of the most efficient of the "exchange sorts" is the *Shell sort*, named after its inventor, Donald Shell. The basic concept of the Shell sort is that during a pass through the data set, instead of comparing and exchanging adjacent records, the sorter maintains a gap of constant size between the records that are compared and possibly exchanged. When no more exchanges can be made for a particular gap size, the gap is narrowed and the compare-and-exchange passes continue. The final series of passes are made with a gap of one, comparing and exchanging adjacent items, just as in the best case of the bubble sort.

The Shell sort is more efficient due to its *partitioning* of the data set by controlling the gap size. The best bubble sort partitions only with a gap of one record (i.e., by comparing adjacent items) thereby limiting record movement with each pass. In the Shell sort, early passes with large gaps exchange records that are far out of position; these records move to near their final positions far more quickly than with the bubble sort. Because of the earlier passes with large gaps, the later passes have much less work to do.

ALGORITHM   The algorithm sorts a file of M records according to key K. The file is represented as an array F with positions denoted F_i where $1 \leq i \leq M$. The key of record F_i is denoted by $K[F_i]$. The additional variable c is defined to count the number of exchanges that occur with each pass through the file. The variable G is defined as the changing gap size. Upon completion, F is defined to be in *ascending order* by key K.

The algorithm is defined as follows:

1. Assign G the integer part of $M/2$ (the starting gap is one-half the size of the data set).
2. If $G = 0$ then stop (the file is sorted).
3. Assign c the value of 0 and i the value of 1.
4. If $K[F_i] > K[F_{i+G}]$ then exchange the values of F_i and F_{i+G}; increment the value of c.
5. If $i < M - G - 1$ then increment i; go to step 4.
6. If $c \neq 0$ then go to step 3.
7. Assign G the integer part of $G/2$; go to step 2.

Close examination of this algorithm reveals that the compare-and-exchange mechanism is identical to that of the bubble sorts. Its uniqueness lies in the partitioning scheme defined.

Different versions of the Shell sort can therefore be defined by using other compare-and-exchange mechanisms within the Shell partitioning.

EXAMPLE   The following Pascal procedure demonstrates an application of the Shell sort algorithm for sorting a 10-element array of real values:

Type Ary = Array[1..10] of Real;

****

Procedure ShellSort (Var A : Ary; N : Integer);
   {Adapted from 'Programming in Pascal' by Peter Grogono,
   Addison-Wesley, 1980}

```
Var Flag : Boolean;
    Jump, I, J : Integer;
    Temp : Real;
Begin
  Jump : = N;
  While Jump > 1 Do
      Begin
        Jump : = Jump Div 2;
        Repeat
          Flag : = True;
          For J: = 1 to N-Jump Do
            Begin
              I : = J + Jump;
              If A[J] > A[I] Then
                              Begin
                                Temp : = A[I];
                                A[I] : = A[J];
                                A[J] : = Temp;
                                Flag : = False
                              End
            End
        Until Flag
      End
End;
```

Heapsort. The *Heapsort* algorithm is an implementation of a *tree* concept to a collection of data stored within an array data structure. It was first described by J. W. J. Williams in 1964.

A *heap* is defined as a binary tree in which the key value of each element (node) is geater than (or less than) the key values of *both* its children. This characteristic is in sharp contrast to the parent-child relationship defined for a binary search tree. This binary tree has the additional feature that it is a *full binary tree*. A node in a heap is said to have the *heap property* since its key value is greater than (or less than) that of its children.

It follows then that the root node of a heap must contain the largest (or smallest) key value of all data items in the heap. The concept of the heapsort is to repetitively express the data collection as a heap and remove the root node of that heap until all data items in the collection have become the root node of a heap.

A heap data structure is emulated as a *vector* (one-dimensional array) using the following convention:

- The key value of the heap root node is contained in the first element of the vector.
- The key value of the left child of a node stored in element *i* of the vector is stored in element *2i* of the vector.

- The key value of the right child of a node stored in element i of the vector is stored in element $2i + 1$ of the vector.

ALGORITHM: The Heapsort algorithm is then specifically defined in terms of the algorithm that rearranges a vector of values into the form of a heap. The algorithm operates on a file of M records according to key K. The file is represented as an array F with positions denoted F_i where $1 \le i \le M$. The key of record F_i is denoted by $K[F_i]$. The variable i is defined to index the records of the file. The variable j is defined to denote the index of the parent of F_i. The variable q controls the number of insertions that occur during the process. The variable r is used to temporarily store a key value.

The algorithm is defined:

1. Assign q the value 2.
2. Assign i the value of q; assign r the value of $K[F_q]$.
3. Assign j the integer part of $i/2$.
4. Repeat through step 6: while $i > 1$ and $r > K[F_j]$.
5. Exchange the values of F_i and F_j.
6. Assign i the value of j; assign j the integer part of $i/2$; if $j < 1$ then assign j the value 1.
7. Assign F_i the value of r.
8. Increment q.
9. If $q \le M$ then go to step 2.

EXAMPLE The following Pascal procedure demonstrates an application of the heapsort algorithm for sorting a 10-element array of real values:

Type Ary = Array[1..10] of Real;

*****

```
Procedure HeapSort (Var A : Ary; N : Integer);
   {Adaped from 'Modula-2 - Programming With Data Structures',
    by Billy Walker, Wadsworth, 1986}
   Var I : Integer;
       Temp : Real;

   Procedure ReHeap (Var A : Ary; I,N : Integer);
      Label Step1,Step2;
      Var J : Integer;
          Parent : Real;
          Flag : Boolean;
   Begin
      Flag := False;
      Parent := A[I];
      J := 2 * I;
      Step1: If J > N Then GoTo Step2;
```

```
      If ((J < N) And (A[J] < A[J+1])) Then J := J + 1;
      If Parent > A[J] Then
                        Begin
                            A[J Div 2] := Parent;
                            GoTo Step2
                        End;
      A[J Div 2] := A[J];
      J := 2 * J;
      GoTo Step1;
      Step2: A[J Div 2] := Parent
    End;
Begin {HeapSort}
  For I := (N Div 2) downto 1 Do
    ReHeap(A,I,N);
  For I := N−1 downto 1 Do
    Begin
      Temp := A[I+1];
      A[I+1] := A[1];
      A[1] := Temp;
      ReHeap(A,1,I)
    End
End;
```

Quicksort. Quicksort was invented by C. A. R. Hoare* in the 1960s. Its concept is that if a *coarse* partitioning scheme is recursively applied to successively smaller subsets of a data collection, the result is a sorted data collection. The *coarse* scheme used only identifies the approximate location of an item with respect to the sorted set, *not necessarily* with respect to other items within the sorted set.

Data sets are partitioned about the median value (the *pivot point*) of the set. Items *between* the partitioned subsets are exchanged based only on comparison with the pivot value, not with comparison to other members of their respective subset. The result is the data set partitioned into three regions, S_1, S_2 and S_3, where

- Items in S_1 have key values less than that of the pivot point.
- Items in S_2 have key values equal to that of the pivot point.
- Items in S_3 have key values greater than that of the pivot point.

This coarse partitioning has the effect that

- The items in S_1 will remain in the region defined by S_1 in the sorted data set (although their positions relative to one another may change).

---

*Hoare, C. A. R., "Quicksort," Computer Journal, v. 5, no. 1, 1962.

- The items in S_2 are already sorted and remain in their positions in the final sorted data set.
- The items in S_3 will remain in the region defined by S_3 in the sorted data set (although their positions relative to one another may change).

Upon completion of the partitioning, the resulting subsets are partitioned in the same manner recursively. It follows that partitioning will ultimately lead to individual items within the data set.

ALGORITHM: The Quicksort algorithm is then specifically defined in terms of the partitioning algorithm. The algorithm partitions a file of M records according to the key K. The file is represented as an array F with positions denoted F_i where $1 \le i \le M$. The key of record F_i is denoted by $K[F_i]$. The variable i is defined to index the subset whose items have key values less than the pivot value. The variable j is defined to index the subset whose items have key values greater than the pivot value. The variable p is defined to designate the pivot value.

The algorithm for the initial partitioning is defined as follows:

1. Assign i the value 1; assign j the value M; assign p the integer value of $(i + j)/2$.
2. If $i > j$ then stop (the file is partitioned).
3. If $K[F_i] > K[F_p]$ then go to step 5.
4. Increment i; go to step 3.
5. If $K[F_j] < K[F_p]$ then go to step 7.
6. Decrement j; go to step 5.
7. If $i \le j$ then exchange F_i and F_j, increment i, decrement j.
8. Go to step 2.

This algorithm is then applied recursively to all resulting subsets with the values of i and j assigned the index values of the boundary values associated with each subset being partitioned. When the partition size reaches zero, the data set is sorted in ascending order.

EXAMPLE 1:   The following Pascal procedure demonstrates a *recursive* application of the Quicksort algorithm for sorting a 10-element array of real values:

Type Ary = Array[1..10] of Real;

*****

Procedure QuickSort (Var A:Ary; N:Integer);
   {Adapted from 'The Design of Well-Structured and Correct
    Programs,' by S. Alagic, Springer-Verlag, 1978}

```
Procedure QSort (Var A:Ary; M,N:Integer);
 Var I, J:Integer;
 Procedure Partit (Var A:Ary; Var I,J:Integer; Left,Right:Integer);
  Var Pivot, Temp:Real
  Begin
    Pivot := A[(Left + Right) Div 2];
    I := Left;
    J := Right;
    While I <= J Do
      Begin
        While A[I] < Pivot Do
          I := I + 1;
        While Pivot < A[J] Do
          J := J - 1;
        If I <= J Then
                  Begin
                    Temp := A[I];
                    A[I] := A[J];
                    A[J] := Temp;
                    I := I + 1;
                    J := J - 1
                  End
      End
    End
  End;
 Begin
  If M < N Then
                Begin
                  Partit(A,I,J,M,N);
                  QSort(A,M,J);
                  QSort(A,I,N)
                End
  End;
 Begin
  QSort(A,1,N)
End;
```

EXAMPLE 2:   The following BASIC program demonstrates an *iterative, nonre-cursive* application of the Quicksort algorithm for sorting a 20-element array of real values. The version of BASIC used in this example supports the logical operators And and Or.

```
100  REM A NON-RECURSIVE QUICKSORT PROGRAM
110  REM ADAPTED FROM 'SOFTWARE TOOLS'
120  REM BY BRIAN KERNIGHAN, ADDISON-WESLEY, 1976
130  REM L AND R ARE ARRAY STACKS TO SIMULATE RECURSION
140  REM P IS THE PIVOT VALUE
150  DIM X(20), L(20), R(20)
160  MAT READ X
170  L(1) = 1
```

```
180  R(1) = 20
190  S = 1
200  IF S < = 0 THEN 560
210  IF L(S) < R(S) THEN 240
220  S = S − 1
230  GOTO 550
240  I = L(S)
250  J = R(S)
260  P = X(J)
270  M = INT((I + J)/2)
280  IF (J − 1) < = 5 THEN 310
290  IF ((X(M) < P) AND (X(M) > X(I))) OR ((X(M) > P) AND (X(M) < X(I)))
     THEN GOSUB 1000
300  GOTO 320
310  IF ((X(I) < X(M)) AND (X(I) > P)) OR ((X(I) > X(M)) AND (X(I) < P))
     THEN GOSUB 2000
320  P = X(J)
330  IF I > = J THEN 440
340  IF X(I) > = P THEN 370
350  I = I + 1
360  GOTO 340
370  J = J − 1
380  IF ((I < J) AND (P < X(J))) THEN 400
390  GOTO 420
400  J = J − 1
410  GOTO 380
420  IF I < J THEN GOSUB 2000
430  GOTO 330
440  J = R(S)
450  GOSUB 2000
460  IF (I − L(S)) > = (R(S) − 1) THEN 510
470  L(S + 1) = I + 1
480  R(S + 1) = R(S)
490  R(S) = I − 1
500  GOTO 540
510  L(S + 1) = L(S)
520  R(S + 1) = I − 1
530  L(S) = I + 1
540  S = S + 1
550  GOTO 200
560  MAT PRINT X
570  DATA 3.2, 5.6, 1.4, 5.8, 3.7, 2.7, 8.5, 9.0, 3.8, 2.1
580  DATA 6.3, 5.9, 1.0, 4.3, 9.7, 2.1, 7.6, 8.4, 2.0, 2.7
590  STOP
1000  T = X(M)
1010  X(M) = X(J)
1020  X(J) = T
1030  RETURN
2000  T = X(I)
2010  X(I) = X(J)
2020  X(J) = T
2030  RETURN
2040  END
```

The left and right parameters for the simulated recursive calls are stored in arrays L and R. The pivot element is initially chosen to be the last element of the array. This is a poor choice for a pivot if the array is already sorted in ascending or descending order. Consequently, this pivot element is compared with two other elements: the first element of the array and the element located at the center of the array. The element that is the median of these three, neither the largest nor the smallest, is chosen as the pivot. This change greatly speeds up the sorting process when the array or a subset of the array is already sorted.

One feature of this version is that at each partitioning, the smaller of the two subsets is sorted before the larger. This minimizes the space needed for storage of the unsorted indices.

Implicit Sorting within Data Structures

The sorting methods discussed to this point are independent of the structure of the dataset to be sorted. The array data structure provides a convenient mechanism for the description of the sorting algorithms, but is not a required form for the data collections.

The definition of the array data structure does not specify relationships between data elements affected by a sorting process. Therefore, arrays provide a convenient data storage area within which sorting methods may be defined. However, other data structures are defined such that the arrangement of their constituent elements with respect to the values (or other properties) of those elements is fundamental to that structure.

Two data structures for which the *sortedness* of the elements within those structures is well defined are (1) priority queues and (2) binary search trees.

A *priority queue* is a collection of data accessed on a basis that depends on some ordering of the data, rather than on a FIFO basis. In this sense, it is not really a queue at all. The procedure that adds elements to a priority queue is defined to add a new element to queue in such a way that the queue is *ordered* according to some data characteristic of the node added. Therefore, the addition of an item to a priority queue data structure is a specific application of an *insertion sort* of an element into that structure. At all times, a priority queue is ordered (sorted) according to some characteristic of each element.

The removal of an element from a priority queue occurs in the same manner described for general queue data structures, always from one end of the structure. However, the definition of the priority queue then assures that elements removed are always the largest (or smallest) elements of the list based on a particular data characteristic.

Priority queues are discussed further and examples given in Chapter 3, Organization of Data.

A *binary search tree* is a hierarchical data structure designed to facilitate a binary search of a collection of data. The procedure that defines the process of inserting an element (node) into a binary search tree also defines a sorting process. This process insures that when the tree is traversed in a specific manner then the element will be orderd with respect to the other elements of the tree according to a specific characteristic of the tree elements.

Binary search trees are discussed in greater detail and examples given in Chapter 3, and in Chapter 10, Searching.

Hashing

Hashing or *address calculation* is the name given to a collection or sorting/searching methods. A survey of hashing techniques is discussed in Chapter 10, Searching.

It is characteristic of hashing algorithms that they can double as sorting algorithms. This is accomplished by defining the algorithm such that if an item being sought in a collection of items is not present within that collection, then it is inserted into the collection at the appropriate location to facilitate future searches.

EVALUATING SORTERS

Several criteria should be considered when selecting a sorting technique for a particular application:

1. Programming effort.
2. Dependence upon size of data set to be sorted (efficiency).
3. Stability.
4. Storage space requirements.

Programming Effort

Sorting algorithms vary greatly in complexity due to such factors as the sorting model used, the description of the collection to be sorted and attempts to improve efficiency by the elimination of redundant operations. Likewise, computer programs implementing these algorithms vary greatly in the programming effort necessary for a particular application. Analysis of sorters indicates that their effectiveness is highly correlated to the quantity of data to be sorted. As a result, some of the ''more sophisticated'' sorting algorithms are no more effective than the ''brute force'' ones under certain circumstances.

It can also be seen that certain of the sorting algorithms are best implemented in specific programming languages. The recursive character of Quicksort makes it applicable the best in languages that allow recursion. Implementation of an iterative form of Quicksort increases the complexity of the application it serves and the storage requirements of the application in such a way that disadvantages can easily outweigh any advantages.

Evaluating Sorter Efficiency

CONCEPT: To define a means of evaluating the efficiency of various sorting algorithms

PROCESS: Processing speed is the first performance measure typically applied to a sort routine or algorithm. However, speed is a relative measure and can be viewed only with respect to the number of data elements in the collection to be sorted. The state of the unsorted collection (i.e., how badly out of sort it is) leads to the determination of ''best,'' ''worst,'' or ''typical'' case behavior of each algorithm analyzed.

For these reasons, order of magnitude analysis (''Big O'') (discussed in Chapter 8) is the conventional method of evaluating and comparing sorting algorithms.

EXAMPLE: The key operation in most sorting algorithms that affects their performance is the comparison of data elements in the collection of data elements to be sorted. As the number of items to be sorted (input) increases, it follows that the number of comparisons will also increase. The effectiveness of a sorting algorithm may therefore be demonstrated by quantifying this relationship between number of items to be sorted and the number of comparisons the algorithm must perform in order to accomplish the sort.

The following is a pseudocode listing of an algorithm for a selection sort.

```
Selection Sort.
Input: an array, A, and its size, N.
Output: the same array A, in sorted order.
begin
   for i: = 1 to n do begin
     m: = i;
     for j: = i + 1 to n do
       compare A[j] to A[m], making j the new m if A[j] < A[m];
       exchange A[i] and A[m];
     end
end
```

The concept of this algorithm is that given a list (array) of items to sort in ascending order, the following procedure may be followed:

1. Scan the list of items, identify the smallest item and exchange it with the *first* item;
2. Scan the remaining list of items (all except for the first item), identify the smallest item and exchange it with the *second* item and so on.

To establish order of magnitude for this algorithm, it is first necessary to derive the relationship between the number of comparisons it will perform and the quantity of data to be sorted.

In an examination of the algorithm for a selection sort, it can be seen that comparisons are performed only when the list to identify the minimum item is being scanned. Therefore one comparison is performed for each of the possible values of i and j. When $i = 1$, j ranges from 2 to N for a total of $N - 1$ values and $N - 1$ comparisons. When $i = 2$, j ranges from 3 to N or $N - 2$ comparisons; when $i = N - 1$, j covers only one value and finally when $i = N$, the j loop is not executed at all.

It can therefore be seen that the total number of comparisons is equal to $(N - 1) + (N - 2) + (N - 3) + \ldots + 2 + 1$.

The sum of this series has the well-known value

$$\frac{N(N - 1)}{2} \quad \text{or} \quad \frac{N^2}{2} - \frac{N}{2}$$

Therefore the number of comparisons performed by this selection sort algorithm as a function of the number of data items to be sorted may be expressed as

$$F(N) = \frac{N^2}{2} - \frac{N}{2}$$

To represent this relationship in "Big O" notation, consider

$$F \leq AG + B$$

This relationship is true given $G = N^2$, $A = 1$, $B = 0$, and $N = 1$. Therefore $F = O(N^2)$ of this selection sort can be said to be an order N^2 sort. Comparable analyses can be performed in a similar manner on other sorting algorithms.

It can be shown that any algorithm that sorts by comparison of items must, for a sequence of N items, use on the order of N $*$ log N comparisons (i.e., $O(N \log N)$). It has also has been shown that some algorithms have worst-case times greater than this, but are still acceptable sorts. Often, the simplest algorithm (i.e., the one requiring minimal programming effort) is the most desirable. For small collections of data, collections of data that are "nearly sorted," or routines of short lifespan ("quick and dirty"), speed may not be an important issue.

Sorter Stability

The concept of *stability* is an important one for a sorting algorithm. It can be described best by means of an example.

Given an unsorted data set in which there exist two or more items with the same key value, consider that these items are present in some order with respect to one another.

Upon sorting, the items with the same key values will be adjacent to one another in the sorted set. If these items retain the same order with respect to one another in the sorted set as they had in the unsorted set, then the sorted method used is defined as *stable*; otherwise, it is *astable*. *A stable sorter will not disturb the relative order of items having the same key value.*

Problems with stability can often be solved by defining multiple sort keys.

Storage Space Requirements

All the sorting techniques discussed in this chapter operate upon data collections in *memory*. This implies that these methods are most effective in circumstances in which there is sufficient storage available to the program during execution to accommodate all the data to be sorted. Program sizing analyses such as those described in Chapter 8 Program Attributes, can be useful in determining the storage requirements for a particular application of one of these techniques.

Additional techniques for file sorting and merge sorts are described the Knuth and Sedgewick books listed in the following references. Such techniques are useful when in-memory sorting algorithms are inadequate.

SUMMARY

Table 11.1 presents a comparison of the sorting techniques discussed in this chapter.

Table 11-1. Comparison of the Performance of Selected Sort Algorithms.

Sorter	Best Case	Worst Case	Typical	Stable
Insertion	$O(N)$	$O(N^2)$	$O(N^2)$	Usually
Selection	$O(N^2)$	$O(N^2)$	$O(N^2)$	Usually
Bubblesort	$O(N^2)$	$O(N^2)$	$O(N^2)$	Can Be
Shellsort				
Quicksort	$O(N \log N)$	$O(N^2)$	$O(N \log N)$	No
Heapsort	$O(N \log N)$	$O(N \log N)$	$O(N)$	No
Priority Queue	$O(N)$	$O(N^2)$	$O(N^2)$	Usually
Binary Tree	$O(N \log N)$	$O(N^2)$	$O(N \log N)$	Usually
Hash	$O(N)$	?	?	Usually

REFERENCES

1. Knuth, Donald E., *The Art of Computer Programming. vol. 3* in *Sorting and Searching*. Reading, MA: Addison-Wesley, 1973.
2. Lorin, Harold, *Sorting and Sort Systems*. Reading, MA: Addison-Wesley, 1975.
3. Rich, Robert P. *Internal Sorting Methods Illustrated with PL/1 Programs*. Englewood Cliffs, NJ: Prentice-Hall, 1972.
4. Sedgewick, Robert, *Algorithms*. Reading, MA: Addison-Wesley, 1983.
5. Wirth, Niklaus, *Algorithms + Data Structures = Programs*. Englewood Cliffs, NJ: Prentice-Hall, 1976.
6. Wirth, Niklaus, *Algorithms & Data Structures*. Englewood Cliffs, NJ: Prentice-Hall, 1986.
7. Press, W., Flannery, B., Teukolsky, S., and Vetterling, W., *Numerical Recipes—The Art of Scientific Computing*. New York: Cambridge University Press. 1986.

CREDITS

The following persons are to be thanked for their willingness to allow the excerpting and/or reproduction of their works:

Chapter 2—Key Topics in Software Design
1. Art Lew, *Decision Tables for General-purpose Scientific Programming*, Software-Practice and Experience, Vol. 13, pp. 181–188 (1983).
2. W. L. McMullen, Jr., *Structured Decision Tables*, SIGPLAN Notices, Vol. 19, No. 4, April 1984; *Improving Process Design Productivity*, Proceedings of the 1984 ACM Computer Science Conference, Philadelphia, PA, February 14–16, 1984; *Decision Tables In Process Control: A Powerful Development Tool*.
3. Georg Raeder, *A Survey of Graphical Programming Techniques*, Computer, 18, 8, 1985.
4. William Rieken, Jr., 'Software Project Methodologies,' notes from a seminar sponsored by the Association for Computing Education Seminars (ACES).
5. Ken Takura, *Program Design Using Pseudocode*, Dr. Dobbs' Journal, March 1984.

Chapter 3—Organization of Data
1. Cahners Publishing Co., *EDN Software Tutorial: Data Structures*, EDN, March 5, 1979, May 5, 1979.
2. Harvey Lynch—personal communication.
3. Nazim H. Madhavji, *Dynamically Structured Data*, Software Practice & Experience, Vol. 11, pp. 1235–1260 (1981); *Visibility Aspects of Programmed Data Structures*, CACM Vol. 27, No. 8, August 1984.

Chapter 4—Generation and Validation of Pseudo-Random Number Sequences
1. Stanford Linear Accelerator Center (SLAC), *VM Notebook Module #18—Care and Feeding of Random Numbers*, author—John Ehrman.
2. Dr. Charles A. Whitney, *Generating and Testing Pseudorandom Numbers*, BYTE, October 1984.

Chapter 5—Simulation & Monte Carlo Techniques
1. Gordon Wright—personal communication.

Chapter 6—Survey of Graphics Techniques
1. Mark Barnett—personal communication.
2. Integrated Computer Systems, Inc., *365—Computer Graphics Course Notes*, Rev. D, 8/79.

Chapter 7—Human Factors
1. D. Verne Morland, *Human Factors Guidelines for Terminal Interface Design*, 1983 ACM 0001-0782/83/0700-0484.
2. Richard Teitelbaum, *Topics in Human Factors*, August 13, 1985.
3. Joan Winters and Tamara Sturak, —Project Managers, SHARE Human Factors Project—personal communications.

Chapter 8—Program Attributes
1. S. Sitharama Iyengar, numerous works, personal communication.
2. Randy Scarborough, IBM, 'Writing Optimizable FORTRAN'.
3. Franz Stetter, *A Measure of Program Complexity*, Computer Languages, Vol. 9, No. 3/4, pp. 203–208, 1984.

Chapter 11—Sorting
1. Roger L. Wainwright, *A Class of Sorting Algorithms Based on Quicksort*, Communications of the ACM, Vol. 28, No. 4 (April 1985).

INDEX

Premature loop exit
  cyclomatic complexity of, 184
  Nassi-Schneiderman representation, 11
  restructured using the Boolean flag
    technique, 43
  restructured using the Duplication of code
    technique, 38
  restructured using the State variable
    approach, 42
Program
  complexity, 181, 186
  dependencies, 177
  efficiency, 173
  good, 2
  graph, 182
  optimizing, 175
  sizing, 190
  testing, 186
Pseudocode, definition and structures, 6
Pseudo-random number. *See* Random
    Numbers
Puzzles
  definition, 195
  magic squares, 196
  mazes, 205

Queue. *Also see* Stack
  emulation, 93
  priority, 80, 123, 235
  and simulation, 121
Quicksort. *See* Sorting algorithms

Random Numbers and Random Number
    Sequences
  definition, 99
  frequency test for randomness, 101
  mixed congruential method of generation,
    100
  multi-dimensional distribution, 105–106
  non-uniform sequences, 109
  periodicity tests, 104
  pitfalls in generation of, 107
  sequence length, 104
  serial test for randomness, 103
  table of, 100
Repeat Until control structure
  cyclomatic complexity of, 183
  decision table representation, 14
  emulation in BASIC, 46
  Nassi-Schneiderman representation, 10

pseudocode representation, 7
  Warnier-Orr representation, 31

Sampling
  definition, 117
  and simulation, 120
Schneiderman, B., 8
Searching algorithms
  binary, 213
  binary tree, 215
  bucket search, 219
  chaining with coalescing lists, 220
  comparison of, 221
  hashing, 216
  linear, 212
  linear probing, 218
  open addressing with double hashing, 219
  threaded binary search, 216
Sequence control structure
  cyclomatic complexity of, 183
  decision table representation, 14
  Nassi-Schneiderman representation, 9
Shell, Donald, 227
Shell sort. *See* Sorting algorithms
Simulation
  definition, 114
  deterministic system/stochastic model, 117
  elements of, 120
  role of time, 121
  shortcomings, 130
  stochastic system/deterministic model, 119
  stochastic system/stochastic model, 119
Software design method
  definition, 4
  restructuring 'unstructured' programs, 37
Software project methodology
  elements, 15
  goals of a, 47
  Hierarchical-Input-Process-Output (HIPO),
    34–36
  Structured Analysis and Design technique
    (SADT), 16–19
  Structured Analysis (Yourdon/DeMarco),
    20–24
  Structured Systems Analysis (Gane/Sarson),
    24–28
  Warnier-Orr method, 28–32
Software science, 186
Sorting algorithms
  bubble sort, 226–227